1

CONGO MY COUNTRY

A

PATRICE LUMUMBA

CONGO
MY COUNTRY

WITH A FOREWORD AND NOTES BY
COLIN LEGUM

TRANSLATED BY
GRAHAM HEATH

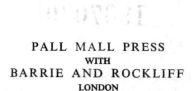

PALL MALL PRESS
WITH
BARRIE AND ROCKLIFF
LONDON

Printed and bound in Great Britain
by Taylor Garnett Evans & Co. Ltd.
London and Watford

CONTENTS

ILLUSTRATIONS

Between pages xvi and xvii
Arriving in London on the way back from New York to the Congo
Returning from the January 1960 Round Table Conference in
  Brussels
At Leopoldville after capture
Arriving in Brussels for the Round Table Conference
In transit after capture
In the hands of General Mobutu's men

Page xxxii
The opening and conclusion of Lumumba's second letter to his
  original publisher

The Life and Death of Patrice Lumumba
BY COLIN LEGUM

I

Nothing that touches the name of Patrice Lumumba is entirely free from controversy. When his book, which was written in 1956-57, was published posthumously in Belgium last year, it raised a fresh outcry both from those who regarded him as a martyred hero and from those who regarded him as evil incarnate. Was it authentic? With what motive did the publishers produce it four years after it had been sent to them? Why was publication held up in the first place? Had the manuscript been "doctored" in any way?

The controversy at least cleared up the question of authenticity: about that there can be little doubt. The manuscript as it stands suits the interests of neither the Belgian colonial authorities, nor of Lumumba's latter-day admirers. It is hardly likely to find its place on the shelves of the library of the Patrice Lumumba Friendship University in Moscow. And even if one accepts at face value some of the more extravagantly phrased tributes, it is hardly a commendation of Belgian rule. What we have here is a remarkable political record of Lumumba's development. One can see his ideas grow and change; towards the end of the book they are almost firm. They bear the unmistakable stamp of Lumumba's mind as I know it from my own conversations with him. Nevertheless, I hesitated before finally accepting the authenticity of the manuscript until I was reassured by Lumumba's own friends. Not all of them, it should be added, approve of its publication now; but many do. They believe it will help to clear away some of the crasser ideas that are held about their leader.

Lumumba's earlier standpoint is that of a "moderate" nationalist; a typical reformer whose attitude is scorned and despised by militant Pan-Africanists. In the three years that he lived after finishing his manuscript, Lumumba had himself discarded some of these ideas. Is it fair, therefore, that this work should be published without revision? I believe it is for several reasons.

It has great importance as a historical document portraying for the first time the attitude of Congolese leaders, about which we know little, on the eve of the great changes that transformed the Congo. It shows the short-sightedness of the Belgian colonial rulers in failing to recognise sooner what was happening. If they had agreed even, say, in 1958, to treat seriously with the Congolese leaders, they would have had the willing co-operation of the politicians, at least in the earlier stages of the transfer of power. "The main aim of my book", Lumumba wrote, "is to bring home to the Belgians and the Congolese the imperative and urgent need to achieve right now a brotherly understanding in order to reach a definitive union." In his appeal to the Belgians, he asks: "If the Congo should obtain its independence . . . tomorrow, why should you leave us, and why should we drive you out *so long as our co-existence gives rise to no friction* [my italics] and so long as we continue to treat each other not as neighbours linked by the mere ties of country, but as true friends in the fullest meaning of the term?"

At times Lumumba clearly wrote with the deliberate intention of engaging the sympathies of the Belgians, flattering them, indentifying himself with their interests, or retreating behind humble prayers of gratitude, in order to soften the impact of criticism that was not easily tolerated at that time.

A second – and perhaps stronger – reason for publication is that for the first time one gets a real insight into the attitudes and feelings of the Congolese élite[1] to Belgian rule. Here is the reality behind the façade of the "model colonial state". It records – usually with a strong sense of piety and puritanism – the social and economic problems in the developing urban society. It conveys the anger and frustrations, the ambitions and the perplexities of the African élite. The Belgians had set out purposely to create a new middle class; but they never understood that this new class – unhappily poised between the illiterate masses below and the white rulers above them – would develop interests of its own. Lumumba himself succumbed to the desire, natural in an evolving élite, to identify himself with the rulers; he wished to be allowed to act as the agent between the government of the Belgian Congo and the masses.

[1]See note on *Evolué* p. 2.

Lumumba conceived his book as a dialogue between the Congolese and the Belgians, with himself as the interlocutor. He explained his attempt to delve into the mysterious of Kitawala, a secret religious movement: "I carried out this little investigation to show how important it is that the Congolese élite who enjoy the confidence of their fellow-Congolese and can communicate freely with them without any stop in their mind, should work in close collaboration with the Belgians to enlighten them on certain questions and thus help them in the conduct of native affairs. It is through the Congolese élite that the Belgians will plumb the depths of the African soul and guide it better."

The tragedy is that neither this nor similar offers were taken up seriously by the Belgian administrators. They knew best. Belgian colonial literature is brimful of expensively-produced nonsense about the supposed wishes of the Congolese. The few Belgians who had any true understanding – such as Father Van Wing – were treated with respect, and ignored. So was Lumumba.

A third valuable aspect of this work is that it tells us about Lumumba himself; not so much about his own life, which he describes briefly, as about his ideas. Those who have formed their impressions about him only from what they have read in the Press (Western and Communist) are bound to be surprised. Is it possible that the Lumumba of independence can have been the same person who wrote with such deep concern about conditions in prisons; the filth and degradation of the detribalized community; the lack of respect shown by the Congolese for their women; the evils of hemp-smoking and drink (vices to which Lumumba himself fell victim); and the need for efficient and courteous police? Here is a side to Lumumba that those who never knew him could never have known existed. Here, too, we are faced with a paradox; how is it that the Lumumba who wrote this book later used his power with such apparently callous disregard for suffering?

It is often wrongly supposed that Lumumba was a half-baked, unsophisicated politician who had only the haziest notion about government and world affairs. This is wide of the mark. His detailed plans for social and political reforms are as valid today as when he first thought them out. Here is a blueprint for those who have survived him to build the structure of a new Congo.

If Lumumba later fell from democratic practice it was not because he neither cared for, nor understood, its importance. "We want democracy," he wrote, "but not a bad democracy." He, who

in the end became so impatient in his demands for immediate
independence, could understand the unwisdom of introducing
"political change prematurely". He understood the "legitimate fears
of the Europeans"; and the consequences for the Congo if the
Europeans suddenly abandoned it. "What would happen if the
Whites left the Congo today? It would be complete ruin. . . . "

Lumumba revealed considerable insight in the passages that deal
with the relationships between blacks and whites, and the role of
African nationalism. He rejected racialism as vehemently as he
rejected tribalism. He demanded "mutual respect", with the pride
born from years of insult. "Let us work together, white and black,
to construct Africa in harmony and mutual affection; these are the
indispensable conditions for any union." There is a jarring, untruth-
ful ring when, at one point, he wrote that the "Congolese élite's
only wish is to be 'Belgians' ". Perhaps Lumumba was describing
the attitudes of his fellow-*evolués*[2] rather than his own; although
it is conceivable that he only later thought his own position through
to the point where he rejected Africans being turned into "carica-
tures of Europeans".

In his conception of the relationship between nationalism and
racialism, Lumumba made a distinct contribution. He differentiated
between what he called true and false nationalism. "A man without
any nationalist tendencies is a man without a soul . . . what we
have to avoid in our country is false nationalism: the cramped
nationalism which conceals forms of racialism and hatred for those
of another race. . . . This struggle against racialist nationalism
can only be effective if we are able to abolish its causes. . . . The
nationalism displayed by the African is often, if not always, the
result of provocations and injustices . . . we see that reactionary
nationalism is always the price paid for a racialist policy . . . the
racialism of the coloured people is always preceded by the racialism
of the colonising country . . . it is always the stronger man who
blazes the trail, and the weaker only follows."

Lumumba emerges from the pages of his book as thoughtful,
reasonable and temperate. "Not all the aspirations of the colonised
people are reasonable of course. . . . To govern people is to guide
and educate them. . . . I favour a policy of prudence. . . .
Precipitate action must be avoided." How very different from the
impression produced by his brief, tempestuous and violent Premier-

[2] See footnote to p. 2.

ship! Can these strongly conflicting impressions be reconciled, or explained?

The easy explanation is that when Lumumba was writing his book he was still a seeker after power; when power was conferred on him it corrupted him. Only those who have been corrupted totally by Lord Acton could be satisfied with this explanation. To understand Lumumba's action we need to understand Lumumba himself and the events that shot him to the top and then quickly destroyed him.

II

There are three distinct phases in Lumumba's development. The first is that of the young man in his twenties with the benefit of only primary school education trying to educate himself, and determinedly forcing his way up the *evolué* ladder to join the Congolese élite. Active in study circles and discussion groups, he chose to identify himself with the Liberals. In the first phase his problem was to find a synthesis between Belgian and Congolese interests.

The second phase came in 1958, with the formation of his *Mouvement National Congolais* (M.N.C.) – the first Congolese supra-tribal nationalist movement – with aspirations towards independence, and the desire to form an independent relationship between the Congolese and the Belgians. His book was written at the crossing-point between the first and the second phase (partly while he was in prison serving a sentence for embezzlement). This would explain some of its contradictions, and the difference in emphasis between the earlier and later chapters. His thinking crystallised as a result of his attending the first All-African Peoples Conference in Accra in December 1958, where he was confirmed in his natural Pan-Africanist inclinations. He returned from that conference, at the end of December 1958, with a new sharpness to his demands for immediate independence. Against the tribalist demands for autonomy, he set himself up as the prophet of a free and unified Congo; a Congo of Congolese, no longer of separate tribes.

In his third phase (1959 up to the time of his death) he was the visionary committed to a single idea.

"For the people I have no past, no parents, no family. I am an idea . . . "

"I have no right to sleep as long as the people are not masters of their own destiny."

"I am the Congo, the Congo has made me. I am making the Congo."

By the middle of 1960, Lumumba's strength was such that, try as they would, neither his Congolese opponents nor the Belgians could resist his claim to become the first Congolese Prime Minister. His success cannot be ascribed only to his ability – there were others more capable. It was because he was the first Congolese to see the need for a *national* leader and, having seen himself in that role, he set himself the task of creating a national-conscious movement to support him. At a time when his contemporaries found it difficult to lift themselves above tribal politics he had already begun to think as a Pan-Africanist. His own peculiar advantage was that he came from a relatively unimportant tribe, the Batetela, a sub-group of the Mongo tribe which has affiliations in three of the Congo's six provinces. From an early age his Christian parents brought him up among the *evolués* of Stanleyville. He was never cribbed by close tribal affinities, nor tied down by particularist interests of a tribal character. He could easily escape from the tribe into the nation; or, at least, into the "idea" of a nation.

Lumumba was often praised for his oratory; but what is less well known was the skilful manner in which he organised M.N.C. and its important network of alliances. Through his association with the Batetela he successfully won to his side all the other groups of the Mongo tribe, which gave him a foothold in Kasai, Orientale and Equatoria provinces. To the minority tribes he offered greater security within a national movement. Among the large tribes he vigorously exploited traditional rivalries – for example, between the Kasai Baluba and the Lulua. After his first attempt to unite them failed, he succeeded in winning first one and then the other to his side. Similarly he used the division between the Katanga Baluba, on the one side, and the Balunda and Beyeke on the other, to forge an alliance, the BALUBAKAT, in powerful opposition to Tshombe's CONAKAT. Success was relatively easy in the Orientale Province where there are no powerful tribes. But his strongest appeal was in the urban centres (other than Leopoldville) where nationalism made sense to many of the *evolués*. Although the M.N.C. won only 33 of the 137 seats in the first independence parliament, it was enough to give Lumumba a great tactical advantage. He had money (collected from many sources abroad) and the gift of many offices in his hands to back up his negotiating strength. But although he succeeded in securing a dominant position in the first Coalition Government,

Lumumba was never strong enough to dominate the rest. Successful leadership depended on two things – keeping the Coalition together while consolidating his own position in the country; and weakening the dangers of tribal secessionist movements. When Lumumba was faced with the spread of secessionism he ignored the first of the dangers to his leadership; and concentrating exclusively on the second, he crashed to his defeat.

III

It was some time after the middle of April 1960 that Lumumba came to be regarded finally as anti-Belgian; by the beginning of July the official Belgian view was to regard him as their arch-enemy. Was he, in fact, anti-Belgian? What is certainly true is that his position changed gradually from being strongly pro-Belgian to being violently hostile to Belgian policy. When I talked to Lumumba at the Round Table Conference in Brussels in January 1960, he was still eloquently optimistic about his relations with the Belgians, despite his very recent imprisonment and ill-treatment as a prisoner. His views about co-operation with the Belgians had changed little from those described in his book. It is clearly recorded that at the conclusion of the Round Table Conference he had said: "The fact that Belgium has liberated the Congo from the colonial régime we were no longer prepared to accept, has won her the friendship and esteem of the Congolese people. We desire this friendship to be enduring and free of all forms of hypocrisy. We shall thus prove to the world that the principle of friendship between nations is one of real significance. . . . As for the Europeans living in the Congo, we would ask them to stay and help the young Congolese State . . . . We need their help. . . . It is with their collaboration that we wish to create the Congolese nation, in which all will find their share of happiness and satisfaction."

I next saw Lumumba in the Congo, at the end of March 1960 – only three months before independence. He was still full of praise for the Belgians, and for their co-operation in the independence elections. Then, towards the middle of April 1960, came his quarrel with the Belgian authorities; they began to describe him locally as "a Hitler". The quarrel is said to have had something to do with the source of the large funds he was receiving. The Belgians knew that some of the money came from their own industrialists; more came from Ghana, Guinea, the U.A.R.; and some, probably indirectly, from the communists. Confidence evaporated; Lumumba accused the Belgians of wishing to dictate to him. What kind of independence was this, he asked? Had the hateful paternalism not yet ended? The quarrel reached its climax when Lumumba – who, as leader of the largest party, had been asked to try and form the first government – was summarily discharged by the Governor General before he had completed his negotiations. Lumumba felt that the Belgians were conspiring to get a coalition government headed by one of his opponents. When that attempt failed, there was no alternative but to call on Lumumba again. Negotitations were prolonged and tough – and Lumumba showed that he could be as tough a negotiator as any. He gave very little away. Although he became Prime Minister, he still smarted under the Belgian attempt to pull the strings. For him the puppet-show was over. At the Independence Day celebrations on 30th June 1960, he made an extremely rude speech about the Belgians in the presence of King Baudouin. "From today we are no longer your *Makak*"! (monkeys). By evening he had sufficiently repented to offer the King a public apology; but suspicions remained.

These suspicions (which incidentally were shared also by Lumumba's colleagues in the government) explain why no negotiations were possible between the Congolese and the Belgians when the Force Publique mutinied within the first week of the Republic's life. There can really be little doubt that the original intention of the Belgians in bringing their troops back to the Congo was not to reconquer it, but to safeguard Belgian lives, about which they were genuinely concerned. The sequel of events, however, caused the Belgians to change their minds; they decided to make secessionist Katanga the base for a campaign to bring about Lumumba's downfall. Notwithstanding the bitterness of events following the revolt of the Force Publique, however, Lumumba still wished to obtain Belgian technical assistance. As late as August 1960, he was appealing to the Belgians to send back the teachers who had fled the country during the revolt. Lumumbaism – while it rejected paternalist Belgian policies and (what is termed) the "official forms of hypocrisy" – always insisted on the importance of Belgian co-operation; provided only that it rested on respect for the true independence of the Congo.

IV

At the height of Patrice Lumumba's career, during the difficult months of July, August, and the first week of September 1960, the instability of his personality and the ruthless impatience with which he worked greatly handicapped effective co-operation between himself, his colleagues, the United Nations and the African States. He lost all sense of time, and, on occasion, of reality itself. On one occasion he issued an ultimatum to the commander of the U.N. forces to secure the removal of all Belgian troops from Leopoldville by 6 p.m. It was then already 6.20 p.m. Not only did he quarrel with every U.N. representative in turn, but he ignored his own friends. Having summoned a Pan-African conference in August 1960 to win support for his stand against Dr. Ralphe Bunche and for his demand that Katanga should be taken by force, he walked out on the conference when it became clear to him that the delegates (with only Guinea dissenting) would reject his proposals.

Lumumba's loss of faith in the United Nations started the moment he discovered he would not be allowed to determine how its forces should be used. He wished them to suppress the Tshombe régime by force immediately. The pity is that this was not done; but at that stage the United Nations was not yet ready to use its force for such a purpose. Lumumba had little or no idea of how the United Nations worked, or of the conventions that applied to the U.N. Emergency Forces. As Premier of the Congo he could understandably only see the three urgent problems facing him in the few fatal weeks that followed independence – to put down the revolt of the Force Publique; to get the Belgian troops out; and to put an end to Katanga's secession. His impatience to see these three objectives quickly achieved brought him into conflict with Dr. Ralphe Bunche and Mr. Hammarskjöld.

Throughout this period he was in a perpetual state of frenzy. He listened to neither argument nor explanation. His personal behaviour was rude and often insulting, especially to Dr. Bunche and Mr. Hammarskjöld. He surrounded himself with a vast horde of advisers from all corners of the world. He seldom slept. He was kept going through his own restless energy, fortified by drink and hemp-smoking (two of the vices condemned in his book).

Lumumba's behaviour drove the U.N. representatives and his friends to despair. Although he had originally made President Kwame Nkrumah his closest political confidant, he began to ignore him once Dr. Nkrumah's advice began to conflict with his own

increasingly unrealistic ideas. Dr. Nkrumah tried in vain to warn
him in a confidential letter (12th September 1960): "You cannot
afford, my Brother, to be harsh and uncompromising. Do not force
Kasavubu out now. It will bring too much trouble in Leopoldville.
. . . Be as 'cool as a cucumber'." In vain Nkrumah urged him not
to rely on the Force Publique after their rebellion, until they could
be disciplined. "Their provincial loyalties are too strong and groups
of them are inclined to follow Ministers from their areas." In this
same letter Dr. Nkrumah pronounced a judgment which was soon
to be justified: "Patrice . . . if you fail, you have only yourself to
blame and it will be due to your unwillingness to face the facts of
life or what the Germans called *Realpolitik*. Your failure will be
a great blow to the African liberation movement, and you cannot
afford to fail. Your policy 'to do away with your enemies now' will
fail; you must adopt 'TACTICAL ACTION'. Remember the forces
pitched against you are legion. But the odds are in your favour, and
you will succeed if only you handle the situation carefully and tact-
fully. God bless. . . ."

But by the second week of September 1960, it was already too
late: Lumumba's mind was made up. All he desired was military
aid from anybody who would help him to achieve what he thought
was right.

Is there nothing at all to be said for Lumumba's point of view?
Nobody was willing to accept Katanga's secession – neither
Lumumba nor Kasavubu, nor any member of the Coalition Government. The U.N. itself was committed to supporting the unity of the
country. Faced with this situation, there were only two alternatives
– negotiations or the use of force.

Negotiations seemed ineffective for several reasons. Tshombe
insisted on a secession or, at best, a confederation, which for him
meant a loose association of autonomous Congolese republics each
controlling its own wealth. There was the danger that unless
Katanga's secession was ended quickly, others would follow suit.
If this happened the power of the Central Government would be
broken, and they would become victims of the tribal secessionists
and their foreign allies. These were not imaginary dangers. When it
became clear that Katanga might survive, Mr. Albert Kalonji proclaimed his separatist state in south Kasai – the Diamond State.
This was followed by a similar but less successful move by the
P.U.N.A.[3] leaders in Equatoria. The rot had begun to spread, and

[3] Parti de l'Union Nationale.

Arriving in London on the way back from New York to the Congo

Returning from the January 1960 Round Table Conference in Brussels

At Leopoldville after capture

Arriving in Brussels for the Round Table Conference

In transit, after capture

In the hands of General Mobutu's men

Lumumba's worst fears were being confirmed.

The other alternative was the use of force. If the U.N. would not help, who would?

V

Since we are here concerned with trying to understand Lumumba, it is necessary to see how these developments looked to him. Why did he choose to act as he did?

Lumumba was clearly in great difficulties. His own forces were too weak and unreliable to be effective, and the U.N. forces could not be used to put down secessionism. The African States, having rejected the use of force against Katanga – at their summit conference in Leopoldville in August 1960 – would not provide troops of their own. What alternatives were open to Lumumba? Fold his arms and hope that sooner or later negotiations might succeed; and meanwhile? Face the fragmentation of his Government's authority and power, as well as of his own?

Mr. Hammarskjöld's answer to Lumumba was that though the U.N. could not help him, there was nothing to stop the Central Government from acting on its own. But the Government had no transport, and barely enough troops. Lumumba's horde of clamouring advisers (by then largely Guinean and Eastern European) urged him to accept a Russian offer of aid since none would come from either the Western or the Afro-Asian states in defiance of a Security Council resolution opposing all direct military aid to the Congo. Russian planes were on the spot, having been used to transport U.N. forces; and a large consignment of trucks (initially intended for distribution by the U.N.) had fortuitously arrived. The Russians were willing to co-operate; the desperate Lumumba thought he saw a way out. Because he knew that his colleagues in the Government would never agree to a proposal to use Russian planes and trucks, he decided to act in secrecy and without their approval. His commander, General Victor Lundula, collected a few units of hand-picked troops and had them flown into Kasai by Russian planes in an attempt first to subdue the dissident Baluba Diamond State, and then to march on Katanga. The campaign itself was a failure; Lumumba's troops were inadequate. Despite a cruel campaign in which thousands of Baluba men, women and children perished, the Diamond State survived. A great cry for vengeance went up from the Baluba in Kasai. As far as they were concerned Lumumba was a marked man; and so were his associates. Later, their capital, Bakwanga, was to become a slaughterhouse for many of them.

It was Lumumba's decision to call directly for Russian support that led to his downfall. The amount of aid the Russians could give him was insufficient for his purposes. He had of course underestimated the amount of force he would need to deal with even the Kasai Baluba, let alone Katanga which was strongly reinforced with Belgian officers. His colleagues in the Government were naturally aggrieved that he should have acted behind their backs. Moreover, as Lumumba might have known, his decision could only precipitate cold war politics in the Congo. By relying on one of the cold war blocs he sinned not only against his Government and the U.N. but against Pan-Africanist doctrines. On his side, it could be argued that the cold war had been introduced before he took his decision: notably through the role of Belgium in Katanga. But at that point none of the major Western Powers (except possibly de Gaulle's France) was backing the Belgians. Although they were admittedly on the alert to intervene the moment the Russians became active, the Western powers were still holding to the policy of giving full support to the African group's initiative in the Security Council. The predictable result of Russian military aid to Lumumba was to turn the Western powers against him. They came to regard him as "a security risk".

All this would have mattered much less in the long run if the Central Government had not broken up. The Coalition Government had all along been an uneasy alliance between the Lumumbaists (who stood for a unitary type of constitution) and the federalists, headed by President Kasavubu. Neither side was capable of governing effectively without the other; both watched anxiously lest the other should gain a tactical advantage. Lumumba's secret deal with the Russians upset his colleagues; what worried them even more was the fear that the Lumumbaists might use the Russians to alter the internal balance of power. On 5th September 1960, President Kasavubu dismissed Lumumba as Prime Minister; in his turn Lumumba dismissed Kasavubu as President. Parliament rejected both dismissals. I have argued the rights and wrongs of this affair elsewhere.[4]

[4] *Congo Disaster*, Penguin Special, 1961.

VI

It seems incredible that so much should have happened in less than ten weeks, the span of Lumumba's rule. Before him was only another eighteen weeks of life. Although he was never able to regain his initiative, he never for a moment accepted his defeat. He fought with astounding courage and, at times, with foolhardy bravery. (His foolhardiness, in the end, proved to be his undoing.) He could still move parliament with his oratory; until Col. Mobutu shut it down. When he found the Leopoldville radio station closed to him on the day he was dismissed as Premier, he swept aside the armed guard, entered the building and commandeered a microphone to denounce President Kasavubu. Ten days later, on 15th September, vengeance-seeking Baluba soldiers set out to kill him. Throughout the day his life was in constant danger; he was forced to seek the protection of Ghanaian soldiers. Thereafter he agreed to accept U.N. protection in his official residence; but until Colonel Motubu threw a ring of soldiers round the U.N. guard, Lumumba regularly ventured abroad. He continued to lay plans for his return to power, using as his intermediary the Ghana Ambassador (until he was expelled), and his own staunchly loyal colleagues. He was seldom off the telephone which was kept open for him by the U.N. Antoine Gizenga and the devoted General Lundula were sent to Stanleyville to re-establish the "legal" government. On 27th November 1960, Lumumba telephoned when I happened to be with a number of his colleagues in their hide-out in the U.N. headquarters. He was in distress over the funeral arrangements for his child who had died in Geneva. He gave not the slightest indication of any plans to escape. But that night he drove straight through Colonel Mobutu's soldiers and disappeared into the night, heading for Stanleyville, four driving days away. His colleagues were incredulous the following morning when I told them of the rumours of his escape.

Typically, Lumumba took no precautions at all. He was arrested three days later at Mweka, near Port Franqui, after delivering an impromptu speech at a café where he had stopped for lunch. News of his speech had spread to the pursuing soldiers, who brutally manhandled him when making their arrest. Two days later, when he was brought back to Leopoldville, he was reported by the U.N. to have arrived "without his glasses and with a soiled shirt; his hair was in disorder, he had a blood clot on his cheek, and his hands were tied behind his back." The next day he was taken to Camp

Hardy, near Thysville. His head had been shaved overnight; his hands were still tied.

Both Mr. Rajeshwar Dayal, the U.N. representative in the Congo, and Mr. Hammarskjöld, vigorously intervened on Lumumba's behalf. Their efforts produced a stinging attack from President Kasavubu. Lumumba, he wrote, was being well-treated in the camp (other evidence shows that this was true; he had his Christmas dinner in the mess with the Camp commander). Kasavubu charged Lumumba with five offences – usurpation of public power; assaults on individual freedom accompanied by physical torture; attacks against the security of the State; organisation of hostile bands for purposes of devastation, massacre and pillage; inciting soldiers to commit offences. "Finally," President Kasavubu said to Hammarskjöld, "you yourself described the organisation of the military expeditions against the Province of South Kasai as a crime of genocide."

Kasavubu drew attention to what had been happening in Stanleyville where there had been "imprisonment of political opponents accompanied by serious torture and brutality, suppression of all individual liberty. . , . The victims include Mr. Songolo, the Minister for Communications, Senators Felé and Fataki, and other provincial and national parliamentarians. Many tribal chiefs have been beaten till blood was drawn, and hundreds of other prominent persons in the Province have had to flee for their lives. . . . You have doubtless communicated this information to the Afro-Asian and East European delegations, whose reactions are unfortunately very slow in manifesting themselves." He ended his letter to Hammarskjöld: "Please regard this question, as I and the entire country do, as a domestic matter. I trust that all who are concerned for Mr. Lumumba's welfare will take the same attitude and will not render too difficult the task of those who wish to restore the reign of justice and respect for human rights in the Republic of the Congo."

It is undoubtedly true that from the start of independence, acts of brutal violence and repression – especially against political opponents and tribal chiefs – occurred in Stanleyville and the rest of the Orientale province. Thirteen Lumumbaist provincial deputies, who had denounced the M.N.C., were imprisoned and severely beaten. Mr. Songolo, the Minister for Communications, temporarily lost the use of his sight after being beaten up. The U.N. tried in vain to get medical treatment for these prisoners. Their treatment did

improve and they were in fairly good shape when they were later
executed as a reprisal for Lumumba's murder. It would be wholly
misleading, therefore, to think that brutality in the Congo was one-
sided. Dreadful crimes were committed by both sides.

The most notorious charge pressed against Lumumba was that
he had sent an official communication on 15th September 1960 to
the Presidents of all the provincial Governments in the Congo,
except Katanga. The text of this letter was presented as evidence
to the U.N. Conciliation Commission by President Kasavubu.[5] It
read, in part:

> Establish an absolute dictatorship and apply it in all its
> forms . . . terrorism [is] essential to subdue the population
> . . . proceed systematically using the army to arrest all mem-
> bers of the opposition . . . imprison the Ministers, deputies,
> senators who sometimes abuse their Parliamentary immunity
> . . . arrest them all without pity . . . treat them with ten
> times more severity than ordinary individuals . . . revive the
> system of flogging and give the rebels ten lashes morning and
> evening for a maximum of seven consecutive days. Double the
> number in the case of Ministers, senators and deputies. . . .
> Inflict profound humiliation on the people thus arrested . . .
> strip them in public if possible in the presence of their wives
> and children . . . imprison repeated offenders in underground
> cells and prisons for at least six months never allowing them
> out to breathe fresh air. . . . If some of them succumb . . .
> which is possible and desirable . . . the truth should not be
> divulged but it should be announced, for instance, that Mr. X
> has escaped and cannot be found. . . . The measures of
> execution that I have indicated above constitute only the first
> stage of the basic régime that we hope will succeed in the
> Congo.
>
> . . . The second stage will be to destroy anyone who criticises
> us.

The letter concludes with a warning that its contents "should be
communicated only to those authorities under your orders in whom
you have complete confidence."

If genuine, this document would show that Lumumba could
hardly have been sane at the time of writing it. But is it genuine?
No proof as to its authenticity has ever been established. Two points

[5] "The Situation in the Congo," *UN Report* A/4 711, 20 March 1961.

of doubt arise. Why should Lumumba have sent such a communication "to all provincial presidents except Katanga", since they were not all his political supporters? The letter is stated to have been sent on 15th September 1960. Yet Lumumba spent that entire day in a military camp threatened hourly by vengeful Baluba soldiers. An enquiry by the U.N., who employed a Swiss expert for this purpose, led them to reject the document as a forgery.

Even in captivity Patrice Lumumba proved to be a grave embarrassment to the authorities. Col. Mobutu showed himself to be genuinely concerned about the prisoner's safety in Camp Hardy. There were no Baluba soldiers there, and the Commander in Charge of the troops holding Lumumba was a close relation of Lumumba's ally, the P.S.A.[6] deputy-leader, Cleophas Kamitatu. In Camp Hardy Lumumba lost no opportunity of haranguing the soldiers and trying to win them over to his side. Soon after his arrival the soldiers did, in fact, stage a mutiny over pay. Col. Mobutu and several Ministers rushed out to Camp Hardy and placated them by offering them more pay. Whether it was thought that Lumumba had succeeded in spreading disaffection, or whether his presence was undesirable for other reasons, is not clear. The Government made several attempts to persuade the Katanga authorities to accept Lumumba's transfer to one of their prisons; but Tshombe persistently refused. There are two reasons to explain the anxiety of Lumumba's opponents to rid themselves of him. The first is that they were terrified of his power; his uncanny ability to dominate any group of which he was a member was a real threat to his rivals, and, secondly, there was a constant danger of a coup by Lumumba's supporters. Shortly before he was finally taken from Camp Hardy the authorities became greatly alarmed by signs of a new rising tide of support for Lumumba. As their anxiety increased, the Government's needs to remove the pivot of the opposition forces became greater. The simple truth of the matter is that Lumumba had an electrifying effect on the Congolese; he was capable of arousing enthusiasm in a way that could not be matched by any other leader in the Congo. That was his strength. The strength of his opponents depended on their ability to neutralise him or, if necessary, to destroy him.

It was from Camp Hardy that Lumumba wrote his last letter, the authenticity of which appears to be fairly well established. The tone of the letter is that of a political testament rather than of a farewell letter to his family; it is the hand of the prophet writing for posterity.

[6] Parti Solidaire Africain.

My dear wife,

I am writing these words not knowing whether they will reach you, when they will reach you, and whether I shall still be alive when you read them. All through my struggle for the independence of my country, I have never doubted for a single instant the final triumph of the sacred cause to which my companions and I have devoted all our lives. But what we wished for our country, its right to an honourable life, to unstained dignity, to independence without restrictions, was never desired by the Belgian imperialists and their Western allies, who found direct and indirect support, both deliberate and unintentional, amongst certain high officials of the United Nations, that organisation in which we placed all our trust when we called on its assistance.

They have corrupted some of our compatriots and bribed others. They have helped to distort the truth and bring our independence into dishonour. How could I speak otherwise? Dead or alive, free or in prison by order of the imperialists, it is not I myself who count. It is the Congo, it is our poor people for whom independence has been transformed into a cage from beyond whose confines the outside world looks on us, sometimes with kindly sympathy, but at other times with joy and pleasure. But my faith will remain unshakeable. I know and I feel in my heart that sooner or later my people will rid themselves of all their enemies, both internal and external, and that they will rise as one man to say No to the degradation and shame of colonialism, and regain their dignity in the clear light of the sun.

We are not alone. Africa, Asia and the free liberated people from all corners of the world will always be found at the side of the millions of Congolese who will not abandon the struggle until the day when there are no longer any colonialists and their mercenaries in our country. As to my children, whom I leave and whom I may never see again, I should like them to be told that it is for them, as is it for every Congolese, to accomplish the sacred task of reconstructing our independence and our sovereignty: for without dignity there is no liberty, without justice there is no dignity, and without independence there are no free men.

Neither brutality, nor cruelty nor torture will ever bring me
to ask for mercy, for I prefer to die with my head unbowed, my
faith unshakeable and with profound trust in the destiny of
my country, rather than live under subjection and disregarding
sacred principles. History will one day have its say, but it will
not be the history that is taught in Brussels, Paris, Washington
or in the United Nations, but the history which will be taught
in the countries freed from imperialism and its puppets. Africa
will write her own history, and to the north and south of the
Sahara, it will be a glorious and dignified history.

Do not weep for me, my dear wife. I know that my country,
which is suffering so much, will know how to defend its
independence and its liberty. Long live the Congo! Long live
Africa!

PATRICE

On 17th January 1961, Lumumba and his two companions – Mr.
Mpolo, former Minister of Youth, and Mr. Okito, vice-president of
the Senate – were put aboard a small plane from which they were
later transferred, at Moanda, to a larger plane. There is evidence to
believe that the plane's original destination was Bakwanga, the
capital of the Baluba Diamond State. (According to the U.N. Commission, which later investigated Lumumba's murder, many prominent Lumumbaists were subsequently sent to Bakwanga, apparently
for security reasons. After the formality of a trial they were all
killed "in horrible circumstances" as a reprisal by the Baluba for
the campaign that had been waged against them. Bakwanga, says
the U.N. report, came to be known as "the slaughterhouse".) Why
the plane carrying Lumumba and his companions did not land there
is unknown; it is possible that the U.N. forces at the airport had
proved a deterrent. Instead of landing at Bakwanga, the plane continued for the last part of its hideous journey to Elisabethville.
Tshombe claims that he did not know that the prisoners were being
sent to Katanga until the plane was on its way.

According to the Belgian pilot's evidence, the three prisoners had
been roped together and were beaten by their captors throughout
the flight. The pilot testified: "They were so severely beaten up that
the Belgian crew was disgusted, and shut themselves up in the front
cabin of the crew." The prisoners could hardly stand when they
were taken from the plane at Elisabethville. They were manhandled
between two lines of soldiers and police who, according to an eye-

witness, clubbed them as they were dragged to a waiting jeep.

Tshombe's evidence to the U.N. Commission was that he had personally seen the prisoners on the night of their arrival (17th January); as a result of the beating and ill-treatment they had received in the plane, they were "in a sad state". Mr. Lumumba, "whose face was all puffed up, had appealed to him, somewhat piteously, for his protection". Two days later (19th January) the Katanga authorities issued a communique saying: "At the request of President Kasavubu and with the agreement of the Katanga Government, the traitor Patrice Lumumba has been transferred to Katanga, as the prison at Thysville no longer offers sufficient guarantees."

From the day of their arrival in Elisabethville, rumours of their death began to circulate. It was not until 10th February 1961, that the Katanga Government put out its crass version of the escape of the prisoners, followed a few days later by the announcement that they had been killed in an undisclosed village. This news was given at a press conference by Katanga's Minister of Interior, Mr. Munongo, in terms (according to the U.N. commission) "savouring of personal spite". Mr. Munongo said: "I know that some people will say we murdered him. My answer to that is: Prove it!"

The U.N. Commission found it impossible to prove anything. The principal witnesses refused to co-operate, and the bodies of the victims remain buried in unknown ground. Tentatively they concluded that Lumumba and his friends had in fact been killed on the night of their arrival in a villa not far from Elisabethville; probably in the presence of Mr. Tshombe, Mr. Munongo and Mr. Kibwe. Suspicion is cast on a Belgian mercenary (whose name is given) as the person who actually despatched Lumumba.

VII

Patrice Lumumba's death was officially anounced on 13th February 1961. He was still only thirty-six years old.

> The news came early in the morning.
> Lumumba is dead
> Lumumba is dead
> Anger split the whole world asunder.

A worker shouts:
  who can murder my age –
  the rails of the trains
        the length of the light of the sun
        we are all Lumumba
Lumumba.

A peasant stamps his feet
  the people never die –
      the heart is in the paddy
      growing along in struggle and song

Freedom that's Lumumba
Lumumba.

                  *   *   *

The news came early in the morning
        Lumumba is dead
        Lumumba is dead
        the earth shook
        the revolution marches on.

              Long live Lumumba.[7]

Black days followed the black deed; black headlines proclaimed;
in London – COMMONS IN UPROAR OVER MURDER OF MR. LUMUMBA;
in Cairo – AFRICANS STORM CAIRO'S DIPLOMATIC QUARTER. WEST
EMBASSIES ATTACK: PALL OF SMOKE OVER NILE; in the Congo –
BLOODSHED FEAR AFTER LUMUMBA'S DEATH; in Lagos – CROWDS
WITH STONES DEMONSTRATE AND ATTACK EUROPEANS; in New York –
FIGHTING AT U.N. OVER LUMUMBA. 'MURDERER' CRIES BY BRAWLING
NEGROES.

Describing the scene in the U.N., Philip Deane wrote[8]: "In small,
private wakes for Patrice Lumumba, the Afro-Asian delegates . . .
swallow their drinks as if there were a bitter taste in their mouths.
. . . They may not all have felt such concern for Lumumba alive
and active; but out of the buried corpse has arisen a powerful
spectre. Here, in the lobbies and corridors and bars of the United
Nations' glass palace, you can hear growing almost hour by hour,

[7] By an Indonesian poet, S. Anantaguna.
[8] *Observer* Foreign News Service, 15 February, 1961.

a menacing myth that could destroy the world organisation itself."

In the end the U.N. survived – was it ever really threatened? – and the Congo struggled back to its feet. Ironically, it now seems as if Lumumbaism has grown greatly in strength in the Congo since Lumumba's death. The mantle of leadership fell not on Antoine Gizenga, but on one of Lumumba's earliest colleagues, Cyrille Adoula. He has proved himself an active exponent of the essentials of Lumumbaism. Having brought together the majority of the surviving Lumumbaists (including General Lundula) and the federalists, he has succeeded by compromise and clever tactics in giving the Congo the stable coalition Lumumba failed to provide. He persuaded the U.N. to commit its troops to break the military power of Katanga – thus achieving eighteen months later what Lumumba had for so long demanded in vain. And he compelled Tshombe to come to him to discuss terms.

What is Lumumbaism?[9] Its essential features are:

(1) An undivided Congo united in true independence.

(2) Fundamental social reforms to eliminate colonial institutions; economic reforms based on socialist principles.

(3) A Pan-Africanist outlook; firm support for non-alignment.

(4) Creation of a supra-tribal national state, based on a nationalist (non-tribal) party and a strong central government; this permits a limited degree of autonomy for the provinces, while maintaining a unitary form of government.[10]

(5) Vigorous insistence on a strictly non-colonialist relationship with Belgium.

VIII

It is still too early to predict that Lumumbaism will triumph in the end. The Congo is not yet out of the woods. The problems that beset the ill-prepared young Republic in 1960 have become much more difficult because of the disaster that overtook it; but these problems have become less intractable.

If, in the end, the Congolese leaders are driven to the conclusion that Lumumbaism in its main essentials is the right policy for the

[9] Immanuel Wallerstein: "Lumumbaism without Lumumba," *The New Leader*, U.S.A., 28th August, 1961.

[10] The M.N.C. Congress at Luluarbourg (April 1960) recognised the importance of "a certain degree of autonomy for each of the six provinces in so far as matters of provincial interest were concerned".

Congo, why did Lumumba fail? The two most important reasons contributing to his failure were the disastrous conditions that engulfed the Congo in the weeks following independence, and Patrice Lumumba's instability.

The situation in the Congo in July and August 1960, demanded a leader capable of thinking quickly and acting calmly, and one willing to listen to tried and experienced friends. It needed, above all, a leader able to think realistically. Lumumba perfectly understood the dangers; but his proposals for dealing with them were hopelessly unrealistic. He took himself and his government from the frying-pan into the fire.

The brief weeks of Lumumba's Premiership were spent in continuous crisis. They would have tested the wisest and most experienced of statesmen; more especially since many of the problems Lumumba was called upon to face were matters with which he could not have been expected to be familiar. He was enmeshed in international politics and in the complex working of the United Nations. There was no time to learn. New crises piled on top of him daily. In sixty-eight days of disaster he faced a mutiny; the secession of two provinces; an incursion by Belgian troops; U.N. intervention; the advent of cold-war politics; a disastrous military campaign; economic chaos; total disruption of the administration, and the breakdown of law and order. Of these several disasters he can be held directly accountable for only two (admittedly two of the worst) – the disastrous military campaign against the Baluba, and the introduction of the Russian element of cold war into the Congo.[11]

Both these mistakes could have been avoided if he had listened to his own friends. But Lumumba's great weakness derived from what was also his strength: his blind confidence in himself. Just as nothing could deter him in his struggle for independence, so nothing

---

[11] Aimé Cesaire, the leader of Martinique, a distinguished Pan-African Marxist and an exponent of négritude has written on this point: "Without doubt one may not approve of all the political acts of Patrice Lumumba. No doubt he made mistakes, not the least of which was to allow himself to be caught in the trap of the cold war, 'this white man's folly'. But how can we fail to admit and understand these faults on the part of a man who was so young, and all things considered, so ill-prepared for the tremendous task which, brutally and overnight, devolved on him, and before which, at least his heart never flinched? At all events, there was one thing which cannot fail to command respect and admiration: that was his prodigious vitality, his extraordinary faith, his love for his people, his courage and his patriotism." *Jeune Afrique*, February, 1961.

could persuade him that he was wrong in the methods he chose to defend the Congo's integrity. He had an inflexible mind. This obduracy was made more difficult by his emotional instability and volatility. Confronted by a total breakdown of government at home, he flew to the U.N. and then made a tour of various capitals in Africa, Europe and North America; deaf to the entreaties of his friends to return home. He roped in advisers wherever he went and allowed them to badger him day and night; in the end he discarded first their advice, and then the advisers themselves. He lived in a perpetual state of frenzy. In a single day he wrote three consecutive protests to Mr. Hammarskjöld. When he was excited his mind seemed to retreat behind an impenetrable glass wall; nothing got through to him at all. It was unnerving. Incessantly he would repeat his own arguments over and over again. He saw enemies everywhere. In the end they destroyed him.

Extracts from the Publisher's Note
to the original French Edition[1]

It was on 17th December 1956 that M. Patrice Lumumba wrote to us for the first time with regard to the publication of the present work.

The manuscript of his book *The Congo, land of the future, is it threatened?* was sent to us at the end of January 1957. Various letters were then exchanged between us. We think it is of interest to reproduce in the following pages the more important letters received from M. Patrice Lumumba.

He had the intention, which we encouraged in order to ensure that the book would not be banned, of persuading some leading personality to write a preface to the book. Months went by without, to our knowledge, M. Lumumba succeeding in obtaining the guarantee he sought.

In the meantime, de-colonisation was speeded up in the Congo and numerous studies were published in the Colony and in the Metropolis, analysing the development of the political structure. M. Lumumba no doubt realised that certain chapters in his work called for modification. Thenceforth political activity seemed to take up more of his attention than this revision.

As it stands, the work is, at all events. extremely interesting, and it seemed to be our duty to pass on this unpublished document to posterity. We publish it without any comment or deletions. We ask the reader to excuse certain mutilated phrases which were illegible in the text. Similarly, we have indicated, without reproducing them, the places where the author has struck out certain passages in his manuscript.

[1] Published by l'Office de Publicité, Brussels, 1961.

P.H.LUMUMBA
B.P.N°29
STANLEYVILLE.   Stanleyville,le 2 février 1957.

            Monsieur l'Administrateur-Délégué
            de l'OFFICE DE PUBLICITE
            16,Rue Marcq
            BRUXELLES.

Monsieur l'Administrateur-Délégué,

            Faisant suite à votre lettre n° P.S./ED/6626 du 23 janvier
écoulé,j'ai l'honneur de vous faire parvenir,en annexe,une coupure
du journal belge "L'Afrique et le Monde" du 30.11.1954,journal
édité à Bruxelles et qui contient mon curriculum vitae comme vous
le remarquerez sous le titre "M.LUMUMBA PATRICE,Président de
l'A.E.S.à l'honneur".La photographie publiée au milieu de cet
article est la mienne.

                            - 2 -

            Je suivis,en 1948,des cours de correspondant en langue française
dans un Institut d'enseignement par correspondance.

            Autodidacte,je n'ai jamais cessé d'apprendre et,actuellement,
j'étudie le Droit,la Philosophie et les Sciences économiques,
administratives.Je suis aidé en cela par des professeurs bénévoles
européens.

            Je prépare actuellement un nouveau livre qui,comme je l'espère,
aura un intérêt sur le plan international.Ce livre traitera de la
colonisation en Afrique Noire,des relations Blancs-Noirs ou entre
métropoles et colonies,ainsi que de l'Avenir eurafricain.

            Les autres livres que je compte publier après celui-ci traite-
ront divers sujets (études,romans etc.) dont le fond est de faire
connaître l'âme noire et le vrai visage de
l'Afrique,raconté et décrit par un Africain.

            J'espère que ces renseignements vous auront suffit pour que
vous ayez une idée sur ma biographie et mes projets d'avenir.

            J'ai toujours été au service du Gouvernement,mais suis actuelle-
ment en disponibilité pour convenances personnelles.Sans aucune
indiscrétion,je compte embrasser une activité libérale et indépendante.
Cela me permettra de mieux concentrer mes efforts pour l'évolution
de mon Pays.et de prêter ma collaboration aux Belges chargés de la
civilisation et de l'industrialisation du Congo.

            Dans l'attente du plaisir de vous lire,je vous prie d'agréer,
Monsieur l'Administrateur-Délégué,l'assurance de ma considération la
plus distinguée.-

*The opening and conclusion of Lumumba's second letter to his
original publisher.*

Letters from the Author to the original Publisher

from Patrice LUMUMBA

Stanleyville
10 January 1957

To the Managing Director
Office de Publicité
Rue Marcq, 16
Brussels

Dear Sir,

Further to my letter of the 31st December and in reply to your letter P.S./ED/6478 of the 10th December 1956, I have pleasure in sending you by the same mail a copy of my manuscript; *The Congo, land of the future, is it threatened?* with a view to publication by your firm.

Should my work be accepted for publication I should be grateful if you would let me know your terms.

My aims in writing my book are as follows:
1. to convey the ideas and aspirations of the Congolese people on the various economic, social and political problems which are of particular concern to them, and on the solution of which—a happy solution, I hope—depend the future of the Congo and the success of Belgium's colonial mission;
2. to enlighten the Belgian authorities in particular, and the colonists in general, as to the way in which the Africans in the Congo envisage their future in the world of today and tomorrow;
3. to give accurate, factual explanations of the reasons for the

B

anxiety and discontent prevailing amongst the Congolese population;

4. to suggest to African political leaders certain reforms which seem to me to be indispensable if the Belgians really wish to avoid a crisis and a loss of confidence among the African population whom they administer;

5. to draw the attention of the Congolese to the bad [a word missing] which lie in wait for our country, and especially to the wicked anti-Belgian propaganda which is already being carried out surreptitiously in the Congo with the direct aim of separating the Congolese from the Belgians;

6. to emphasise the need for a harmonisation of social relations between Belgians and Congolese;

7. to defend Belgian sovereignty in Africa, for the Belgian colonial mission has become the joint mission of Belgians and Congolese.

It is desirable that all sections of the Belgian public, at home and in the Colony, should know what the Congolese are thinking about the problems raised by the presence of Europeans in their country. It is essential that they should also know exactly what are the wishes of their wards. It is equally desirable that they should understand the need for sincere and frank discussion between the two races involved.

At the same time, it is desirable that the opinion of the Congolese, in their capacity as Belgian citizens and as subjects of Belgian administration, should be heard by all those entrusted with the study of African problems. It is a matter which involves the interests and prestige of the Belgian Administration.

For your guidance, I take the liberty of pointing out that for some years now I have been concerned with the development of my fellow Congolese. As a former President of the Association of *Evolués*[1] and of various cultural and occupational groups (not to mention my share in the establishment and running of inter-racial Clubs for

---

[1] *Evolué*. A term used to describe Congolese who "evolved" through education from a purely tribal way of living. They had been taught to speak French, embraced Christianity and renounced polygamy. They were the emergent "middle class" which Belgian policy aimed to produce. They were mainly civil servants, teachers, priests and parsons, white-collar workers and artisans. They were regarded by Belgians, and looked upon themselves, as the élite: the urbanised, partly westernised "new men" of the Congolese society.

Belgians and Congolese), I have had frequent opportunities of discussing, both with the colonial authorities and with the Congolese, the various problems which I have dealt with in my work. I have studied them very fully and the conclusions I have drawn are the fruit of long experience.

I have written this book after carrying out a careful investigation into various problems of general interest in the development of the Belgo-Congolese community. These articles, as Mr. Songolo says in the attached copy of *L'Afrique et le Monde* have always been valued by all readers, both European and African, and I have in my possession a large number of appreciative comments on them.

In 1948, I took a correspondence course in the French language organised by a correspondence college.

I am self-taught and I have never stopped learning. At present I am studying Law, Philosophy, Economics, Social Science and Administration. I am helped in this by European teachers who give their services free of charge.

At the moment, I am working on another book which will, I hope, be of international interest. This book will deal with colonisation in Tropical Africa. relations between Whites and Blacks, or between home countries and colonies, and with the future of Euro-Africa.

The other books which I hope to publish after that will deal with various subjects (studies, novels, etc.) the aim of which is to make known the soul of the African and the real face of Africa, told and described by an African.

I hope that these details will be adequate to give you an idea of my career and my future plans.

I have always been in Government service, but at present I have no commitments, for personal reasons. Without being indiscreet, I may say that I hope to take up independent work in one of the liberal professions. This will enable me to devote all my efforts to the cause of the development of my country and to collaborate with the Belgians, whose task it is to civilise and industrialise the Congo.

Looking forward to hearing from you, I remain,

Yours faithfully,

[signed] Patrice LUMUMBA

from Patrice LUMUMBA

Stanleyville
2 February 1957

To the Managing Director
Office de Publicité
Rue Marcq, 16
Brussels

Dear Sir,

Further to your letter No. P.S./ED/6626 dated the 23rd January last, I have the honour to send you attached herewith a cutting from a Belgian paper *L'Afrique et le Monde* dated 30 November 1954, published in Brussels, in which you will find details of my career under the title, "M. Patrice LUMUMBA, Honorary Chairman of the Stanleyville *Evolués* Association". The photograph published in the centre of this article is of myself.

I think it might be helpful to give you a few further details concerning my biography.

I am the founder-President of the *Amicale des Postiers* [Post Office Workers' Friendly Society]. Since 1955, this association, which originally catered only for native Post Office workers, has included European and Congolese officials in the postal services.

After being Secretary of A.P.I.C. (Association of Native Public Servants)—a union which includes all native officials in the African Administration (Eastern Province), I was elected President in 1955 and I still hold that office.

In addition, I am a founder member of the Committee of the BELGO-CONGOLESE UNION in Stanleyville, an inter-racial association which includes Belgians and Congolese.

With regard to my family, I now have three children of whom the older two [boys] attend school along with European children at the Stanleyville Royal Athenaeum.

I am one of the first Congolese to be granted *Immatriculation*[2] and given equal status with Belgians.

I was a member of the delegation of Congolese leaders who visited Belgium in 1956 at the invitation of the Minister for the Colonies, and at the end of my study tour I made a statement to the *Agence Belga* in Brussels which was reproduced in papers in

[2] *Immatriculation*: see p. 51.

Belgium and the Congo, to the great satisfaction of Belgians and Congolese.

I was presented to King BAUDOUIN during his visit to Stanleyville in 1955, and had a long talk with him.

With regard to my intellectual and social activities, apart from being chairman of several cultural groups for Africans, I am a regular contributor to several newspapers in the Congo and also to *L'Afrique et le Monde,* a Belgian newspaper published in Belguim. In addition, I am chief editor of the post office journal *L'Echo,* the quarterly publication of the Postal Workers' Friendly Society for the Eastern Province. It was at my request that the Governor General authorised me, by his decision issued in the Official Bulletin of the Belgian Congo, to publish this journal. I may, therefore, be ranked amongst the journalists editing newspapers in the Congo.

For more than six years I have been publishing articles dealing amongst the various social strata of the native population.

I hope you will have been able to appreciate that since last year Belgian circles have been somewhat uneasy regarding the confused situation in the Congo.

To speak bluntly, a stormy future lies ahead of the Congo. In this book I hope to offer both a solution and a remedy to the existing uneasiness, hesitation, confusion and doubts. If the reforms which I have recommended here are put into effect within a relatively short time, this will do much to remove the present difficulties which separate White and Black in the Congo.

I am convinced, and in this I have the support of leading people who have studied my manuscript, that if my book is published it will be a great success in the Congo with both Africans and Belgians.

The main aim of my book, as I see it, is to bring home to the Belgians and the Congolese the imperative and urgent need to achieve forthwith a brotherly understanding which will lead to a definite union. This union will be cemented by the affection which Congolese and Belgians must display towards each other.

Finally, I should be most happy to have your suggestions as to the presentation of the book. I should like the cover to represent some aspect of Africa which I leave you to select.

I look forward to hearing your decision and remain, with thanks in anticipation,

Yours truly,

[signed] Patrice LUMUMBA

AIM OF THIS WORK

Author's Introduction

The aim of this work is to make a contribution towards the search for a solution for the present and future problems of the Congo. I do not claim to offer the solution, since there are others more competent and qualified than myself, namely the rulers of the country and those responsible for Belgian colonial policy. My aim must be interpreted merely as a desire to take part in the free discussion of the complex problems confronting the country, since the clash of ideas produces light. It is as a citizen of this African continent that I wish to take part in the debate which is now opening.

For a long time past the Belgians have constantly been appealing for the collaboration of the Congolese élite.[1] It is in reply to this appeal that I have undertaken to study some current problems which affect our everyday life; I reserve the right to return to them later or to study certain other questions of general interest which sometimes escape the attention of our rulers.

My intention is not to teach our rulers, or show them the way to go—that would be presumptuous—but to enlighten them on the mysteries of the African soul: what the Congolese think of the hard facts of life, of their future and their union with the Belgians.

When I said that certain questions sometimes escape the attention of our rulers I did so advisedly, for it is not easy to plumb the African soul. Colonists who have undertaken a study of Bantu philosophy know only too well that the African does not easily confide in a "foreigner".

Amongst many other examples, we have recently experienced

[1] élite: see note on *Evolué* p. 2.

something which confirms this instinctive mistrust of the Congolese for the white man: the practices of the Kitawala,[2] this politico-religious sect which has been often spoken of in the past and is still the subject of passionate debate.

What are the motive forces, the mystic elements upon which that sect is based? Is it hatred of the white man, the attempt to find a religion appropriate to their mentality, Moslem proselytism or what? Such are the questions which the white men ask themselves —questions which have already been answered by investigators who have studied the problem on the spot.

Although this movement may be stopped for a short time—at least in its outward manifestations—it nevertheless continues in the soul of those who practise it; when they are arrested and interned, they are always replaced by other neophytes. This is a vicious circle.

In an endeavour to satisfy my curiosity and to obtain a clear idea about the basis of this movement, I approached some followers of the Kitawala sect and asked them some precise questions. My request was given short shrift, as they took me for an emissary of the Whites. Finally, after using much skill and diplomacy to prove to them that this was not the case, and that I was their "blood brother" and could not betray them, they decided, with some hesitation, to reveal the mysteries of their sect.

I asked them to tell me sincerely if what they had told me was exactly the same as what they were telling a representative of the Government who was carrying out an investigation among them at that time. They replied: "Not at all. No amount of pressure will ever make us tell him what we have just told you; on the contrary we shall merely tell him generalities; we shall say nothing more even if he interrogates us a hundred times."

I am convinced that they have never revealed to a white man some of the things which they told me in confidence, precisely because of that mistrust caused by the fear of reprisals. What they told me with great conviction is the opposite of what certain

---

[2] *Kitawala.* A religious sect outlawed by the Belgian authorities. Two of its leaders 'Jesus Christ' and 'Hallelujah' were hanged in 1943. The word is a dialect form of Watchtower—a splinter religious organisation emanating from the United States. It has followers in many parts of Africa, and is one of the numerous religious sects that have sprung up in the Congo—the best-known being Kibanguism. Father Van Wing has written of these sects: "In the countryside and in the big towns and workers' settlements hatred of the White (man) is propagated mainly by the politico-religious sects called Kibanguism, Kitawala and others, which can operate only in secret."

people allege.

I carried out this little investigation to show how important it is that the Congolese élite, who enjoy the confidence of their fellow Congolese and can communicate freely with them without any *arrière pensée*, should work in close collaboration with the Belgians to enlighten them on certain questions and thus help them in the conduct of native affairs. It is through the Congolese élite that the Belgians will plumb the depths of the African soul and guide it better.

After this little digression, I must now return to my theme.

This study covers a number of questions which are in the minds of the Congolese, questions which I have investigated by means of a wide survey of public opinion.

The variety of my experience in the social field has enabled me to establish many contacts with various sections of the population, in the course of which I have discussed numerous social and political questions concerning the future of the Congo.

My investigations have not been limited to the *evolué* class; they have also been carried out among the working-class and the traditionalist leaders—the chiefs, nobles, and others. I have established contact with people of all types and all shades of opinion. In consequence, I feel competent to summarise the various opinions which were expressed without going too wide of the mark. To these opinions I shall add my personal reflections on the problems concerned.

I make no claim to speak here on behalf of all the Congolese; that would be presumptuous, for there are many others who possibly do not share my opinion. Besides, no one has a monopoly of truth or wisdom. As I emphasised at the outset, this is merely a contribution towards the search for the effective solutions and new methods which are essential in view of the evolution of the Congo.

Precisely at this moment, when heated controversy is beginning to rage between the colonisers and the colonised on the principles of administration and the shape of the new society which is being constructed, and when the Congo is entering its new phase, it is important to study all sides of the problem, to pick out the basic principles, and to reform what is outmoded, so that whatever action is taken may be suited to the needs of the hour.

This vast programme requires the collaboration of all those who are willing to put their experience, intelligence and sound judgment at the disposal of the Government in its difficult task.

My ultimate aim is certainly not to dictate to the Government what measures it should take, but to try to find a constructive basis for discussion, a discussion which is so much desired and has been so long awaited; a sincere, frank discussion which will enable Whites and Blacks, colonisers and colonised, to understand each other, and to say freely, as friends and brothers, what they think and what they want, without mincing their words.

This discussion must obviously not be made for the occasion for sterile and heated argument; on the contrary, it must be constructive and intelligent, in order to overcome—for the common good—many difficulties which arise from a failure by the two parties to understand each other.

CHAPTER I

The Purpose of Colonisation

Recently there have been heated discussions about the Congo in Belgium, in the Congo itself and abroad. There are strong differences of opinion and outlook among the protagonists. Some make accusations against the Belgians and belittle their work; others pay tribute to Belgium for its great achievements in Africa; others again demand independence, autonomy, integration, either immediately or in a few decades; the Government itself advocates the integration of Belgians and Congolese in the great Belgo-Congolese community.

Who is right? What attitude should be adopted towards these proposals? This it what I propose to consider, avoiding all bias and inspired only by a desire for objectivity and for the good of the country.

Why are the Belgians in Africa? What is the political system which they have chosen in their colonisation of the Congo? What is the final aim of that colonisation?

The Belgians have a twofold aim in Africa: economic and humanitarian.

According to the definition given by M. Fallot, colonisation is "the influence of a civilised people on a people of lower civilisation, exercised with the aim of steadily transforming the latter by the development of its natural resources and by the improvement of the moral and material condition of the native people".

Belgium itself has defined its policy as follows (*Code* page 29):

"Belgium's mission in the Congo is essentially a civilising one. It has a twofold aim. On the moral plane, it is to ensure the well-being of the native population and their development by the broadening of individual liberty, the steady relinquishment of polygamy, the development of private property and the support of institutions and undertakings promoting native education and giving the natives an understanding and appreciation of the advantages of civilisation (*Colonial Charter*, Article 5). On the economic plane, Belgium's mission is to achieve the development of the colony for the benefit of the natives and, to this end, to work towards an increasingly complete organisation of the country which will strengthen order and peace and guarantee the protection and expansion of the various branches of economic activity: agriculture, commerce and industry."

If we glance back over the past and compare the lot of the African in the Free State[1] with his lot in the year 1956, contrasting the Congo of yesterday and today, we can freely admit that Belgium has not failed in its mission and that, apart from a few mistakes which are inherent in any human activity, much that is fine and great has been achieved and is still being achieved.

We would urge those who are only willing to see the bad side of colonisation to weigh up the good and the bad to see which is the greater.

To whom do we owe our liberation from that odious trade practised by the bloodthirsty Arabs and their allies, those inhuman brigands who ravaged the country?

At a time when our people were suffering from these atrocities, when they were being decimated by sleeping sickness and by that grim tragedy which was taking place in Manyema[2] and throughout the Congo, when thousands of the inhabitants of the country were being carried away in chains to be sold like cattle in gruesome markets, other countries—which were more powerful than Belgium —remained indifferent to our fate and left us to perish.

Belgium, moved by a very sincere and humanitarian idealism, came to our help and, with the assistance of doughty native fighters, was able to rout the enemy, to eradicate disease, to teach us and to eliminate certain barbarous practices from our customs, thus restoring our human dignity and turning us into free, happy vigorous, civilised men.

The former dark continent, travestied in so many pictures, has today become one of the most beautiful countries of Africa, this

[1] In accordance with the Treaty of Berlin, 1885, Leopold II of Belgium held the Congo as his personal property under the name of the Congo Free State. He bequeathed it to the Belgians in 1908.

[2] *Manyema*: a great slave-trading stronghold active even at the end of the nineteenth century.

wonderful land of the Congo in which the African people are developing even more rapidly than did the Belgians themselves.

This rapid development is explained easily enough by the fact that the Belgians had to toil for centuries to reach their present stage of development whilst we are merely benefiting from the fruit of their experience and work. Hence our development will be much quicker than theirs.

To whom do we owe this fortunate situation? To the Belgians. Any genuinely humane and reasonable man must show gratitude and respect for the immense work achieved in this country at a cost of incalculable material and human sacrifice.

As regards the mistakes which were made, I have already said that they are inherent in any human activity, be it in Africa, Europe or any other country of the world; this is virtually a truism.

In my humble opinion, there is absolutely no point in constantly raking up these mistakes from the past. What matters now is to find new solutions. Does that mean that I excuse the Belgians or blindly take up their defence? No. I only excuse what is excusable and I only defend what can be defended.

Let us stop railing against these few mistakes.

Our only aim should be to fill out the gaps, close the cracks, and work out together the solid foundations for the Belgo-Congolese community in a spirit of harmony, humanity and justice.

This Belgo-Congolese community is in process of establishment and I recall with pleasure the declaration made by His Majesty King Baudouin, our well-loved King, that "Belgium and the Congo constitute a single nation". The King's thought is clear: Belgians and Congolese are all citizens, just like Walloons and Flemings, and they must live side by side in true brotherhood. This is the goal towards which we are all striving, and we cannot doubt the sincerity of our King's intentions.

We must jealously defend our joint achievements; that defence can be nothing other than a better understanding between Belgians and Congolese, a firm union which will be cemented by mutual affection.

Let us beware of doubtful "Liberators" who think of us only at harvest time; for all we know their aim may be to pocket our wealth and plunge us back again into even more abject misery! But when anyone discusses our affairs disinterestedly, let us thank him sincerely.

Paternalism

There are many people who criticise this system of tutelage and only see its bad side. But it provides protection for the native against the encroachments of certain unscrupulous people; its object is to improve the moral and material condition of the natives.

The guardianship of the courts, the Commission for the Protection of the Natives,[3] the mother and child welfare system, free medical services in the hospitals and clinics (payment is now being introduced), the establishment of the Native Welfare Fund and various other funds, the baby clinics, etc., all these, in my view, are important measures produced by the system of tutelage.

I readily admit that this system is out of date as regards a certain class of the population which is rising to emancipation, but it is still necessary for the uneducated masses who are unable to defend themselves and look after themselves. In all our discussions, we ought to devote particular attention to them, as they still form the majority of the population.

[3] See p. 38.

CHAPTER II

Economic Integration

Equality in the labour market is the dream of all the Congolese; it is a legitimate dream which is in accordance with Article 23 of the *Declaration of Human Rights*: "Everyone, without any discrimination, has the right to equal pay for equal work. Everyone who works has the right to just and favourable remuneration, ensuring for himself and his family an existence worthy of human dignity, supplemented if necessary by other means of social protection."

In general, the Congolese worker has not yet reached his due standard of living. As Governor General Ryckmans has stated recently in an article published in the Colonial press, it is admitted that the wages paid to the natives are still inadequate. At the present time, the majority earn less than 500 francs a month;[1] this can be confirmed from the tariffs of legal minimum wages in various areas; only in Leopoldville can workers earn anything approaching a thousand francs.

The same unsatisfactory state of affairs is found in the various trades, both in the public and private sector. There is ample evidence of this in the recent fiercely-supported wage claims.

My little investigation on this subject has led me to the conclusion that the minimum necessary to sustain life—the absolute minimum for an unskilled worker without a family—is 1,300 francs for food alone, made up as follows: 3 francs for breakfast (one cup of coffee with a few native fritters), twenty francs for the mid-day meal and twenty francs for the evening meal, making a total of forty-three francs per day. This is, of course, on a diet only of manioc leaves or spinach, as a kilogramme of meat of the lowest quality, (generally called servants' meat), costs not less than forty

[1] 140 francs to £1.

francs.

For a salaried worker of medium social status—the status to which any educated Congolese is entitled—the average monthly household expenditure will vary between 3,000 and 5,000 francs, depending on the size of his family.

Let us see exactly what will be the expenditure, without any luxury, of a middle-grade, *evolué* salaried worker, the father of two children—a household of four; his way of life is no longer primitive and his native diet has been substantially improved by the addition of some items of European diet: coffee, tea, milk, bread, sweet-stuffs, potatoes, vegetables, fruit, meat, etc.:

Breakfast	5 francs per day for four persons =	20 francs
Lunch	30 francs per day for four persons =	120 francs
Dinner	20 francs per day for four persons =	80 francs
		220 francs

Monthly expenditure 220 × 30 days = 6,600 francs

To the cost of food, we must add the other requirements of a family and the education of the children.

The under-nourishment of the Congolese is due solely to the inadequacy of their diet. How is it possible to obtain a varied diet, rich in vitamins, without the necessary financial resources?

The physical and mental health of the people demand an increase in wages.

It should also be noticed, to take an example, that some Congolese *evolués* whose children go to schools belonging to the European system, have to feed and keep their children at virtually the same standard as the children of Europeans of modest means—particularly in regard to clothing. This is in order to avoid harming the children psychologically in their contacts with their European fellow pupils by an excessive difference both in clothing and diet.

These children cannot go to school in rags, barefoot, with pieces of ҫhikwang[2] in their hands, since all the children are required to maintain a very high standard of cleanliness, both in regard to their clothing and their persons; they cannot breakfast on *Chikwang* in the classroom while their European comrades are eating bread and jam; besides the teachers would never allow it.

[2] *Chikwang*: A cheap cereal food that forms part of the subsistence diet of the poorest people.

There is a real duel between employers and workers over wages. Employers claim that the Blacks are already earning enough, that their output is inadequate, and that, in these conditions, any increase in wages is unjustified. What is to be done in the face of this clash of interests? In my view, a compromise is essential. The employers undoubtedly have the right to require from their workers a higher output to match the wage which they are claiming. The workers also have the right to demand a fair wage from their employers. If no agreement can be reached between employers and workers, logic requires concessions from both sides.

If the output of Congolese workers is really inadequate, how is it possible to explain the Congo's great economic development? Those vast and prosperous plantations scattered over the country, the roads, bridges, large blocks of flats and other buildings, the operations of the big mining companies, the management of local tax and post offices, etc., all these are surely the product of African labour.

The Europeans bring to the Congo their capital, their intelligence and their experience, whilst the natives supply their energy, muscle and labour power; the European supervises and directs, while the African works hard, loyally and willingly. It is thanks to this steady work and loyal co-operation on the part of the Congolese that these colonial projects are making such progress.

We agree that some workers disregard their contractual obligations and do not improve their output; but we must avoid the sweeping generalisation that the output of the Africans is poor.

Under this heading of productivity, there are two closely-linked conditions which must be fulfilled in order to obtain a better output from all manual or salaried workers:

1. *A good vocational training,* without which it is difficult for an employee to acquire a conscientious attitude to his work. It has been proved that Congolese who have received a suitable vocational or technical training—such as medical and agricultural assistants, trained postal-workers from the postal school, trained male nurses, radio operators from the tele-communications school, and skilled workers from the higher and intermediate vocational schools—are on the whole above the average in efficiency, and most conscientious workers.

Their greater efficiency is due, not only to practice, but also to the fact that they know the technical details of their trade and can solve certain questions on their own without the help of their employer—questions which a mere routine worker would often be unable to solve without that help.

In the interests both of the employers and the workers of the Congo, it is essential to establish the maximum number of vocational and technical schools for trade apprentices so that, in the near or distant future, every worker may become a specialist in his trade. That would provide firms with a body of first-class workers.

A man should not be a jack-of-all-trades as is the case at present in the Congo, where Africans move from one type of employment to another, so that a man who yesterday was a labourer may today become a checker, clerk, male nurse, cashier, stoker, or what have you.

2. *An adequate and fair wage,* a real incentive without which it is illusory to hope for a better output from the workers.

Some manual and salaried workers have said to me: "What is the point of working hard, toiling away uselessly, when our efforts will not be rewarded by an appropriate wage."

I explained to them that, if the manual and salaried workers, as a whole, improved their efficiency, that would increase the profits of the firms and, in consequence, would lead to a raising of wages; for it should not be forgotten that employers are afraid that an increase of wages without a compensating increase in productivity might ruin them. But they made short shrift of this argument: "If your thesis is valid and practicable, how is it that the few top-grade manual and salaried workers who have now reached a standard of efficiency equal to that of European workers are not paid on the same basis as the latter, and do not even receive half the lowest wage paid to Europeans? As those workers are not paid correspondingly, although at present they are only a minority and would not place a heavy burden on the employers, we think it would be Utopian to dream of a general regrading of Congolese wages, even if the Congolese were to double their efficiency."

I would urge those who may try to do slipshod work, on the pretext that they are less well-paid, not to lose heart in this struggle for a better life: that sort of conduct merely weakens our position. The more we increase our efficiency and observe our contractual obligations, the stronger will be our claim. Discouragement does not help the development of a nation. Whatever may be the difficulties which confront us, and they are difficulties with which every nation is familiar, we must continue our efforts with an unshakeable will and with absolute confidence in ourselves.

We shall never be able to improve our situation by laziness, but only by an unyielding and ever-increasing common effort. The men of good will – and there are many of them – must give the lead to the others.

As it is admitted that present wages are inadequate, the most elementary justice demands that this collective claim for higher wages should be granted as far as possible.

The Congolese ask for nothing better than to earn 100 francs a month, provided that, with those 100 francs, they can live more or less decently, meet their children's requirements adequately and have something left over to put aside for the future.

How can a man improve his standard of living, secure decent conditions for his family, pay for his children's education and, in general, enter the ranks of the civilised, with such an inadequate income?

How many really deserving Congolese, to whom the card of civic merit[s] has been granted because their way of life was virtually the same as . . . [illegible] . . . it must be realised that, owing to their straitened circumstances, they are living in huts or rented houses, without the bare minimum of comforts and with their children inadequately provided for, etc. . . .

And how bitter is their disappointment when they find that other people, wealthier but less civilised than themselves, are easily able to obtain those cards which are so much desired by the élite, cards which grant their holders equal status with the Europeans in certain matters?

Is it realised that the main cause of dishonesty among many Congolese (cashier-foremen, tax collectors and officials handling public funds) is their low rate of pay, on which they cannot possibly make ends meet, even with the best will in the world? In these circumstances, even the most honest will not always maintain their standards. Overwhelmed by the problems of living and by hunger, they are less able to resist temptation and they often end by succumbing. Some cashier-foremen are paid from [words illegible] to [illegible] per month and, to crown it all, they are only paid several months in arrears.

It would not be correct to deduce from this that an increase in salaries will automatically eliminate all dishonest practices, and that no African will ever be able to steal or embezzle money, but it has to be admitted, in all objectivity, that the number will be

[s] The Civic Merit Card: See p. 45.

considerably reduced, since the main cause for these malpractices will thus be eliminated.

In the interests of security itself, consideration should be given to the possibility of removing all the factors which may encourage or give rise to crimes of any kind.

It is admitted that some Congolese do earn a good living, but they are only a minority whom I shall ignore since I am concerned with the majority and not with special cases.

It should also be pointed out that the Congo is not the only country in Africa in which the Blacks are less well-paid than the Whites. On the contrary, we are amongst the best administered and happiest colonies in the African continent. Our standard of life is far superior to that of the Africans in some other countries. But that ought not to prevent us from moving forward all the time, since the ambition of Overseas Belgium is to be amongst the leaders in the march towards progress and a humane life.

The Congolese élite have no wish to ignore what has been accomplished; they only wish to be "Belgians" and to be entitled to the same well-being and the same rights, given equal merits, of course. This desire is praiseworthy and in accordance with human justice.

I should also like to reply to the argument which is often put forward by some people according to which (a) Congolese workers already earn much more than workers in metropolitan Belgium and (b) Congolese wages should be based on the Belgian scale.

In regard to the first point, this is true only for a tiny minority. Let us examine the position more closely. In Belgium, the monthly wage of a young clerk with a lower secondary education (i.e. who has not studied classics[4]) varies between 50,000 and 77,000 francs or more, plus cost of living allowance, plus an increment of 1,800 francs every two years, plus promotion every two years if he has a good report. The monthly wage of a servant boy or night watchman varies between 44,200 and 55,400 francs, plus an increment of 800 francs every two years, plus family allowances, plus all other benefits.

In the Congo, the basic wage of a native clerk who has had the same full lower secondary education (four years of secondary school under the Congolese system) as his Belgian colleague, is fixed at 15,000 francs plus thirty per cent cost of living index, plus family allowance, plus promotion every three years, plus annual increment

[4] Lumumba is referring to academic subjects such as those referred to on p. 26.

of two, three or three-and-a-half per cent depending on whether his report is good, very good or excellent.

I agree that the general standard of education of a Belgian is superior to that of a native who has had the same schooling in the Congo; that is a question of curriculum.

This comparison between the wage of a Belgian clerk and a Congolese clerk, both of whom have had the same schooling, is sufficient in itself to rebut the assertions of certain people who oppose an increase in African salaries under cover of specious arguments.

As regards the second point, I do not think that it would be quite fair to apply the Belgian salary scale in the Congo, for the simple reason that the cost of living in Africa is higher than in Belgium (with the exception, of course, of the mass of the people who live on a lower diet), and because the Blacks pay more than the Europeans for many articles imported from Europe. That may appear strange at first sight, but it is a fact. Whereas Europeans are often granted discounts in the shops (e.g. for large families) these are never granted to the Africans, who always buy at full price and are frequently cheated by unscrupulous foreign traders who profit by the ignorance of the Africans by putting their prices up during the first three days after each pay day.

In short, wages in the Congo should be based not on the Belgian scale but on local requirements. It is impossible to compare two sets of circumstances which are fundamentally different.

To sum up:

1. The wages of all African workers should be increased to keep pace with the cost of living, in view of the fact that this is increasing much faster than wage rates;

2. The democratic formula "equal pay for equal work" should be applied, in order to get rid of any idea of racial discrimination.

As I wish to be conciliatory, I shall admit that it is fair for a European, who is leaving a distant country to come and offer his services in the Congo, to be paid a separation allowance for a certain transitional period, just like a Congolese going to work in Belgium. Encouragement must be given to the people of good will who come not merely to earn a living but also to co-operate disinterestedly in the development of the Congo and of its inhabitants. We must take into consideration the humanitarian as well as the purely financial aspect.

This special allowance should be calculated, however, only on the base salary and not on the other benefits (cost of living allowance, family allowance, lodging allowance) since, in many cases, the expenses which the Europeans have to bear are the same as those for the Africans, particularly in the case of the African élite who have the same standard of living as the average European. How high should this expatriation allowance be? I shall leave that to the authorities and employers. I shall simply give an opinion in order to provide a basis for discussion.

As there can be no question of reducing or increasing present European salaries in order to regularise the position, the pay of a Congolese worker whose efficiency is equal to that of a European should be not less than three-quarters of the pay of a European of the same grade. If the pay of the European is 100,000 francs, the African will receive three-quarters of this, i.e. 75,000 francs.

This principle of equality should be applied without any reservations, since Belgian colonial policy has always professed itself opposed to any kind of racial discrimination.

Those Congolese who merit it are entitled to demand that the Government of their country should put into practice this principle which has been laid down by Belgium. As Belgian citizens, they are entitled to a fair wage.

In an article published recently in the Belgian press and entitled "The Common Destiny of Belgium and the Congo", M. Marcel de Courte defends the principle of equality in these few moving words: "If then it is true that collective advancement is absurd and that individual advancement is an absolute obligation, the African who has reached his full individual development must be given the individual place which is his due in accordance with his personal capacities in the Belgo-Congolese community."

It is essential that he should recieve exactly the same treatment in regard to pay and civil rights as a White of the same level.

This criterion is not an empty concept of equality but a concrete fact of service rendered to the community. Our Congolese policy will never be fruitful unless we make use of the competition between Blacks and Whites for the benefit of the community. The prize will go to whoever is best in his own right irrespective of racial group. In this connection, I can easily visualise an African capable of giving orders to a less competent European. That is both reasonable and just.

" . . . more than ever we need a completely realist policy for the Congo, which will prevent us all from going mad."

Pending the establishment of a uniform employment policy in the Congo, two special pieces of legislation should be enacted for the benefit both of employers and the best elements of the Congolese élite; one would apply to unskilled manual and salaried workers, and the other to Europeans and *assimilés*,[5] but the benefits of the latter would be open to any other Congolese who, by his industry and competence, shows himself capable and worthy of benefiting. By *assimilés*, we mean all élite manual and salaried workers of the same status as European employees.

To make this integration more concrete and viable, competitive examinations would have to be arranged in all branches of employment, both in the public and private sector, at half-yearly or yearly intervals; those who were successful would be admitted to the European employment group. European employees and *assimilés* would be promoted to the various grades of this group without any discrimination in accordance with the conditions laid down in the regulations.

The competitive examinations for admission to the European employment group would comprise vocational tests and a test of maturity; the latter would be designed to assess the intellectual ability and degree of mental training of the employee.

As part of this programme, it would very useful to establish in the Congo a college of administrative and social training containing various sections; it would give a suitable administrative, vocational and social training to those African employees not in possession of the diplomas or certificates required for immediate admission into the European employment group. At the conclusion of the period of study – which would be not less than six or twelve months – this institution would issue diplomas entitling their holders to be admitted to the European employment group in the public and private sectors.

Competent workers who wished to do so would be authorised to leave their employment temporarily in order to attend these courses, just as certain employees of the fourth grade of the African Administration, when they are on leave in Belgium, attend courses at the Colonial School with a view to their transfer to a higher grade.

Those Congolese who had had a higher education (at secondary school or at a university, etc.) would automatically be admitted to the European employment group and each one would have the grade appropriate to his examination certificate.

[5] See *Immatriculation—Assimilation*, p. 51.

This would seem to be the most realistic formula if we genuinely wish to facilitate the advancement of the Congolese élite.

If admission to the European employment group or promotion to responsible posts is restricted only to those Congolese who have been to university or who hold secondary school examination certificates, African integration will be held up and there will continue to be an atmosphere of discontent among the élite. These members of the Congolese élite, although they have not had the opportunity of a higher education or university training, have considerably improved their education by private study.

In this connection, it should be noted that the two Congolese universities are of recent creation, and that the few secondary education courses which existed in the Congo for Africans were only open to theological students destined for the priesthood. Thus, in practice, no serious courses of study were available until the last few years. It would be unfair, therefore, to refuse social advancement in the Belgo-Congolese community to capable persons who, by experience, practice, self-education or correspondence courses, have reached a degree of competence bringing them up to the level of the middle-grade Europeans for the sole reason that they do not hold a particular examination certificate.

Is it their fault if they do not hold this certificate and if they have not studied particular subjects which were not available at the time they were at school?

Moreover, it must be borne in mind that, even if this higher education had been available at the time, the majority of Congolese intellectuals would not have been able to benefit by it for one reason or another; experience has proved this even in the Western countries which have reached the highest level of civilisation. The same phenomenon can be observed amongst employees in the public and private sectors, where university graduates form only a small minority, the great majority consisting of those who have only had secondary education.

In any sphere of employment what counts is not an examination certificate but *Efficiency* and *Productivity*. In the Congo, as in Europe, there are people of little education who, from the point of view of efficiency and ability, are superior to those who have spent many years at the school desk.

An examination certificate does, of course, give a presumption of ability, but there are other factors which must be borne in mind.

In Belgium, too, there are people who have not had the opportunity of higher education but who win promotion by perseverance, private study and increased efficiency and by making use of the many facilities put at their disposal in the form of competitive examinations, further training courses, etc.

If such post-school competitive examinations and courses can be organised in Belgium, there would seem to be little reason why similar examinations should not be arranged in the Congo, a young and developing country in which secondary and primary education have only recently been improved by the establishment of state schools, and in which the Congolese élite are eagerly seeking to acquire and assimilitate the knowledge which is essential for their full development and their integration in the wider European community.

This is the goal which the African élite wish to achieve whatever the efforts involved.

In this new country, the great Western principles and the subtleties of Western law (stating for instance that a particular certificate is *essential* for anyone wishing to take up a particular occupation) should not be applied rigidly, because the inhabitants of this country have not yet acquired the same mental outlook and background as Europeans.

We assume that the qualifications required today from Belgians for the recruitment of Civil Servants are not the same as those which were in force in 1800.

Hence the conditions for the admission of Africans into the various European employment groups should be somewhat more flexible, becoming steadily stiffer as the intellectual development of the country proceeds. The same procedure was followed in regard to the auxiliary personnel in the nineteen forties; persons who had only had primary education were admitted to those grades after a probationary period. That procedure was justified by the fact that, at the time, it was impossible to find a sufficient number of candidates with post-primary education. Since then the position has changed, as there has been a considerable output from the inter-mediate and secondary schools and the training colleges; for this reason the conditions of recruitment of auxiliary personnel were altered in 1947. At present, only those who hold a certificate of post-primary education issued after the full four-year period of study can be employed.

Why could not the same be done at the present time with regard to the recruitment of élite personnel into the African Civil Service?

Is it really essential to know algebra, trigonometry, Eastern philosophy and Roman history in order to be a good African civil servant?

This does not by any means imply that such knowledge, or any other knowledge, is not essential for Africans. The reverse is true. We merely wish to show that certain administrative posts do not, in practice, require a profound knowledge of all these subjects which are basically of use to the individual and not to the organisation. A sound vocational training, sufficient maturity of mind and a good knowledge of French are fully sufficient.

The Congo already has a fair number of African civil servants who are kept in the background and who are confidently looking forward to being given posts commensurate with their ability; their number is still small but it is probably not less than 300 for the Congo as a whole. They are quite capable of competing today with the average European on the labour market if given the opportunity; they are eagerly awaiting that opportunity.

In view of their specialised training, their theoretical knowledge and practical experience, Congolese are at present capable of taking over the following jobs: health officials (e.g. medical assistants who – as the doctors admit – are better trained than the European health officials and nurses), district officers, postal officials (Congolese are already in charge of important Post Offices on their own responsibility as assistant-postal officials), administrative secretaries, secretary accountants, draftsmen, heads of zones, agricultural officials, (as agricultural assistants), teachers, masters on duty, mechanics, journalists, wireless announcers, surveyors, civil-police officers, radio operators, ships' pilots, etc.

Some of these posts are already filled by Africans unofficially.

These people do not normally hold the same educational certificates as European officials but they have the required skills which some of them have been able to demonstrate and of which others, who have not yet had the opportunity, will give proof when the opportunity is offered to them.

Equality in Employment is claim number one put forward by all the Congolese élite.

It is the subject of heated discussion everywhere: in offices, workshops, on the roads, in everyday conversations. If you mention this burning topic to the *evolués* you will be aware of their distress of mind: how, they say, can we enjoy the benefits of civilisation, bring

up and educate our children, shape our lives with dignity, humanity
and a minimum of self-respect, and pull ourselves out of the rut if
our incomes are too low?

As in all human societies, there are some who exaggerate their
grievances but that does not invalidate the basis of truth in their
arguments; there is something in what they say.

Amongst those who are well-paid, there are some who waste
their money on extravagances instead of improving their standard
of living; there are others, however, who use their money wisely
to care for their families and who make praiseworthy economies.

The Advantages of Implementing the Principle of Equality.

The introduction of equality in employment would have the following advantages:

> It would go far towards eliminating the causes of tension and
> discontent amongst competent people who feel that they are
> the victims of discrimination solely on account of the colour
> of their skins;

- it would prove to everyone that there is no question of racial
  discrimination but only of social discrimination, which exists
  in every country in the world and is based mainly on the
  merits and aptitudes of the individual;
- it would rid certain Europeans, who are not fully aware of
  their role as educators, of a superiority complex in their
  relations with the Africans, a complex created not by the
  colour of their skin but simply and solely by their superior
  economic position;
- it would bring to the labour market a healthy competition
  which would act as a powerful spur to productivity and would
  benefit both employer and worker;
- it would spur on those who are discouraged and lazy;
- it would remove any doubt as to the sincerity of the policy of
  non-discrimination professed by Belgium, a doubt which
  exists (often wrongly) in the minds of quite a number of
  people;
- it would prove to all that the Belgo-Congolese community
  and the principle of the equality of its citizens is not an empty
  phrase but something which is steadily being put into
  practice;
- it would firmly rebut the cynical allegations which certain

people tend to put forward to the effect that the Government's policy is a policy of talk and half measures; allegations which are intended to sow confusion in the minds of the Congolese and discredit Belgian achievements in Africa;

- it would facilitate a speedier integration of the native élite;
- finally, it would strengthen trust, understanding and solidarity between Belgians and Congolese and thereby increase the authority of the Government.

CHAPTER III

Political Integration — Political Rights
Sharing of Power

In the previous chapter we considered, purely from the point of view of employment, how and to what extent the Congolese élite could take part in the running of the public services. Let us now look at the other side of the question: participation in the running of public affairs by representation on committees and official councils.

The Congolese are unanimous in their wish to take part more effectively in the running of their country and to serve on all the committees and councils dealing with the interests of the Belgo-Congolese community. This is a legitimate desire, in harmony with the views of the Government, which is devoting very careful consideration to this question.

Ought political rights to be granted immediately to the Congolese?

In principle, everyone has the right to take part in the running of his country's affairs.

Jacques Maritain says that "Aristotle's famous dictum that man is a political animal does not merely mean that man is naturally made for life in society; it also means that men naturally wish to lead a political life and to take an active part in the life of the political community.

"This assumption with regard to human nature is the basis of political liberty and political rights and, in particular, of the right to vote. It may be easier for men to renounce active participation in political life; in some cases they may have led a more carefree and happier life by being political slaves in the city or by passively handing over to their leaders all responsibility for the running of the community. But by so doing, they are surrendering a privilege which meets a need in their nature, one of those privileges which, in one sense, make life harder and involve some degree of toil, tension and suffering, but which are an expression of human dignity. A state of civilisation in which men freely appoint those in authority over them is an inherently more perfect state. For it is true that the essential purpose of political authority is to guide free men towards the common weal; it is normal for free men to make their own choice of those who are to lead them; that is the most elementary form of active participation in political life. For this reason, universal suffrage, under which every adult person has the inherent right to express his opinion on the affairs of the community by voting in the election of representatives of the people and leaders of the state, has an absolutely fundamental political and human value and is one of those rights which a community of free men can under no circumstances relinquish."

Must these great principles of European democracy be applied immediately and without restriction in the Congo?

Before replying, we must examine all sides of the question.

The inhabitants of the Congo, both Belgians and Congolese, have as yet no political rights. But they sit together in the various consultative councils established in the country (provincial and governmental councils, the permanent representative body, works councils, etc.) in which they can express themselves freely in the defence of national interests.

The African representatives in these bodies are appointed by the Government without consultation with the people and without the consent of the people.

Reforms are now being worked out and will shortly be published. But we do not yet know exactly how far they will go.

For reasons of prudence and wisdom, no political rights in the full sense of the term were granted to the inhabitants of the country; this cannot be attributed to bad faith as some people allege.

I noted in an article which appeared in an American journal (the *Minneapolis Times*) over the signature of Mr. Carl T. Rowan, some criticisms levelled at Belgian colonial policy: " ... The sole aim of this policy is to perpetuate the white man's domination in Africa by refusing the African facilities for political expression and by purchasing his consent through economic and social benefits."

Is this correct? I should like to know. Although I am not acquainted with the inner workings of colonial policy, being of colonial status myself, I shall glance at the situation from a realistic point of view.

In the early days of Belgian penetration into central Africa wisdom advised that native society should not be revolutionised by the brusque and wholesale application of new democratic methods which ran counter to the old methods of tribal life and were liable to produce negative, if not dangerous, results. Therefore, in working out any far-sighted political policy worthy of the name, it was advisable to take account of traditional requirements and a whole series of local circumstances.

Logically, the enjoyment of political rights (the right to vote) presupposes that the beneficiaries have an adequate understanding of public affairs, an appreciation of the general interest and of Government regulations – all of them qualities which the Congolese did not possess at that time and which only a minority possess at present.

To introduce the ferment of political life prematurely among the ignorant and irresponsible masses in response to a craving for modernisation would be to introduce the ferments of discord and dissension; it would not be a victory for the democratic idea nor would it lead to such a victory; it would open the way to a return to the old tribal concepts with each person wishing to be head of the new tribe; this would give rise to petty quarrels which would be detrimental to harmonious social relationships. It has proved necessary to give the people peace and happiness instead of disorder and wrangling, disguised as democracy.

On the other hand, to grant political rights solely to the European inhabitants who, at that time, were the only people capable of using them effectively, would have meant sacrificing the interests of the natives to a certain number of unscrupulous persons (I make no generalisations here). It is for that reason that neither the Belgians living in the Congo nor the Congolese themselves were allowed to have political rights.

When we consider all that has been achieved and is still being done in this country for the development of the African, it is difficult to believe that Belgian colonial policy is secretly aiming at a perpetual domination of White over Black, a sort of disguised slavery; that policy would run counter to the moral obligation which *Christian* Belgium has taken upon itself to raise the status of the native population to that of the citizens of metropolitan Belgium.

The moving speeches made by His Majesty King Baudouin at Leopoldville on 17 May 1955, and on his return from the Congo at the African Royal Circle, together with the policy followed by our Minister for Colonial Affairs, M. Buisseret, and the Governor General, M. Pétillon, particularly during the last two years, give us firm grounds for hope.

Can our King be deceiving us? Have we any right to doubt the sincerity of his love for us, the sincerity of his most humane intentions? Are we to doubt the sincerity of our great Minister for Colonial Affairs and of the Governor General and of all the great Belgians in the Mother Country who wish to make of us not mere servants but Belgians of the same status as those of Europe, or rather civilised citizens made in the image of the great human family?

The Congo cannot, of course, escape the laws of nature; it will follow the same course of development as Belgium, and finally its inhabitants will have to enjoy political rights. I believe that it would be possible, in the relatively near future, to grant political rights to the Congolese élite and to the Belgians of the Congo in accordance with certain criteria to be laid down by the Government. In my view, there would be no question of granting these rights to people who were unfit to use them, to dull-witted illiterates; that would be to put dangerous weapons in the hands of children.

We are well aware that some Europeans have doubts – justifiable doubts – about granting these rights to the Congolese, for fear that they may abuse them or turn them against the Europeans. These opinions reflect either a sincere care for the welfare of the Congolese themselves, or pessimism, or exaggerated or unfounded fears.

Those in authority should always be guided by wisdom in all their decisions and actions, but it is important to avoid an excessively conservative policy which is out of touch with the state of development of those under authority and which can give rise to difficult situations.

The *status quo* could be maintained for the uneducated masses who would continue to be governed and guided – as in all countries – by the responsible élite: the White and African élite.

We suggest below the categories of Congolese to whom political rights could be granted if this should one day be possible:

   – all those who are able to read and write, a fact which would

have to be proved by the production of a certificate or of a document certifying that the person concerned has had a full primary education; such documents to be established in accordance with local regulations;
- chiefs, nobles and native judges (in the case of illiterates, the vote would be registered by a representative of the Government or by a jury formed for that purpose in each centre or commune). It would be bad policy to refuse the vote to native authorities, even if illiterate, unless the administration should decide otherwise.

That would form the first transitional step towards universal suffrage which would come with the introduction of universal education.

Whilst awaiting this distant time – very distant, since we still need several years before illiteracy is eradicated from our country – we must be patient, let things develop and start with *ad hoc* measures.

The Machinery of Government

In addition to the various official committees and commissions which already exist, I shall indicate below the various councils on which Congolese could take an effective share in power, starting from the lowest and going up to the highest levels. This little plan has been drawn up in accordance with my own ideas since, as I have already said, I do not know the Government's intentions in this matter!

Local area council (*rural commune*): under the chairmanship of the head of the local area. All the chiefs of the traditional groups within the local area would belong to the council *ex officio*.

[Here follows a passage which has been crossed out by the author.]

The other members would be appointed directly by the population by means of free elections.

The clerk of the local area administration should have had a secondary education, in order to facilitate relations between the Government and the local area. These clerks would be recruited as far as possible only from amongst people trained at the Colleges of Administration which have just been established in the Congo.

C

The authority of the local area council would be limited to matters of local interest within the area.

The council would be organised entirely on traditional lines.

Decisions would have to be submitted for the approval of the Territorial Administrator, who would have the right of veto. In case of dispute between the Administrator and the council, the latter would have the right of appeal to the District Commissioner.

Territorial Council: under the chairmanship of the Territorial Administrator. All the heads of the local areas within the territory would be members *ex officio*. The other members would be elected by the population. The territorial council would also include settlers and missionaries resident in the territory, elected directly by the population.

The *evolué* club or clubs, which are officially recognised in the territory, would be entitled to submit candidates.

Terms of reference of the council: all questions of local interest concerning the territory.

The secretary of the council would be either a European or a well-educated Congolese.

Decisions would be put into effect automatically or submitted for the approval of the District Commissioner if the importance of the subject justified it. The District Commissioner would have the right of veto. In case of dispute between the Commissioner and the council, the latter would have the right of appeal to the Provincial Governor.

District Council: under the chairmanship of the District Commissioner. All the territorial Administrators and the heads of the local areas within the district would be members *ex officio*. The other Congolese members would be elected by the people. Representatives of the settlers and missions would be elected by the people.

Decisions would be put into effect automatically or submitted for the approval of the Provincial Governor if the subjects concerned were of sufficient importance. The Provincial Governor would have the right of veto.

Council of the Commune (in towns and non-traditional centres): under the chairmanship of the mayor. All the members would be appointed by the population.

[Here follows a passage which has been deleted by the author.]

In the case of a mixed council, covering both white and black communities, the membership would include an equal number of Whites and Congolese in order to ensure that one group could not dominate the other.

In the case of two separate communities, as, for instance, in the chief town of each Province where there are two distinct townships – a European and a native township – the town commune would be administered by a European mayor and the suburban commune by an African mayor assisted by a Civil Servant adviser.

European technical officers would be seconded to the administration of the African township as is the case today with officers attached to the non-traditional centres. It would only be necessary to change the names: the administrator representing the protecting authority would become the administrative adviser of the head of the township who would be given the title of mayor.

The mayor would have to have a good mental background, a good training in administration, politics and social affairs, and should have completed a probationary period which would enable the authorities to judge whether he was competent to carry out his functions or not.

If the head of a particular African township was incapable, he would be removed from office and replaced by a more capable person. A head who had been removed from office on the grounds of incompetence could be given other duties commensurate with his abilities.

These new communes would enjoy a certain measure of administrative autonomy suited to the circumstances of the Congo.

Provincial Council: under the chairmanship of the Provincial Governor as at present. The European councillors would be appointed in accordance with criteria laid down by the administration. The system would have to be changed in regard to native representation: the heads of the local areas representing native constituencies would have to be chosen only among literate chiefs who were able to express themselves suitably in French. A knowledge of this language would have to be compulsory owing to the fact that all the debates in the Provincial Council take place exclusively in French.

If an important chief who is illiterate and does not speak French had to belong to the Council for political reasons, he would himself appoint a deputy who would represent him on the Council.

There are, at present, some chiefs in the Provincial Councils and the Government who are only there as a matter of form: they should be replaced.

Native Provincial Councillors should be chosen in the following manner:

- either by the members of the District Council, each District Council electing from amongst its members its delegates to the Provincial Council,
- or by the Province as a whole, each District voting by limited suffrage restricted to literate electors and the established authorities.

Decisions would be put into effect automatically except for matters coming within the sphere of the Government which would be submitted for the approval of the Governor General. The Governor General would have the right of veto.

Governmental Council (*Congolese Parliament*): the chairman would, of course, be the Governor General.

The African Councillors would be elected either by the members of the Provincial Councils or directly by the population by means of free elections.

Decisions would be put into effect automatically except in the case of matters coming within the sphere of the Minister of the Colonies who would have the right of veto.

Colonial Council: It would be very desirable for some Africans, selected from among the pick of the Congolese élite, to belong to this high assembly in which the problems of the Congo are discussed. Representation would be given not only to Africans, but also to those Belgians who have definitely settled in the country. This step is fully justified by the establishment of a Belgo-Congolese Community,[2] which is intended to enable overseas Belgians to work closely with the Belgians of the Mother Country in controlling the destinies of the young "Belgium in Africa".

The settlers have often expressed this wish. In my view it can only be fulfilled in so far as it is compatible with the higher interest of the country. There should be experienced native advisers grouped round the various administrative departments of the colony and the

[2] See Chapter XV.

Colonial Department. At the beginning they would, of course, lack the necessary skill; they would need some time to become adjusted to the work and to learn their job. This they would do under the enlightened guidance of their educators.

The presence of these future African deputies in the various administrative and legislative assemblies would often give useful guidance when decisions had to be taken in regard to native policy.

Living as they do side by side with their fellow Africans in the Congo, they are more closely in touch with the development of the African mentality than are the Europeans, and they have a better knowledge of the problems affecting the life of the natives and of all the currents of opinion which sometimes escape the authorities; much can be learnt from them because they have the confidence of the peoples to whom they belong.

Some members of Parliament in the Home Country often have superficial and incomplete views on the problems of the Congo which they have obtained either from official reports, which do not always give a true picture of the problems, or from lightning visits which do not give them time to make a thorough first-hand study of these problems; such people would find the African deputies and councillors very valuable collaborators.

In every forum where the Congo is discussed, be it in the Congo or in Belgium, the inhabitants of the country, Civil Servants, settlers, missionaries and Africans, should be invited to state their point of view, not in order to put forward claims but to collaborate in running their common Fatherland.

The participation of the élite in the running of the country, from the suburban council up to the highest spheres, would provide a symbol of Belgo-Congolese unity.

There is no practical difficulty in carrying out this plan; it depends solely on the will of the country's rulers, those who are responsible for Congolese policy.

I am convinced that, if this was to be done, one of the main causes of misunderstandings between the Government and the people would be removed; the settlers would be content and so would the Congolese élite. In short, this step would play an effective part in building up confidence and a fruitful, enduring collaboration between the colonial and home authorities on the one hand and the Congolese and white élite – representing the Belgo-Congolese Community – on the other hand.

The Commission for the Protection of the Natives

Under Article 6 of the Colonial Charter, a permanent Commission was established by Royal decree dated 1 June 1912, to ensure the protection of the natives and the improvement of their moral and material conditions of life throughout the whole of the colony. This commission is composed of eighteen members and meets under the chairmanship of the Attorney General of the Appeal Court in Leopoldville. A sub-commission was set up in Elizabethville by a Royal decree dated 7 May 1923.

Each year, the Commission sends to the King a collective report on measures which should be taken for the benefit of the natives.

In addition, the members have the right to report to the Public Prosecutor's office any abuses and illegal practices carried out at the expense of the natives; they may do this in their individual capacity.

The Commission for the Protection of the Natives has been, and continues to be, of the greatest assistance to the native community in its allotted sphere of action; it also keeps a close watch on the actions of the Government and often points out to the Government the lines which it should follow in its colonial policy.

In my view: (1) a sub-commission should operate in the principal town of each province, or there should be one sub-commission for every two provinces, which would give a total of three sub-commissions in the Congo as a whole; (2) the number of native members should be increased.

If it is impossible for the Commission to be made up of an equal number of Europeans and Congolese, the latter should number not less than eight whilst the number of European members should be reduced to ten.

The native members should be chosen only from among the intellectual élite who have a broad outlook and whose loyalty, social and intellectual activity, have proved that they are interested in the welfare of the community and in the harmonious development of the Congo.

The fact that a man is a head of department or a chief clerk in a particular service, does not guarantee that he will have the ability and skill which are required – though not, in fact, demanded – in order to carry out this noble mission of protection.

There are many people who, by good luck or by faithful service, have found their way into certain posts which place them high on the social ladder, yet they lack the intellectual and moral capacities which are required to carry out a particular social or administrative job demanding a certain level of education.

No one should be appointed to any office unless he has the necessary aptitude.

According to reliable information certain native members of the Commission have sometimes paralysed its work by their narrow-mindedness.

At the close of the last session of the Commission for the Protection of the Natives which was held in Stanleyville early in 1956, I had an interview with the President of the Commission. Replying to my request for an increase in the number of Congolese members, he declared, in the presence of a delegation of *evolués*, that this was not yet possible for the simple reason that the few members serving on the Commission at present had not acquired sufficient maturity and that it would only make things worse to increase their numbers. In debate, their views are sometimes limited and some of them cannot always distinguish local or particular interests from the general interest. There would be no objection to increasing the number of Congolese members if their competence could be guaranteed.

Native Representation: In the previous chapter, I touched on the problem of native representation. I shall pause for a moment to go further into this important question.

Briefly, the Congolese complain that they are represented in the various official councils and commissions by incompetent people whom they neither trust nor respect.

Speaking of the reform of the consultative assemblies in one of his speeches at the opening of the Council of Government, the Governor General, M. Pétillon, spoke somewhat as follows: "These native representatives have been chosen by us because of their successful careers and their characters, but what guarantee have we that they really represent the natives?"

With few exceptions, the part played in these meetings by the present representatives is purely symbolic. Their speciality is dumbness and pointless exuberance. During discussions of general problems, they make a brilliant display of prejudice, defend special interests and say "Amen". The Government complains about them (some Civil Servants have admitted this to us) and so does the African population. They have been badly chosen. And yet there are capable people who could fulfil this task with competence and dignity.

When Congolese representatives are to be chosen for a particular council or to make a study tour in Belgium, the selection often seems to be made on political grounds (which should not be the case) and it generally favours people who are to the liking of their local superiors; in the eyes of the Congolese, this selection often has the appearance of a prize rather than an objective recognition of competence and merit. "Greenhorns" are preferred; they are given the coveted title of "native representatives" solely in order that they may further some particular interests because they will never say, No, when a particular person says, Yes, because they can be made to do what they are told, because they can be made to sign any declaration. For political reasons the selectors pass over competent people who have quick and critical minds, who can argue; because they cannot be influenced, they will not blindly do what they are told or say what others want them to say, because they will raise controversial matters (however constructive in ... [illegible] truth). This has been said to me over and over again by *evolués* in the course of my enquiry.

I myself have often witnessed unfortunate situations which prove that the selection is sometimes ill-advised. To take only one example amongst many:

In the course of my study tour of Belgium, made at the invitation of the Ministry for Colonial Affairs, the majority of the distinguished people (we were sixteen) were very sober, level-headed, and estimable people, who had rendered notable service to the administration, but they were not equal to their task. The reason: lack of training and lack of maturity. Others did not even submit to the Ministry for Colonial Affairs the end-of-mission report which they were asked for; others again merely filled their report with trivialities.

Difficult though it is to believe, the report submitted by one of these distinguished persons consisted of a bare six lines, made up of two personal pleas: he aked the Minister to use his influence in order to procure him a civic merit card and children's allowances (benefits which might possibly have been refused him by the local authorities).

I was dumbfounded when my travelling companion showed me his report, which he intended to submit to the Minister. I could hardly believe my eyes! I advised him to tear up this trivial report which was unworthy of him; I suggested that I should draft another report for him in a rather more serious vein, dealing with questions of general interest, but my companion fought shy of my advice, believing that it was inspired by jealousy because I was discouraging him from claiming advantages for himself . . .

A distinguished person who does not know where to apply in order to obtain his civic merit card and family allowances, and who uses a study tour of Belgium to talk nonsense and bring the Congolese élite into discredit, is not worthy to be numbered amongst this élite, whatever his grade of employment and however good his record.

And what can one say of those people who go to Belgium only in order to rhapsodise over the wonderful food, to stand and admire the Brussels illuminations, the Belgian coast, the museums, the trams, the Cabinet building, the coalfields, the Palace of Justice and the natural beauties of Belgium, and who, on their return to the Congo, forget all that they have seen, all that has been shown and explained to them, retaining only this impression: the Congo Belgians are Germans, they do not like us, whilst in Belguim, we were popular and we dined with the "High-Ups" (this is what one distinguished person said to me at a reception given by a highly-placed official of the Colony who asked the travellers to give their impressions of their trip, and he is not the only one). They take no notice of the information given to them during their sightseeing trips, they are bored, they fall asleep; all they ask is to return to the hotel.

Their curiosity is aroused only by trivialities . . . [illegible] but when constructive or instructive matters are involved they become mere spectators and dreamers . . .

In order to please a White who asks for their impressions of the trip, they will give the parrot cry: "People work very hard in Belgium" (it remains to be seen whether they are sincerely convinced . . .); but in private and hushed discussions, when they are among their cronies who ask eagerly for news of the Celestial Empire, they tell stupid little anecdotes about what they have seen, mentioning only the bad side of things – the petty defects – forgetting (if indeed they were ever aware of it) that Belgium is not a paradise and that the essential purpose of their mission is to learn, to observe, to study everything that is good and worth-while so that they may spread amongst their immediate circle the intrinsic values and the intellectual, moral and artistic values of Western civilisation.

Of the sixteen distinguished persons there were at least six who made it their business to remedy this situation, to fight daily against the inaccuracies and blunders of the others; and our guides had no easy task, either.

In short, in all these study tours of Belgium made by distinguished persons, the number of genuine élite always seems to be far too small.

These tours should not be given as a reward: instead of throwing away 50,000 or 100,000 francs or more in order to give recognition to the merits of an old servant, a chief, a noble or a clerk, in the form of a princely voyage to Belgium, it would be better to buy him a small villa where he could rest in peace, buy him five or ten head of cattle for stock-rearing, a tractor or some agricultural tools, etc. . . . This reward would cost less than a tour of Belgium in which many of the participants are lost and bewildered by the ostentation of the West; it would be much more valuable for these old servants and they would appreciate it more.

The organisation of ceremonial tours as a form of reward must be avoided; they are not in the public interest and they are against the interest of Belgium herself.

The achievements of the Belgians are judged in Belgium and abroad by the quality of the élite who travel in the country or live or study there.

On the other hand I am most anxious that a large number of Congolese élite should be allowed to explore the Mother Country; people who can profit by the experience of getting to know the Belgians and can return to pass on this experience to their own people. There are many deserving young people employed in both the public and private sector who could be chosen without any hesitation, provided that they offered all the requisite guarantees.

I should also be proud to be accompanied by intelligent and capable chiefs – such as Chief . . . [illegible] . . . who would be the senior members of the team.

In writing the foregoing I am not attacking my comrades; that would be a betrayal of the Congolese élite of which I am a part. I am only pointing out these few anomalies because they are likely to bring discredit on the Congolese élite and the achievements of civilisation, because I wish to see an end of these anomalies and because I share the desire of all *evolué* circles that every Congolese who is called upon to represent his fellow countrymen should represent them worthily and effectively and contribute to their development by his deeds, his example and his social and intellectual activity. The *evolués* are dissatisfied and no longer wish to be represented by false ambassadors.

I apologise for having dealt with the question in somewhat plain terms. On the other hand, I have kept silent on certain matters as it is not my custom to pour oil on the flames.

Legal Integration of the Congolese: The legal integration of the Congolese élite is being carried out by stages. Up to now, only the *immatriculés* and holders of the civic merit card have been legally assimilated with the Europeans and only in connection with the following matters:

- the application of the co-ordinated decrees on judicial organisation, procedure and competence, granting holders of the civic merit card the official right to damages;
- penal proceedings, entitling holders of the civic merit card to the reduced rate of legal costs and exemption from the payment of a deposit;
- the application of the decree on the restoration of civil rights to convicted persons;
- the stepping-up of fines (only for *immatriculés*) – an extremely disadvantageous measure which the *immatriculés* consider to be UNJUST (see their protests on this subject in various articles which have appeared in the press) because they earn as much as the Europeans with whom they are being assimilated in this connection, and also because their financial situation is exactly the same as that of the holders of the civic merit card or of any other Congolese of traditional status; conditional sentences

[They have also received] exemption from certain regulations which are applied specially to natives:

- restricted movement during the hours of darkness within the urban districts and European centres;
- imprisonment in the native district prisons;
- punishment by flogging in prison;
[and it gives them:]
- the right to attend all cinema performances;
- the right to hold property (a privilege which is also granted to all Congolese, *immatriculés* or not, under the Decree of

          10 February 1953);
      – unrestricted purchase and consumption of alcoholic beverages;
      – Hospitalisation in European clinics (only for *immatriculés*).

Social Integration: The subject of social integration is at present being studied in competent quarters. Considerable leeway has to be made up here as soon as possible.

The four aspects which we have just examined, i.e. economic – political – legal and social integration – are very closely connected and form an indissoluble whole.

To what extent and by what date will the complete integration of the Congolese be brought to a stage where we shall no longer have in the Congo ordinary natives, holders of the civic merit card, *immatriculés* and Europeans, but simply CITIZENS, all enjoying the same rights and advantages without any discrimination whatsoever, as is the case in Belgium?

Immatriculation does not automatically result in the complete integration of the Africans; the *immatriculés* are not assimilated with the Europeans either economically, socially or administratively. Does this imply that this category of élite citizens, whose degree of civilisation is officially recognised as equivalent to that of the average European, is still not worthy to be integrated socially into the European community? Will he have to submit to still further tests in addition to those at present laid down for *immatriculation* in order to be fully assimilated with the Europeans? What exactly must he do in order to be treated on an equal footing with the European?

These are some of the questions to which the Congolese *evolués* are eagerly seeking an answer.

After mature consideration, I have rejected collective integration, because such an over-simplified formula would hamper the development of the Congo. What would actually happen today if collective integration were introduced by law? Everybody: *evolués* and non-*evolués,* civilised and uncivilised, being automatically assimilated and enjoying complete equality of rights and benefits, would regard this assimilation as charity or prodigality: no one would take the trouble to improve his mind, character or skill. It would be the end of all idea of duty and effort.

Moreover, collective assimilation would be tantamount to moral coercion, a kind of psychological poisoning, for the effect would be to introduce a single status (of the Western type) and identical laws for Whites and Africans. The results for the Africans would be the replacement of their traditional status, to which many of them are still attached, by a European status, which would not accord with their traditional way of life.

In the interests of all concerned, therefore, integration must be individual. Under these conditions, we consider that it would not be fair to refuse anyone the status which he claims, which best meets his aspirations and suits his way of life, and with which he wishes fully to identify himself and his children.

On the basis of legislation at present in force, this integration can be secured only by the issue of the civic merit card and by *immatriculation*.

But what will be the position of the deserving Congolese who are not *immatriculés* or do not possess the civic merit card and who, for personal reasons, do not wish to apply for these cards?

Let us study these two items of legislation separately in order to bring out some facts which might serve as a basis for discussion.

Civic merit card

This card is granted, after a thorough investigation, to any Congolese, literate or not, who is aged twenty-one years (or at least sixteen years in the case of minors), monogamous, and who "shows by his good conduct and habits that he sincerely desires to attain a more advanced degree of civilisation".

The card is issued by a Commission under the chairmanship of the District Commissioner and composed of nine to eleven members. It may be withdrawn temporarily or permanently from anyone who: (a) does not fulfil the conditions laid down for the granting of the card, (b) does not give the children under his care adequate instruction or education, (c) has misused his card by lending it to a third person or in any other way.

The card is held personally.

The Civic Merit Card was conceived as a transitional stage in the process of integration; it marks an intermediate stage between native society as yet undeveloped and civilised society, composed of Europeans and those who have been legally assimilated.

The preamble to the decree instituting the Civic Merit Card reads as follows:

"Whereas the degree of development, both intellectual and moral, attained by the majority of the natives does not as yet allow of their assimilation;

"Whereas, pending the preparation of a statute for the civilised Congolese population (i.e. a statute for the *immatriculés*), the existing laws and regulations recognise that certain special rights accrue to natives whose degree of civilisation justifies this;

"Whereas, in order to facilitate easy identification of these natives, it is essential that they be given a special identity document".

This provision, therefore, clearly explains that the civic merit card does, in fact, represent a transitional stage towards *immatriculation* or assimilation, the last stage of integration in the civilised community.

To ensure that the assimilation or integration of the Congolese is not a fiction, it would be desirable to review the existing conditions or rather to review the procedure for the granting of the civic merit card so that the benefit of this card could be more easily extended to the deserving members of the population. At present there is an impression that the granting of this card is somewhat restricted.

Many people do not wish to apply for this card for the following reasons, which they have explained to me:

1. Some state that they have been shocked and discouraged by the rebuffs sustained for no valid reason by certain applicants whom they considered to be deserving; they add that, under these conditions, they do not wish to subject themselves to the same affront and to the risk of being publicly humiliated;

2. Others say they would prefer the Government to *take the initiative* one day in recognising the merits of its awards by adapting its legislation to the degree of civilisation attained by the latter and granting them appropriate rights of its own free will;

3. The third group say: "It is ridiculous and presumptuous to claim from the Government by means of a special request official recognition of a state of civilisation which one already possesses and which is naturally recognised by the public". They also add that the cards are quite useless.

4. Finally, the fourth group say naively that as long as these cards bring no *material advantage* (but only a large number of obliga-

tions and duties) and as long as their holders are not ECONOMIC-ALLY subjected to the same terms of employment and the same salary scale as the Europeans, they can see no real advantage in holding these cards and will never make application for them. On the contrary, they say, it would only be a matter of disappointment to them and would deprive them of the advantages which we enjoy today and which are specially reserved for "low wage earners", ordinary natives and minors who are still under the protection of the authorities.

These are the opinions which I have collected in the course of an enquiry into this matter.

There is something strange about the excessively small number of holders of the civic merit card: either there are restrictions on the issue of the card or the *evolués* do not wish to apply for it for the reasons stated above.

This is a paradoxical situation when one notes that in the EIGHT YEARS since the card was instituted, from the 12th June 1948 to the end of 1955, the *total* number of civic merit cards issued was only 884 (eight hundred and eighty-four), whereas among the twelve million inhabitants of the Congo there cannot, at the present time, be less than one hundred thousand genuine *evolués* who deserve to benefit from this distinction.

At this rate – the equivalent of 110 cards a year for the whole of the Congo – it is going to take ten centuries or *one thousand* years before we have 110,000 officially-recognised *evolués* in the Congo; and, before all of our 12,000,000 inhabitants can obtain their certificate of integration, we shall have to wait at least a thousand centuries or 100,000 years!

As I have frequently stated in the course of my investigation, I am a supporter of the policy of progressive development adopted by the Government. It is this principle which makes me believe that it would be a breach of faith to refuse a deserving Congolese the benefits of statute law which he seeks, thereby indirectly forcing him to flounder in backward customs (I am not speaking here of the good customs, which must be retained but of backward native customs), to be ruled, *against his will*, by traditional law with consequences which are often disastrous for the *evolués*.

The first aim of colonisation is to bring to the colonised people the benefits of modern civilisation and a new system of orderly government.

When a native of a colonised country, who has been educated by his civilisers, wishes to bring up his family in the state of civilisation which he has chosen, he should not be thwarted in this desire by draconian measures which might unintentionally hold up the evolutionary process of native society.

I do not say that this evolution is being hampered at present; I merely wish to draw attention to these matters in order that the institution of the civic merit card shall not end in failure.

Since the civic merit card only represents a transitional, intermediate stage, its benefits should be widely granted to all who can fulfil the minimum conditions, without going into a lot of useless detail.

The evolution of the Congolese should certainly not be rushed. It must follow its normal course, but without hindrance.

Coming down to details. I should like to set out below the categories of Congolese who might well be awarded the civic merit card without too much administrative red tape:

(a) Every Congolese who has successfully completed a full course of post-primary studies (including secondary school, intermediate school, instructors' school, schools for medical auxiliaries – medical assistants, nurses, veterinary assistants, health inspectors – post office and telecommunications workers, schools of meteorology, and surveying, agricultural intermediate and high school, higher trades training school, etc.), who has received a good character training and holds, in addition to his diploma, a certificate of good character given by the territorial authority.

In my view, once a man has received a sound general, vocational or technical education over a period of ten or more years, and the territorial authority, *after enquiry,* has given him a certificate of *good character and citizenship,* this is ample justification for granting him the civic merit card. If the applicant subsequently proved to be unworthy, the Authority would withdraw the card in accordance with the provisions of Article II of the Law instituting this card.

(b) All skilled manual or salaried workers who possess a recognised qualification and a certificate of good character.

(c) Chiefs who are performing their duties to the satisfaction of the Administration, and who hold certificates of good character, as well as certain native nobles and judges whose character is satisfactory.

(d) All single women who have completed a full course of primary education or hold a certificate of home and domestic training given by the principal of the *Foyer Social* and who have a certificate of good character given by the territorial authority.

There is no provision under the law for the card to be granted to single women; this is an omission. It is not every woman who is fortunate enough to find a husband, and there is no reason for consigning them to the bottom of the social scale merely because they are unmarried. They have a right to the same status as married women, to the protection of the Government and to emancipation. The evolution of African women must include all women and not merely married women.

If a single woman has been given a good schooling by her White teachers, and if her conduct is above reproach, I see no reason why she should be refused the civic merit card.

(e) All clerical workers in the African Administration who have been granted official status and who fulfil the conditions necessary to be members of the Government service – i.e. being of irreproachable conduct, monogamous, and holding a certificate to show that they have completed four years of post-primary education, etc.

(f) The wives and children of card-holders; following the same procedure as for *immatriculation* the granting of the civic merit card to the head of a family would automatically extend the same advantages to the members of his family (wife and children under age in his care).

If the *immatriculation* of a Congolese automatically includes his wife and children, the same should apply to the issue of the civic merit card.

If a man is acknowledged to have reached a certain degree of civilisation, this recognition should also extend to his wife and children with whom he shares his life and whom he educates in accordance with his own ideas. It would be inconceivable for a husband and wife to enjoy different legal status, as this could create complications in the household – especially in case of legal action.

The principle that a wife adopts the status of her husband has been pointed out in the course of discussion on *immatriculation* and is a general principle of law. Family stability demands a common status for all its members.

This question deserves to be re-examined in the light of the foregoing.

As far as native nobles and judges are concerned, I believe that to make the issue of the card dependent on a period of twenty to twenty-five years of "good and loyal service" is to give the impression that this is a reward, a kind of "matabiche" or honorary award rather than a recognition of a degree of civilisation which has actually been attained. This long waiting period of twenty to twenty-five years – even though they were to show themselves worthy to hold a card before the expiry of this period – seems to bear heavily on judges and illiterate workers.

In my view there is a distinct difference between the mechanical rendering of good and loyal service and the possession of the capacity or aptitude which is necessary to enjoy the rights and carry out the obligations laid down by the law, rights and obligations which stem from the civic merit card.

For instance, a progressive young noble, of high intelligence, after five years of continuous contact with civilising influences, may end up by reaching a higher stage of civilisation than certain intellectuals. Is it fair to refuse him the card which is due to him by reason of his degree of development for *the sole and only* reason that he has not yet completed twenty or twenty-five years' service in accordance with the stipulations of the law?

I am convinced that to put into effect the few modifications suggested above would greatly encourage the progressive and more realistic emancipation of Congolese society.

I have every confidence in the effectiveness of the measures suggested, as experience shows that those who hold the civic merit card make a serious effort to advance towards civilisation for fear of losing their rights and their privileged position in society – a deprivation which would be officially denoted by the withdrawal of their cards if they behaved badly or ceased to fulfil any of the conditions. The moment the highly coveted card is issued, life changes for the holders; society benefits greatly from this, as there is now one more member of the élite to strengthen the vanguard of Congolese advancement.

In view of the excellent results obtained so far, it is now perfectly safe to move forward resolutely, without defeatism or demagogy, from the experimental stage to more positive measures. Following this line of reasoning, therefore, we must abolish all the direct and indirect restrictions which hamper the harmonious development of the Congolese population.

As for the procedure for withdrawing cards, it seems to me unfair to withdraw a card *permanently* as laid down in the decree under Article II. Withdrawal should be *temporary* and not permanent, and the period of withdrawal should be clearly stated, as is done in Belgium when a citizen is deprived of the enjoyment of his political and civic rights.

As the law in Belgium does not *permanently* deprive a citizen of his rights – even if he is a criminal – it should not do so in the Congo, where we have to be guided by the law of the Home Country. The Congolese must have the same rights under the law as their fellow countrymen in Belgium.

The fact that a civilised man, an *evolué*, has been guilty of an infraction of the law, whatever its nature and however serious, does not mean that he is no longer a civilised man or an *evolué*.

A policy of permanent deprivation of rights unwittingly discourages the persons concerned from mending their ways as they might do if they had the hope of recovering their rights and reputation after a given period.

Immatriculation—Assimilation

The *immatriculation* (registration) of the Congolese was promulgated by a decree of the 17th May 1952.

On reading this decree, we find the following preamble, which explains the precise significance of this doctrinal reform:

"*Immatriculation*, according to the Colonial Charter, is an instrument by which certain Congolese are assimilated with non-natives in regard to their civil status by being made subject to civil laws of the European pattern. According to the explanatory statement, the immediate aim of the decree is to grant the benefits of *immatriculation* only to those of the native élite who have genuinely adopted the Western form of civilisation. But this reform is only a first step in an official policy of gradually replacing the racial criteria on which a large part of Congolese legislation is based at present by criteria reflecting, in the main, the degree of civilisation of the various elements in the local population. This policy implies that the legal assimilation of Congolese *immatriculés* with non-natives is carried into effect not only in regard to civil status *but in all spheres of the law where common rules of life require it.*"

In order to be granted *immatriculation*, the applicant must:
1. have come of age as defined by the law, i.e. reached the age of

twenty-one;

2. show, by his education and way of life, that he has reached a stage of civilisation at which he is capable of enjoying the rights and fulfilling the duties which are laid down in the written law.

In order to define these criteria clearly, the report of the Colonial Council points out that it is not sufficient to have a European education; the applicant must show by his actions that he is guided by that education and follows its tenets. It is not sufficient to live more or less in the European style; he must have a training which will enable him to understand civic life as regulated by the law.

Procedure

A Congolese who desires to be granted *immatriculation* must submit to the President of the Court of First Instance a petition to which is attached:

1. A birth certificate or, failing this, an identity certificate, for himself and each member of his family,

2. A certificate of good character and a declaration of his family status,

3. A statement of his wife's consent, drawn up by the Magistrate's Court,

4. Any other documents (educational certificates, employers' testimonials, etc.) which will show that the appropriate conditions are fulfilled,

5. The sum necessary to pay the costs of proceedings and of the publication of the application in the Administrative Bulletin.

The petition is then passed on to the King's Attorney who arranges for its publication and assembles all relevant information. The application is published in the following manner:

1. A notice is posted up on the door of the Territorial Administrator's office in the applicant's town of residence;

2. The same notice is inserted in the Administrative Bulletin of the Belgian Congo as stated above.

The notice mentions the period within which the King's Attorney will proceed with his enquiry into the *identity* of the applicant; the public are invited to submit any comments or objections.

3. The employer is asked to give confidential information regarding the applicant in order to determine his vocational and intellectual ability and his social and moral qualities;

4. The territorial authority conducts an enquiry into the private and public life of the petitioner. Visits are made to his home: every room in his house, from the sitting-room, bedroom and kitchen, right down to the W.C., is throughly investigated, in order to bring to light anything which is incompatible with the requirements of civilised life. This domestic investigation is intended to enable the investigator to determine his standard of living, his family relationships (the care and education of the children, the care of the house, etc.) and the degree of development of the applicant. Information regarding his private conduct is assembled from all sources. The sum total of all these statements and all this information should enable a decision to be made, in full knowledge of the facts, as to whether or not the petitioner has reached a degree of civilisation comparable to that of an average European. The file is then re-transmitted to the Clerk of the Court, accompanied by all the information which has been accumulated and by detailed and reasoned opinions.

The Court fixes the date for the formal hearing, and the petitioner and his wife, possibly accompanied by their children, are summoned by registered letter thirty days before the date of the hearing.

The hearing is presided over by the Presiding Judge of the Court of First Instance, assisted by four assessors.

The petitioner and his wife submit to a very close cross-questioning, including some extremely complicated questions, some of which constitute a dangerous trap. Amongst these are: What do you understand by *immatriculation*? What is your object in applying for it? What are its legal advantages? What do you do in your spare time? What sort of friends do you consort with? What books do you read and by what authors? If you had a disagreement with your husband, would you leave your husband in order to go to your relatives? How do you share your meals with your husband? Does he beat you? What does your husband do with the money he earns? Does he entrust you with the management of the home? etc.

This interrogation enables the Court to acquaint itself personally with the personality and maturity of the applicants.

The petitioner is admitted to the register only if he has adequately proved that he has reached a degree of civilisation equal to that of a European.

By its very conception, *immatriculation* remains an exceptional measure from which "only the élite who have genuinely adopted the Western form of civilisation" can benefit. It is for this reason that, from May 1952, until the end of December 1955, the number of heads of households admitted to the register in the whole of the Congo was 116.

Assimilation of the immatriculés

Once admitted to *immatriculation,* the person registered is assimilated to the Europeans in regard to the application of the civil law and in those matters defined under the heading "Legal integration of the Congolese". He has roughly the same rights as a holder of the civic merit card.

To tell the truth, the *immatriculés* are deeply disappointed and, as a lawyer wrote recently in an article which appeared in the local press, *the Africans are no longer attracted by the beauties of immatriculation. Le Courrier d'Afrique, L'Avenir* and other journals in the Congo have often complained of the unfavourable position of the Congolese *immatriculés.* In a recent article entitled "Crisis of Confidence" which appeared in *L'Avenir* dated 25th August 1956, this journal wrote, amongst other things: " . . . we need no further example than this inglorious affair of *immatriculation,* a sort of hoax in which the Government has once again lost face by promising much and giving nothing unless it be the dust thrown in our eyes".

From the many other articles of protest published in various journals over the signatures of both Africans and Europeans who are concerned about the interests of the native population, I shall quote only two, which appeared recently in *La Voix du Congolais* of September 1956, under the title "The Problem of the *Immatriculés* and *Evolués* in general", and in *Le Courrier d'Afrique* under the heading "Where do the Congolese *"Immatriculés"* stand in the Social and Economic Sphere?":

"The *immatriculés* complain that their status confers on them more obligations than advantages. They consider that these two aspects should be at least equal, and they desire complete social equality between themselves and those whose way of living and thinking they have adopted. This is only fair. Since the way of life which they have adopted compels them to satisfy needs which are identical with those of Europeans, it is only fair that they should be given equal treatment in every sphere of life, legal, social and economic. There are privileges which it is normal to grant exclus-ively to non-natives, because of the considerable sacrifices they have made in coming to live abroad . . . But to establish a distinction based not on individual merit but solely on the colour of the skin or on egotistical claims appears in the eyes of the natives to be an insult to human dignity. The discontent which prevails among the *immatriculés* has inevitably spread to the mass of the native popu-lation, especially the developing urban classes of society."

Article from the *Courrier d'Afrique*:

"It is truly deplorable to note that the Congolese *immatriculés* have many duties but fewer advantages . . .

"Certain of the Congolese *immatriculés* who work for companies or firms are now employed under contract, as the employers have taken note of their work, their responsibilities and their duties, but those who are in the employ of the Administration are at the mercy of their superior officers . . . The Congolese *immatriculés* in Leopoldville have formed an Association with a view to claiming their social and economic rights . . . Recently they sent to the Governor General a list of claims, which they confirmed a month later to M. Buisseret, Minister for the Colonies. These demands remained unanswered. In order to keep them quiet, the authorities granted them the green card which is given to non-natives – That is not good enough – Much more far-reaching measures must be taken – For the Congolese *immatriculés* are the creation of the Belgians – The Belgians ought to be proud and happy to see the fruits of the work they have accomplished in Africa in seventy-five year.

"If certain Congolese have today succeeded in attaining a standard of living equivalent to that of the average European, it is thanks to the persevering efforts of Belgians of good will. Are these results, which have been achieved in the face of innumerable difficulties, to be regarded as valueless? . . . We ask that those Congolese *immatriculés* in the employ of the Colony, who are efficient and have a good record (excellent or very good), especially those in respon-sible positions, should be paid at the same rate as locally-engaged Europeans – and that they should travel in the same conditions as the European temporary staff . . . If the Government will not give encouragement to the Congolese *immatriculés*, they will at the same time be hindering the progress of the Congolese masses –

because the masses have their eyes fixed on the *immatriculés* to see what the Government is going to do for them and whether *immatriculation* is an advantage or not . . . At present there is a marked decline in the number of applications for *immatriculation* . . . . We ask the authorities: do they envisage assimilation for the *immatriculés* only at the legal level and not at the social level?"

The many disappointments experienced by the *evolués* have been confirmed and explained in the declaration made by the Reverend Father Van Wing, an eminent member of the Colonial Council and a specialist in African questions, on returning from his last study tour of the Congo, in the course of which he had many discussions with the *evolués* on the subject of *immatriculation* and other relevant questions. In the course of debates in the Colonial Council on a draft Bill on the assimilation to non-natives of the Congolese *evolué* of Ruanda-Urundi in connection with an increase in penal fines, he declared that the *evolués* of Leopoldville had told him that they regarded *immatriculation* as a useful piece of Belgian propaganda at the U.N. (See the summary records of the proceedings of the Colonial Council).

The unrest created by immatriculation can be understood when the following points are considered:

Congolese *immatriculés* have the same duties and responsibilities as Europeans, but not the same rights and privileges; thus there is equality of duties but not of rights.

The obligations incurred by the *immatriculés* are as follows:

- the duty to provide for their children instruction and education similar to that of the Europeans; all *immatriculé* children are required, by a decision of the Governor General, to attend European-type schools. In addition, *assimilé* parents are in duty bound to provide for their young people a first-class training and education to prepare them for a better future in the coming Belgo-Congolese Community, where they will have to work side by side with their Belgian comrades. Failing this, the children of the *immatriculés* will revert to an undistinguished life, and *immatriculation* will lose its social value, in the eyes of both Europeans and the Africans themselves;
- the duty to pay school fees and fares for the school bus to convey the children to school, and to pay for the purchase of school books, etc.
- the duty to save modest sums: (a) to enable them to pay

boarding-school fees when children are obliged to leave the parental roof to continue their secondary education elsewhere (which frequently happens in the case of inhabitants of the bush) – (b) so as not to have to live by their wits in case of prolonged illness or unemployment – (c) finally, to avoid the dangers of improvidence – especially after the death of the head of the family;

- the duty to obtain a decent home for the accommodation of his family, and to furnish it in accordance with their needs, as the Congolese are not generally housed by their employer;
- the duty of contributing by his example, behaviour, actions able appropriate to their level of education, at the social as well as the family level;
- the duty to pay the same scale of fines as non-natives, and even the same taxes;
- the duty to continue to improve his mind and character by studying and reading, which means that he has to buy books and subscribe to newspapers and magazines;
- the duty of contributing by his example, behaviour, actions and full collaboration, to the work of civilisation and development of the Congo.

The *immatriculé* like any other man, civilised or not, is subject to the natural law *that a minimum of comfort is necessary for the practice of virtue.*

Unfortunately, in spite of his legal status, his standard of living, his social position, his real needs – needs which are inherent in the life of every civilised man – and his professional competence, the Congolese *immatriculé* is, with very few exceptions, on an equal footing, both economically and socially, with every other Congolese; in the labour market he is subject to the conditions of the old labour contract (Decree of 16 March 1922), whereas he ought strictly to benefit – in the same way as the recognised "coloureds" – from the provisions of the employment contract applied to non-native employees.

The decree of the 25th June 1949 dealing with the employment contract stipulates that the Governor General may extend the benefits of this decree to any native of the Belgian Congo or of Ruanda-Urundi whose degree of evolution justifies assimilation, which means in practice the *immatriculés,* whose degree of evolution has been indisputably proved.

The report of the Colonial Council, which stresses the special position of the *immatriculé,* states that "the present decree in no way aims at establishing racial segregation in a disguised form; it proclaims the principle of non-discrimination as far as this is compatible with the present degree of evolution of the natives".

If we compare the recognised "coloureds" and the Congolese *immatriculés,* amongst whom some "coloureds" are also included, from the point of view of civilisation, education and professional skill, we find that the position is as follows: taken by and large the Congolese *immatriculés* are in advance of the recognised "coloureds" for easily understandable reasons: the Congolese *immatriculés* owe their status to their personal abilities and their degree of civilisation, of which they have been able to give adequate evidence, whilst the "coloureds" owe their position, not to their degree of evolution or their education, but to the generosity of their fathers who recognised them.

The recognised "coloureds" are treated, solely by reason of their legal status, on the same footing as the Europeans, and benefit by the same provisions of the employment contract as the latter; this is a right acknowledged to be theirs by law. The law prohibits their employment at native rates, just as it prohibits the engagement of non-natives (legally, recognised "coloureds" are non-native) under the conditions of the employment contract or statute applicable to the native population.

Now, what difference is there, from the point of view of civilisation and efficiency, between a recognised "coloured" and a Congolese *immatriculé*? It should be noted that many of the recognised "coloureds" – if not the majority – have been educated in native quarters by their mothers and taught in the same schools as the native population.

With the exception of certain recognised "coloureds" who were taught and educated either in Europe or in Africa *by their fathers,* all the other recognised "coloureds" are neither more civilised nor better educated than the Congolese *immatriculés.* Far from it. Some "coloureds" would never even have been granted *immatriculation* if they had had the misfortune not to be recognised or adopted by their fathers.

Nevertheless, the recognised "coloured", regardless of his intellect, character or skill, is, by the simple fact of his birth or adoption, treated legally and socially as a "Non-Native" and remunerated as such (on the same basis as a locally-engaged European), whilst the black or "coloured" *immatriculés,* whatever their degree of civilisation and training, and however well educated, are treated on the same footing as their *non-evolué brothers.*

What objective factors are taken into consideration to justify these distinctions: colour of skin, social ability, competence or efficiency in employment?

I ask this question because I know that governmental policy does not permit any racial discrimination. Are there perhaps other factors which we have overlooked, and which the Congolese have not appreciated? If so, they should be brought to light in order to avoid any possibility of misunderstanding.

For my part, I consider that in accordance with the principle of non-discrimination, the act of *immatriculation* should have the same legal effect as a deed of recognition or adoption, and that the Congolese *immatriculés* and the recognised or adopted "coloureds" in the Congo should, therefore, be treated on a footing of perfect equality, socially, economically and legally.

Every European, even if he has an inferior education or lower qualifications, has the right, *as a civilised man,* to a certain minimum remuneration fixed by the Administration. This minimum, which is granted to him by law, is calculated by reference to his legal status and his essential needs as a civilised man, because if he were paid a wage below this minimum he would be reduced to a standard of living which would be below his station in life and therefore intolerable.

With the object of protecting the employee, the Decree on the employment contract provides that "if the remuneration falls below the fixed minimum, proceedings may be instituted for breach of contract within ten months of termination of contract, and these may result in compensation."

As for the minimum granted to non-native employees, the law fixes this – for locally-engaged employees, including "unskilled" workers and temporary officials – at seventy-five per cent of the lowest monthly wage awarded to Administration officials, i.e. a basic 75,000 francs plus fifty-five per cent cost of living bonus, plus various other allowances.

It seems to me logical that the average European, the recognised "coloured" and the Congolese *immatriculé,* should be treated on the same equal footing and be entitled to the same rate of pay.

In short, *immatriculation* should be regarded as the final stage in integration.

It would be a serious political error to practise a policy of "the half-open door" with regard to the *immatriculés,* and such a policy would be likely to give rise later to awkward psychological repercussions among the native population. It would be denounced as discrimination, and would lead to a loss of confidence among the Congolese, to racial hatred and to a fanatical, reactionary nationalism.

The establishment of an Association of Congolese *Immatriculés* the chief aim of whose members is to claim their rights, is inevitably a prelude to this regrettable nationalistic tension between Whites and Blacks. The Association is pursuing eminently praiseworthy aims – the dignified and orderly defence of lawful interests of the *immatriculés* – but it would never have been established if the latter had been satisfied with their lot and if there had been a degree of amicable understanding between them and the Europeans.

Is any thought ever given to the long-term consequences of this policy – consequences which are certainly not the fault of the founders of the Association, but which may ultimately arise if matters do not take a different turn?

The work of colonisation undertaken in a country cannot be crowned with success or achieve its ends without the whole-hearted collaboration of the élite of the country, the leaders of the mass of the population.

The native élite, whose loyalty and level of civilisation have been officially recognised by a decision of the High Court, should be regarded as genuine allies, valuable collaborators of the Belgians, with whom they should form a united and dynamic team to continue the work of civilisation and to defend their common interests. They must be closely associated with the achievements of the Belgo-Congolese Community and act as intermediaries between their people and the colonisers, by taking an adequate share in the conduct of public affairs and the direction of national policy.

The assimilation of the élite to the Belgians must not be a one-sided affair of *Duties* and no rights; assimilation must not be partial, but *Total* and *Complete*.

The resolution on the full assimilation of the *immatriculés* was submitted to the Permanent Deputation of the Government Council in 1953 by the Congolese deputy and native representative on the Council, but it was rejected at the time because, it was stated, *public opinion (European opinion) was not favourable towards it.*

I think it advisable to recall here some generous ideas which were expressed by the honourable members of the Colonial Council during debates on the draft decree on *immatriculation* and which show that the principle of full assimilation of the *immatriculés* was acknowledged by the distinguished persons who preside over the destinies of Belgian Africa.

One eminent member urged that "the necessary legislative measures to ensure the progress of native society should be accompanied by the appropriate economic and financial measures".

Another member emphasised the importance of the draft decree which, he declared, was likely to exert a direct influence over the development of relations between the Belgians and Congolese. The controversy to which it gave rise showed that there was no dispute over the aim to be achieved but only over the means to be employed. Moreover, much of the criticism was based on an inaccurate interpretation of the word "assimilation". Here, it refers to putting the *immatriculés* and the Europeans on an equal legal and social footing. That is a great advance. The Government's policy on this point meets a human aspiration: it is unthinkable that we should grant only a part of our rights to the élite who stretch out their hand to us and show themselves worthy to enjoy the same legal system as the non-natives. *This would be a violation of human dignity, a capitulation to colour prejudice and the death-knell of our work and our aims.*

"It is, therefore, essential," he continued, "that we should be able to count on the loyal and whole-hearted collaboration of the élite and that no effort should be spared in combating individual and group colour-prejudice and removing its cause. A campaign must be started to fight this scourge."

Another member was concerned about the spirit in which the Decree would be applied. "The majority of those who have spoken on the draft Decree are in favour of the evolution of the natives, but," he declared, "they are unanimous in recommending prudence and usually appear to be opposed to their political and legal emancipation. In those fields where the possibility of assimilation has been considered, as in the case of the employment contract and the insurance and pension scheme, the administration appears to have made no use of the powers granted to it. Similarly, it is to be feared that the Decree on *immatriculation* will be applied in a reactionary way and will remain a dead letter." In conclusion, he asked for a statement concerning the number of natives who would be able to benefit from *immatriculation* and the spirit in which the

Decree would be applied.

Another member expressed himself in these terms: ". . . The general adoption of common customs, laws and ideals is one of the striking phenomena of our age. The natives who can truly claim to be *evolué* must be given the opportunity to take their place with not only Congolese citizens but also with the citizens of that universal nation called humanity. The native who has been conditioned by European ideas, won over to our philosophical, religious and social concepts, and who refuses *immatriculation* would be a deserter from civilisation and an unfortunate example to his fellows."

I cannot conclude this chapter without some discussion of the position of native priests and our future university students.

In accordance with the Decree on *immatriculation* every Congolese, whether he be a priest, bishop, university student, doctor, engineer, or provincial governor, *must*, if he wishes to be regarded as a civilised being enjoying the same legal status as the Europeans, submit his written petition to the Court of First Instance in the same way as any other native. The principle is not bad in itself merely because legal procedure is involved. But let us consider what it really means in practice.

The Congolese priests, who rank amongst the foremost civilised Africans, will not apply for *immatriculation*, not because they reject it but because they wish to avoid being slighted.

These humble apostles of God do not wish to humiliate themselves by the slighting procedure of *immatriculation*, a procedure which seems incompatible with the dignity, modesty and humility of Christian ministers.

No one disputes the level of civilisation of the native priests. After twenty years of study, including six years of primary education, six years of secondary education, three years of philosophy and five years of theology, the African priests have a completely European way of life: day and night they share the life of the European priests with whom they live on a footing of complete equality. There is absolutely no outward difference or differentiation between them and the Europeans: their assimilation is an undisputed fact, and no other Congolese – *immatriculé* or V.I.P. – enjoys the same consideration, prestige and esteem in the sphere of inter-racial and social relationships as do the priests.

It is most desirable that these priests, who are *de facto assimilés*, should be granted *immatriculation* automatically on production of documents establishing their status.

When discussing the African élite of the Congo we must bear in mind the native priests, the first élite in the country; I say first élite because from the outset of the process of colonisation the native priests have been the *only* Africans to receive a complete higher education in the training colleges, and because they have lived side by side with the European for many years, in contrast to the secular élite who live on the other side of the barrier.

Their education, character and way of life have undoubtedly brought the native priests to a degree of civilisation equal to that of the European priests whose life they share, and it seems to me that there is little justification for subjecting them to the same procedure as the ordinary Congolese whose level of development may be in doubt.

There is no question of favouring them to the detriment of other Congolese, but only of recognising their merits and absolving them from procedures which are obviously quite unnecessary in their case.

Each individual would, however, be free to adopt the system of *immatriculation* or to refuse it.

With regard to university students, I have had discussions with some of these who are at present studying in Belgium on the subject of the integration of the African élite. They were unanimous in stating that they would not apply for *immatriculation*. Some went so far as to hope that the decree would be completely abrogated, stating (quite rightly) that if justice were done and if everyone were treated fairly and according to his merits, *immatriculation* would cease to have any justification. We prefer social justice to outward show, they told me.

The law stresses that intellectual training does not constitute civilisation. "A workman who is a little more than illiterate but who has been brought up by Europeans may be completely won over by our customs, whilst a university student may have retained the traditions of his family." (Report of the Colonial Council.) This is true. It is an indisputable fact which cannot be gainsaid. Both in Africa and in Europe individuals can be found in all strata of society who, although not well-educated, are more civilised than a good number of university graduates. But looking at the question objectively, we must strike a happy mean, avoiding extremes one way or the other.

Other things being equal, it will be admitted that a man whose mind and character have been soundly trained at a university is, generally speaking, sufficiently mature to know how to behave as an upright man in accordance with the disciplines he has been taught.

We are convinced that no *evolué* – and *a fortiori,* no university graduate – has anything to gain by preserving degrading ancestral customs which are incompatible with those standards of modern civilisation, to which all members of the Congolese élite aspire.

The argument that Congolese university graduates might preserve family traditions is based on probabilities rather than on reality.

What would happen later on if the Congolese university graduates – the future leaders of the native population – were not legally assimilated to the Europeans because they had not been admitted to the "register of the civilised population?" From the legal point of view they would be subject to the legislation appropriate to the *non-evolué* mass of the population who still retain the traditional customs. This would place the university élite on the lower rungs of the social ladder, whilst the Europeans and the Congolese *assimilés,* many of whom would not have had the same training as these university graduates, would form the civilised, privileged aristocracy of the Belgo-Congolese Community.

To mention only one branch of the law, these university graduates would be tried by courts, specially designed and set up for the non-civilised (native courts, police courts, magistrate's courts and district courts), whilst the Europeans and legally assimilated would be tried by special courts for non-natives (Court of First Instance and Appeal Court). In passing, we should note that the Court of First Instance also hears, as an Appeal Court, judgements given in the first instance by the District Court or in disputes between a native and a non-native.

In the case of conviction, for example, every university graduate who is not *immatriculé* and not *assimilé,* whether he be administrator, doctor, engineer, agricultural expert, magistrate or barrister, would suffer the same prison conditions as non-white prisoners. They might perhaps benefit from the special conditions for *evolués* which, basically, are not very different from those to which the other native prisoners are subjected, whilst the Europeans, the *immatriculés,* the Asians and the Hindus are kept under different conditions reserved for civilised persons.

Such a situation could not fail to stir up strong reactions among the university-trained élite. Their self-respect would be wounded by this contrast, they would regard this treatment as an insult, and would follow the slippery slope straight into the ranks of the dis-contented – embittered men who will finally rise up against the other group with the sole aim of protesting against these injustices.

All the human revolutions which have taken place since the human race began have been caused by *latent discontent,* which finally breaks out if the causes which provoked it are not removed in time.

The attitude of the African university graduates – like that of the entire élite – will be determined by the attitude of the colonisers.

It is essential to avoid psychological and political errors which may make Jomo Kenyattas – leaders of revolt – out of Congolese university students; such errors may occur either as a result of imprudence or by over-attachment to subtle points of western law which are not always understood by the Africans. These revolts are not always caused by hatred of the Whites as some people would often have us believe, but are the consequences of political errors, discriminatory measures and injustice of which the élite of the country are the victims.

I believe that there is not a single Congolese university graduate who would refuse to adopt a status which would assist his wife and children to develop to the full and to advance to the status of civilised beings – a status which would guarantee that his family would not be dispossessed by the clan after the death of the head of the family.

As a safeguard, the *immatriculation* of university graduates might even be delayed for a certain period which could be laid down by the Administration (perhaps a year or two) at the end of which the authorities could note whether or not the applicant's way of life justified legal and social *assimilation.*

I think that this category of African élite could be trusted without much need for hesitation or formalities.

Nationality

What will and what should be the nationality of the *assimilés* or of the Congolese in general? This legal problem cannot be tackled without the support of some legal texts on the subject.

Article 1 of the Decree of the 21st June 1904, on Congolese nationality states: "Every Congolese native, as long as he resides on State territory, retains his Congolese nationality, is subject to the laws of the State and is treated as a subject of the State, particularly

D

in regard to penal jurisdiction, extradition and deportation, even if he claims to have obtained foreign nationality by naturalisation, residence abroad or in any other way, or to have put himself under the protection of a foreign power."

According to jurisprudence, since the annexation of the Congo by Belgium on 18th October 1908, Congolese nationality has ceased to exist, and Congolese nationals have acquired Belgian nationality without being Belgian citizens; they are "Belgians with colonial status".

On the other hand, in accordance with the Belgian Constitution, only the following categories of persons can be Belgian:

1. Children born of a father who has Belgian nationality at date of birth;
2. Children born in Belgium of parents who are not legally known. Children born in the Colony or abroad of parents one of whom has or had Belgian nationality, may – among others – acquire Belgian nationality by choice. It is by virtue of this provision that "coloureds" who are recognised by their fathers possess Belgian nationality.

Foreigners may also acquire Belgian citizenship by naturalisation; but Congolese may not do so since they are already Belgians with colonial status.

Such is the legal aspect of the problem, which can be summed up as follows:

The Africans of the Congo are neither Congolese (because they have lost their Congolese nationality as a result of the annexation of the Congo by Belgium) nor Belgians (because they do not have Belgian citizenship), but simply Belgian *subjects.*

Basically, there is a serious conflict between international law and the Belgian Constitution.

According to international law, any colonial territory loses its own nationality by its annexation to the occupying power, and adopts that of the colonial power; it is by virtue of this law that the native people have lost their Congolese nationality, which they still had whilst the Congo was a "FREE STATE". But the Belgian Constitution runs counter to this international law by not granting Belgian nationality to the Congolese and not permitting them to choose Belgian nationality.

As a compromise the natives have been classified as "Belgians with colonial status". [. . . here follows a phrase which has been struck out by the author.]

The fact that those Congolese who live in Belgium and have elected to make their home there do not enjoy political rights is clear proof that the natives do not have Belgian nationality.

It follows from the foregoing that the natives of the Congo are virtually "stateless", since it is impossible to claim to have a nationality if, legally, one does not enjoy the rights and advantages attaching to that nationality.

In my view the Congolese, as members of human society, must have the same right as the citizens of other nations to change their nationality if they so wish, and must no longer be deprived of their own nationality.

This question of nationality must be settled because it is of prime importance. Everyone should have a nationality and not be treated indefinitely as a member of a subject race.

I fully agree that the policy pursued by Belgium in the sphere of political emancipation has been a very wise one; to have rushed things and indiscriminately granted the Congolese the same rights as the Belgians, before they had attained the required degree of maturity, would have been a political error of another kind, detrimental to the very system of democracy which it is desired to set up in this country, a system which must rest on a firm and stable basis.

But for all that I do not think that we must wait until all the inhabitants of the country have attained the required degree of maturity before they can be granted Belgian citizenship, especially those who have expressed a real wish for it.

Whilst awaiting a general solution to this problem which can be applied to the whole of the Congolese people, we must limit ourselves to the fundamental principle of progressive and individual emancipation based on individual merit and ability. It seems to me that the time has come to grant to the Congolese élite who desire and are worthy of it (in practice the *immatriculés*) full rights of citizenship on a par with the recognised "coloureds" and naturalised foreigners; without this right of citizenship the Congolese will not enjoy the same rights and prerogative as their Belgian compatriots from the Mother Country.

It is in this spirit that, when discussing the problem of *immatriculation* and *assimilation* of the Congolese, the Commission for the

Protection of the Natives, at its meeting held in Elizabethville in 1951, considered (see note at foot of Resolution No. 31) that "to grant full equality to these *assimilés* (the *immatriculés*), it would be sufficient to grant them Belgian nationality of metropolitan status, a solution which would put an end to all discussion."

The solution to this problem depends only on the will of the Government.

This solution is not premature; it meets a real need and is in conformity with the policy for integration of the élite, a policy which has been clearly defined by the Government in all its official declarations. This policy ought to be laid down quite clearly now, in view of the existence of a group which already meets the required conditions (as regards education and maturity).

To grant the right of citizenship to the African élite – a right which would put them on the same footing as the Europeans – would be an act of justice and would also call forth in the Congolese people as a whole feelings of national pride and of friendship towards Belgium, for the *evolués*, rightly or wrongly, are no longer willing to regard themselves as members of a perpetual subject race or as victims of racial inferiority (which moreover does not exist biologically); they consider themselves to be true citizens, the equals of the Belgians, both in dignity and in civic rights.

CHAPTER IV

Justice — Native Institutions

In the Congo there are two distinct legal systems; one applicable to the Whites and *assimilés*, the other to the natives. This distinction is not based on colour, as some would like to maintain (since native *assimilés*, *immatriculés* and holders of the civic merit card are subject to the same legal system as the non-natives), but solely on the degree of civilisation of the citizens, taking into account the status of each individual.

By this distinction, the natives have the great advantage of being defended by their protector, the King's Attorney, and of benefiting by a reduction in legal fees.

Let us consider chiefly the native courts (in the chieftaincies, sectors, Centres[1] and territories).

In these different sets of courts all differences are settled in accordance with local custom. The Government has no desire to disturb native social and political organisations and leaves the courts to function according to the old Bantu ideas.

But in view of the present state of development of the Congo, after more than seventy-five years of contact with civilisation, I wonder whether a closer examination could not be made of the position of these old native institutions, some of which seem to have hampered progress. Many customs are out of date, have fallen into disuse or have been overtaken by progress. Consideration should, therefore, be given to the possibility of abolishing them in the interests of the harmonious development of the Congolese people.

New customs, half European and half Bantu, have arisen as a result of contact with the European, and these have been grafted on to purely traditional customs. These new "extra-traditional"

[1] Extra-traditional Centres, i.e. self-governing townships.

customs which can be observed in all the industrialised townships, should be codified by experts to form a new code of Congolese traditional law, in conformity with the realities of the new situation and with the state of development of the African population.

I am in favour of retaining good customs, as I have a distaste for any policy which would involve making Africans poor imitations of the Whites. We are proud to *remain* what we are, but we are also civilised Africans, imbued with respect for our personalities, our traditional institutions, and our moral standards – in so far (of course) as they are consistent with the principles of human civilisation towards which the Congo is irresistibly advancing.

In the rural districts, the life of the inhabitants is almost exclusively coloured by traditional rules; this is no longer the case in many of the industrialised regions where these traditional laws no longer retain their original form; under the influence of Christianity and many other civilising factors they have been considerably modified. This is becoming more and more noticeable in the townships where many detribalised Congolese have lost almost all their connections with their traditional background; others have broken with tradition either partially or completely.

Many Congolese who are established in these European centres have definitely chosen to live there and no longer intend to return to the country districts from which they came. Their children, who have been born in these centres, and have become parents in their turn, do not know their parents' native village or their dialect, unless it happens to be the official vernacular language of the place where they live (Lingala, Swahili, Kikongo or Kiluba). After the death of their parents, these "uprooted" people who have never seen the native village from which their parents came, remain permanently established in the European centre where they were born and have grown up. They know nothing of ancestral traditions, under which they have never lived. And what are their customs? They are "extra-traditional" customs which bear little relationship to the traditional customs of the village.

Many Congolese *evolués* who have been strongly influenced by European standards are determined to order their lives according to new ideas; they also wish to be tried not according to tradition, but according to European written law.

Unfortunately they are not able to do this, because the courts established in the extra-traditional centres are organised in the same way as the courts in the traditional areas.

Why cannot "extra-traditional courts" be established in the "extra-traditional centres"?

The *evolués* are dissatisfied with this situation.

The auxiliary officials of the Administration and the soldiers of the *Force Publique* are privileged, being under the sole jurisdiction of the territorial court presided over by the Administrator of the territory or his representative, where they have every likelihood of being tried directly by a European civil servant, and understood. But those in private employment, regardless of their degree of evolution, are tried by the courts of the Centre presided over by native judges who have had little or no education and whose judgments often require review either at the request of the defendant or on the instigation of the territorial authority.

In the case of auxiliary officials or military personnel the courts in the Centres or chieftaincies only hear exceptional disputes falling within the competence of traditional law; but this rarely happens. They also hear cases between private persons and government officials, but only when the latter are the plaintiffs.

This discrimination between Congolese employed by the administration and the army and those working in the private sector has given rise to serious and justifiable dissatisfaction [illegible] *evolués* who declare that the administration should not protect its own employees to the detriment of the employees in the private sector, instead of establishing justice for all its wards, State employees as well as employees of private undertakings.

The territorial courts are swamped by appeals because the Congolese have little confidence in the decisions of the native courts which are sometimes biased and which often impose disproportionate penalties or violate the elementary rules of justice.

The defects in the courts of the Centres which are the subject of complaint (I am speaking here in particular of the extra-traditional centres) are these:

- except in a few towns, the Judges and Counsellors of these Courts are semi-literate or illiterate; in general they are former soldiers and pensioned workmen, servants, orderlies, whose appointment is often a form of reward for some service or other. Having had no education, they lack the capacity for reasoning, objectivity, synthesis and independent judgment in reaching their decisions;
- lack of legal and ethical training required for the exercise of

the duties of Judge and Counsellor;

- almost complete ignorance of the particular traditions of each tribe (some of them being detribalised), which form the basis for the sentences. They do not even take the trouble before settling a complicated dispute to seek information (have they been instructed to do so?) from qualified persons in the Centre who are better acquainted with the traditions of a particular region – especially in the case of a dispute between two *non-evolué* natives who still observe their respective traditions.
(We recognise that the Bantu traditions have a common basis in many spheres, but they differ on certain points.)

- being paid very little – miserably paid, if we may say so – they are easily corrupted; this explains their proverbial venality, for which the natives have various words; thus the Judges can be bought and these bribes, known in Swahili country as "Kanyaka", ensure them a valuable addition to their modest fees.

This venality is mainly due to the miserable salaries paid to the Judges. Without this "greasing of the palm" they would have great difficulty in making ends meet. This is very regrettable.

Would not European judges succumb to the same temptation if they were inadequately paid? The Counsellors, instead of backing up the Administration in its task, are there only for appearance sake (although there are exceptions); some have no contact with the inhabitants they represent, whereas Article 10 of the co-ordinated decrees on the extra-traditional Centres stipulates that "the Centre Counsellors shall individually assist the Chief of the Centre and the representative of the protecting power in the exercise of their duties by keeping them informed of the wishes of the inhabitants".

During the debates of the central council they often support the "Yes" or "No" of the Chairman of this council without understanding its import. Many counsellors – especially those who are illiterate – have not even any idea of the democratic nature of the discussions and imagine – quite mistakenly – that to say "No" when the Administrator has said "Yes", or to make a quite proper observation when they have not understood the question, would result in their dismissal or would "put them in the bad books" of their chief. This is an error of judgment but a very common one!

The administrator asks nothing better than to be enlightened by his judges and counsellors.

All this explains why the action of certain judges and counsellors is valueless, and why the inhabitants lose patience when they see themselves being sentenced and represented by persons who are not fitted for this task.

There are other judges who are extremely honest and conscientious, but their number is unfortunately very small. [Further defects in the courts of the Centres are:]

-   the clerks employed in these courts are very poorly educated (their education has generally not been continued beyond the primary stage). Some judgments are badly drawn up, the main forms of procedure are not fully observed, the registry not properly kept. The majority of these clerks of the court are not equal to their task.
-   the judgments delivered are not always put into effect and little trouble is taken to see that they are put into effect. Persons sentenced to the payment of damages are not always imprisoned for debt in case of non-payment by the expiration of the stipulated period (they only need stand the judge or clerk a drink to obtain an extension of the time-limit).
-   cases on the list for trial often drag on for months without being heard, not because of shortage of staff but because of carelessness on the part of certain judges. During debates an enormous amount of time is wasted in unnecessary chit-chat (this is a common fault with the Congolese: they palaver too much . . .), failure to observe regular hours for hearings and unpunctuality on the part of judges.

In the course of my inquiry I noted that the judges of one court did not arrive together at a fixed time but each one arrived at a time to suit himself and proceedings could not begin until one or other of the judges had arrived. As a result, instead of delivering ten judgments per day, only three or five are delivered.

I have also discovered a lack of method in working and a lack of initiative.

Prison sentences are often imposed for minor offences which call for a caution or merely a fine. Fines, too, are often severe and out of proportion to the gravity of the offence even in routine offences.

All the anomalies which I have just mentioned are more striking in urban Centres.

In traditional areas excellent judges are to be found; very wise, upright, influential and honest, respected and trusted by the inhabi-

tants. They are traditional judges, and they have a thorough knowledge of the laws which they are called upon to apply. Generally
speaking they are in easier circumstances than the low-salaried
judges in the European Centres who are burdened by innumerable
troubles and financial difficulties and resort to extortion.

To protect the inhabitants from the whims of the judges, the
native courts ought to have a penal code like that of the European
courts, laying down the punishment for any particular breach of the
law with minimum and maximum penalties. All the offences which
come within the competence of these courts should, therefore, be
listed.

The excessively long drawn-out and rigorous application of
ancestral traditions in the extra-traditional towns is no longer justified in certain spheres – especially in regard to the evolving class
which desires to free itself to some extent from tribal law.

There is no question here of artificial Europeanisation or of withdrawing from one's own people, but of a progressive adaptation to
the process of evolution.

As M. Georges Brausch, Doctor of Colonial Science, has written,
traditions ought to be recorded. In the same survey, published by
M. Brausch in *Problèmes d'Afrique Centrale* No. 20 (1955), we
read the following resolution, submitted by the Symposium organised from the 13th to 15th April 1955, by the Afrika Institut of
Leyden:

"If it is desired that traditional law shall be a dynamic factor in
the future progress of the African peoples, it must not be isolated
from the main stream of justice as is the case in the territory. The
responsibility for applying traditional law should not be regarded
as an exclusive duty reserved to a certain category of court. On the
other hand, it is important that the responsibility for applying the
law should be entrusted to judges whose qualifications and duties
enable them to consider the question in the light of wider considerations. This presupposes not only an improvement in the legal
training given to the Africans but also more care in ensuring that
the African courts are supervised and directed by persons who are
specially qualified to do so by reason of their knowledge and
experience."

If this aim were achieved in the Congo – and we hope it will be –
the present anomalies would be greatly reduced, the people would
have competent judges worthy of their title, and finally the Administration would gain a body of valuable collaborators who would

make an effective contribution to the evolution of the country and to the fair application of the law.

The situation can be improved immediately in the large centres, such as Leopoldville, Coquilhatville, Luluabourg, Matadi, Stanleyville, Bakavu, Elisabethville, Usumbura, Kindu, etc. A simple decision by the competent authorities would suffice to replace incapable judges by more competent ones. A number of Congolese have specialised in an elementary study of the written law, traditional law, the judiciary system, the principles of native policy, etc. These future stipendiary judges and counsellors can be recruited from amongst the officials attached to the Record Office and the public Prosecutor's Department, the counsels for the defence at the native courts, and employees of the Government and the private sector who show the necessary aptitude and who could leave their departments to enter the service of the native divisions.

It would be essential for these people to receive a remuneration in keeping with the dignity of their duties, which would also ensure that they were not exposed to the temptation of corruption or extortion as is the case at present. The same scheme of pay and promotion could be applied to them as to auxiliary officials of the African Administration.

It would be advisable to set up a special grade for this category of officials, called "Judiciary Personnel Grade in the Native Divisions" with seniority as for other State employees. Included in this grade would be: judges, counsellors and clerks of the court.

The social and economic evolution of a people must be accompanied by legal evolution.

CHAPTER V

Equality before the Law — Prison System

Ideally, there should ultimately be a single legal system applicable to both Whites and Africans. At present, it can be seen that in punishing offences the sentences are lightened for the Europeans – enforcement is sometimes suspended (stay of execution), whilst for the Blacks sentences seem to be more severe and usually include prolonged imprisonment. Similar breaches of the law are thus punished differently depending on whether a Black or a White is involved: in the case of the latter the minimum penalty is often imposed, whereas the maximum penalty is imposed in the former case.

This is the general impression of the Congolese on this subject.

Experience shows that an excessively long period of imprisonment by no means assists the re-education of the prisoners. On the contrary, as a result of prolonged contact with offenders of all types, prisoners are often exposed to harmful influences which affect them for the rest of their lives; others contract vices which they did not have prior to their imprisonment. There is no more unhealthy place than the interior of a Congolese prison; the prisoners have no topics of conversation beyond recounting their exploits, teaching each other the tricks of the trade, indulging in violent criticism of both the legal and administrative authorities who have condemned them, and hatching plots.

To console themselves in their misery they devise all kinds of immoral diversions: men change themselves into women and the majority of the influential prisoners each have their "special" woman. Many prisoners follow this path, either willingly or under skilful compulsion. This is common currency in prisons. How scandalous this is! Those who did not smoke hemp outside prison smoke it inside. In spite of the most careful searches, hemp circulates in prisons in large quantities. The morale of the prisoners is undermined by it day and night.

The separation of prisoners into special categories is purely theoretical, with the exception of the "dangerous" category (generally captured escapees or troublemakers inside the prison), who are confined together; but in spite of everything, they have contacts with other prisoners and continue the same malpractices.

It is certain that imprisonment does not have the same moral effect on the Congolese as it does on Europeans. The latter regard imprisonment as a dishonour and an ineradicable stain on their reputation; this is not the case with the ordinary Congolese.

My survey shows that the *evolués* are to a certain extent affected in the same way as the Europeans.

It is essential, on the one hand, to establish equal justice for all men regardless of colour, and on the other hand, to modify the method of punishing offences where natives are concerned.

To ensure that imprisonment will have an emotional as well as an educative effect on the Congolese, the traditional concepts held by the Africans with regard to imprisonment should be taken into consideration when pronouncing the sentence. European concepts do not always have the same effect where the Congolese are concerned. The aim of the prison must be to rehabilitate the prisoners and not to punish them in such a way as to make them worse than they were before their imprisonment.

Before the arrival of the European, no one had ever been detained in prison for a period of years or for the whole of his life. Offenders were punished expeditiously, and these old methods had a greater effect than the European methods.

Our people have never known the outbreaks of offences which are prevalent in the Congo today, and this trend is continually increasing. Can it be that colonisation has led to a loosening of standards?

Theft, for instance, was rare before the arrival of the Europeans. You could close your house with a piece of string and go off on a journey lasting several weeks without fear of anyone breaking in. I believe that the new needs created by civilisation and the difficulties of obtaining what is required for subsistence, are the main causes of theft. The same applies to prostitution. How can single women from poor families, who have never had the opportunity to find a husband, live unless they commit misconduct? No one wants to do this, but how can they live otherwise? Can public charity feed them,

house them and keep them for the whole of their lives? Many
people complacently condemn prostitution (we also condemn it
because it is a social scourge) without suggesting any remedy. Prostitution seems to be the price paid for civilisation; we do not know
how it can be successfully eradicated.

You do not find girls selling their services in the country villages
as is the case in towns.

Finally, the punishment of offences deserves to be re-examined.

Prisoners should live in rather more humane conditions, more in
keeping with human dignity. In certain prisons, the meals served
to prisoners are practically uneatable, meals such as even a primitive
and poor native would not eat at home. Some *evolué* prisoners do
not eat these meals, and fast except for a grilled banana. What is
worse, prisoners are forbidden to eat home-prepared meals brought
to them by members of their family on visiting days.

What does the diet consist of? In the morning a few groundnuts;
at midday a dry *chikwang* which is very difficult to chew (it should
be noted that many Congolese do not eat *chikwang* which is a
special food of *certain* tribes only); at four o'clock, rice, badly prepared in large dirty casks, or very dark manioc flour,[1] with the addition of unwashed salted fish, badly cooked. Each evening the prison
refuse bins are filled with uneaten meals thrown out by the
prisoners. Some are compelled to eat by hunger because there is no
other food.

Prisoners in small prisons in the interior are better fed than those
in the large centres.

They are not allowed to wear vest, trunks or shoes; only holders
of a special permit supplied by the doctor are allowed to wear shoes.
They sleep on boards, laid on the ground.

Non-recognised "coloureds", merely because of their brown skin,
wear shoes, have suitable clothes, sleep on beds provided with a
mattress, sheets and mosquito nets; they eat well, and are attended
by other prioners who act as servants; yet other Congolese prioners,
who have reached a higher level of civilisation and evolution, live
in indescribable conditions far below that level.

Why are distinctions drawn between prisoners on grounds of
colour instead of their degree of evolution and civilisation?

There are four categories of prisoners: 1. Europeans and
assimilés; 2. non-recognised ("coloureds"); 3. Congolese *evolués,*

[1] *Manioc*: tapioca.

termed "special class of *evolués*" and 4. non-*evolués*. This classifica-
tion seems faulty, and it gives rise to justifiable criticism. The
"coloureds" category ought to be abolished, because it gives the
obvious impression that the Government is practising racial discrimination, at the very moment when a battle is being waged
against such discrimination.

The non-recognised "coloured" who is not an *immatriculé* and
does not hold the civic merit card, is a Congolese just like any other
and should be treated as such. We have a good deal of sympathy for
the "coloureds" both recognised and non-recognised, and we are
not attacking them, but we do protest against the practice of racial
discrimination because this unjustifiable discrimination is not authorised by any law.

We see no objection to the "coloureds" benefiting by special
treatment, in fact we welcome it as an act of humanity towards
these children who were abandoned and rejected by their fathers.
But it must be conceded that there is something wrong when an
important Chief, a supervisory clerk in the Administration, a distinguished employee or a Congolese of superior education, are
treated in prison as common individuals, deprived of their clothing
and their respect, whilst the non-*evolué* "coloured" taxi-driver,
docker, apprentice mechanic or waiter are treated with consideration
because their skins are not black. I think that the Congolese *evolués*
are more deserving than non-*evolué* "coloureds" and that they have
at least the right to the same consideration as that accorded to the
latter.

Prisoners who are granted the special diet for *evolués* only have
the advantage of eating slightly differently from the other prisoners;
the food is the same but it is slightly better prepared. In regard to
clothing and accommodation there is no difference; bare feet, board
beds, flogging, solitary confinement, etc.

The right to an *evolué* diet does not depend on the prisoner's stage
of cultural development or any merit, but on the goodwill of the
prison officer; it is not a right but a favour, which can be granted
even to a non-*evolué;* ninety per cent of the genuine *evolués* who
should benefit by this diet do not do so, with the result that Sector
Chiefs, skilled workmen and office clerks are put together with other
non-*evolué* prisoners, whilst others, less culturally advanced, benefit
from the special diet.

The *evolués* seem to be looked on with less favour than the other
Congolese.

The decree on prison diet states, in Article 17, that "exceptionally the district commissioner or his delegate may take into consideration the social status or the degree of civilisation of a non-white prisoner when making such changes in favour of the prisoner as he deems fit with regard to accommodation, clothing, food, work and discipline. In this matter he will conform to the instructions of the Governor General or the Provincial Governor".

This is too theoretical since it is more honoured in the breach than in the observance. Apart from legal *assimilés,* I have never seen a Congolese prisoner who has benefited from improvements in regard to accommodation, clothing, discipline, etc. I have seen with my own eyes leading *evolués,* invested chiefs [illegible] of the Administration, living in exactly the same conditions as any other non-white prisoner. Improvements may be made in the other centres which I have not visited, but I think that the situation is more or less the same everywhere.

Prison is always a prison, a place of punishment. The Congolese do not wish to live in luxury, but they wish to serve their sentence under rather more suitable conditions and to be treated with respect like the "coloureds" because they all have a right to the same consideration and to the same respect for human dignity.

Flogging

In my view, taking into consideration the state of mind and the cultural development of the native population, it is time that flogging was abolished as a punishment in the Congo. This primitive punishment is a relic which is no longer appropriate in the present day and age.

I share the view that prison conditions should be strict, with the object of re-educating the offenders. If desired, convicts could be sentenced to hard-labour rather than continue to be subjected to a punishment which involves tearing human flesh by the whip even for minor offences; hard-labour will exert a greater effect on prisoners than the whip.

The Congo ought not to be the only African country where natives continue to be flogged mercilessly.

The law punishes people who torture or maltreat *animals,* and human beings ought not to be cruelly treated under the pretext that they have committed an offence.

The majority of Europeans in the Congo are not in favour of the abolition of flogging. I have had discussions with many of them on this subject, and they all say: "If flogging is abolished that will be the end of disclipine among the natives; they will no longer stand in awe of the Europeans and the representatives of authority, there will be disorder, etc."

Are these arguments valid? I do not think so. You do not win the confidence, respect or obedience of a subject people by wickedness, cruelty or harshness, but by good administration, respect for the rights of citizens, and just and humane treatment. In such conditions respect comes *naturally* and willingly, and authority is based on a solid foundation. A chief who is respected and obeyed because he is feared has no influence over his subjects and his actions have no effect; he will be respected and obeyed as long as he is seen but when he is absent he will no longer be respected or obeyed; even what has been done and built up in his presence will be destroyed.

I do not believe that the whip is the reason why the Congolese have so far remained attached to the Belgians; it is not because of the whip that the Congo has been built up; it is not because of the whip that native workers come and offer their services to the European, it is not because of the whip that these large and flourishing plantations and the colossal enterprises which are scattered all over the Congo have enriched their owners; it is not because of the whip that the Belgo-Congolese Community will be built up, but through mutual esteem and mutual trust.

Any form of militarism is incompatible with a firmly-based union.

Moreover, Circular No. 1/Just. dated 31st August 1947, prohibits the flogging of native authorities and judges, NCOs in the *Force Publiqué,* members of the native clergy, *evolué* native officials. The abolition of the whip for these categories of Congolese is evidence of the consideration shown by the Government towards the various classes of the Congolese élite. But unfortunately, the intentions of the Government are not always translated into action by the executive officials, and these difficulties can often be traced back to the officials.

I have been able to ascertain, from first-hand reports and personal observation, that this prohibition is a dead letter. Former NCO's of the *Force Publique,* clerks in the Administration, and *evolués* of high standing, who benefit by the "special system for *evolués"* in prison, are flogged, in spite of the fact that attention has frequently been drawn to these instructions by the higher authorities.

The Government is making a considerable effort to improve the prison system for the Congolese by setting up trade apprenticeship workshops, holding cinematographic shows of an educational and recreational nature, organising courses, etc. I can thus state that prison is not always a place of punishment, but is also a place of rehabilitation, the main purpose of which is to restore the offenders to a normal life.

Punishment by flogging was more appropriate for Arab slaves; the Arab era has passed away and this degrading form of punishment should now be completely abolished.

CHAPTER VI

Reforming the Police

The recruitment of illiterate policemen should be discontinued, and the syllabus of the police schools should gradually be strengthened. The only way to secure educated and competent policemen is to make the policeman's career rather more remunerative than it is at present. Otherwise we shall always have second-rate people without a trade, who enrol in the police force as a last resort, like despairing men enrolled in the Foreign Legion.

The Congolese police force is at present composed almost exclusively of military personnel discharged from the *Force Publique,* the majority of whom can neither read or write; all the former military intellectuals (NCO cashiers, operators, office clerks, workmen, etc.) find employment elsewhere.

The majority of our present policemen have no clear conception of what their job involves; instead of the police being servants of the public and adopting a courteous attitude to members of the public, it is the public who are in the service of the police and often witness regrettable scenes between police and citizens; arbitrary arrests, abuse of authority, extortion, etc.

I have come across bands of police who regularly arrest people at night – even before curfew – with the sole object of "getting their own back".

They are often guilty of making slanderous statements in front of government officials, and, as they are often trusted, their victims pay dearly. This is not always the case; besides I have refrained from comment, as that would give the impression of drama. This is personal experience. Some uneducated people do, of course, behave incorrectly towards the officers of law and order; I sincerely regret this. But the fantasies of our policemen have become proverbial, and the reason for this lies in their illiteracy and lack of ethical principles.

Every policeman should be able to read and write in order to check the documents of persons apprehended and to perform other minor clerical duties connected with their work. Sometimes policemen are given summonses for distribution in the city and, not being able to read, they have to ask passers-by to show them the address indicated in the summons; this is the only way in which they can reach the addresses. Sometimes summonses will be thrown away by an illiterate policeman who has not succeeded in finding the addressee, and in this case the latter is in trouble with the authorities for having *refused to comply with a summons*, when in actual fact he has never received it.

It would be an excellent thing, too, if a Police College could be set up later on in the Congo, open to holders of a diploma in the humanities or secondary education. This College would provide a sound legal and administrative training which would fit its graduates for the duties of police commissioners and judicial police officers. They would be assistants to European police commissioners at the very least! The task of the latter would thus be eased.

CHAPTER VII

Freedom of Movement

Curfew in the townships

It is being increasingly borne out, by articles published by Congo-lese in various papers and by numerous statements issued at meet-ings of cultural associations, that whilst conceding the need for measures of public security, everyone would like to have rather more liberty of movement at night.

"Europeans can move about freely in their quarters from six o'clock in the evening until six o'clock in the morning and the same should apply to us. The principles of individual liberty should be observed in our case, too. The rights of honest citizens should not be sacrificed because of the misdeeds committed by a few footpads who work under cover of darkness. We pay taxes, and this money should be used to engage as many policemen as is necessary to enforce the law. *Immatriculés* and holders of the civic merit card who have been given permission to move freely during the night are not the only Congolese *evolués* to benefit from this measure. We do not wish to go into the European quarter at night, unless it is for a good reason, but we do wish to be free in our own township, as the Europeans are in theirs, and as other Congolese are in the country districts where there is no prohibition on movement at night. We are not chickens to be shut up in our houses when we have no desire to sleep. We do not ask for freedom in order to steal during the night or commit crimes, but to avoid trouble with the police who often infringe our personal liberty without adequate justification."

These are the views of the Congolese on this matter. In Leopoldville, Elisabethville, Stanleyville or elsewhere the theme is always the same.

The control of movement at night is a police measure taken in the interests of the inhabitants, with the object of protecting them against footpads. The curfew hours differ from one area to another, because this is a local measure taken by the local authority in each township.

In my view, as soon as an adequate number of policemen can be made available to ensure order, both by day and by night, it will be possible to allow freedom of movement for all.

CHAPTER VIII

The Congolese in the Towns

The reasons for the exodus of Congolese to the towns are as follows:

1. to escape from poorly paid forced labour and from the harshness of certain Chiefs;
2. to seek work with a view to earning the money they need to get married and enjoy a modicum of comfort (to buy a bicycle, a gramophone, clothing, footwear, etc.);
3. to have a little more freedom than is possible under the yoke of traditional laws and obligations from which some wish to escape;
4. to obtain a good education.

1 and 2 are the main and most common reasons, especially the second.

It is certainly deplorable to see whole villages being emptied and the population pouring into the large towns where many Congolese are often completely out of their element.

The majority of the Congolese who leave their village have no trade except that of a farmer. When they arrive in the large towns – very often with the aid of a false or forged Change of Residence Permit – they usually join the ranks of the unemployed, the parasites and finally . . . the footpads.

But the reasons for their exodus are understandable and legitimate; every man has the right to seek to improve his lot by honest means, or to leave his native heath to seek his fortune elsewhere if he cannot find it at home.

In spite of extremely severe regulations controlling the issue of Change of Residence Permits and the right to reside in the extra-

traditional Centres, the exodus goes on undiminished: the population of the Centres increases at the same pace, and each year sees
an increase in the number of unrecorded and unauthorised immigrants. In many of the villages in the interior you will no longer
find any young people; although removal from one district to
another is forbidden, they provide themselves with Change of
Residence Permits.

Sometimes the irregularities are discovered by the Administrative office at their place of destination. The persons concerned are
imprisoned for forgery and sent back, on their release, to their
native village; but they are astute enough to infiltrate amongst the
regular inhabitants (harboured, of course, by their "ndeke"[1]) and
they always manage to regularise their position one way or another.

All these regulations for the issue of Change of Residence Permits and permits to stay in the Centres have proved to be ineffective.

The territorial officials administering the native townships and
the extra-traditional centres know quite well that there are large
numbers of unauthorised immigrants in their areas; men and
children from villages in the interior, carrying forged passports or
lacking any identity documents. Not a week passes without some
unauthorised persons being arrested and convicted.

In spite of the good intentions of the administration, and regular
round-ups all these efforts are doomed to failure. The exodus continues at an increased rate.

Other remedies must be sought, since those which have been tried
so far have failed to produce the desired effect.

Do not these restrictions on movement from one area to another
constitute in some degree an infringement of the individual liberty
of the Congolese? And what will happen when the natives have the
right to move freely within their country and to establish their home
where they wish?

If the exodus is to be slowed down, the living conditions of the
natives in the country districts must be so improved that they no
longer envy the city-dwellers. In my opinion, the measures to be
taken are the following:

-   prohibition of unpaid work, except for certain traditional
    obligations which are essential for the maintenance of the
    social balance.

[1] *Ndeke*: literally 'bird', but used to describe relations; 'brother',
in the African sense, that is people coming from the same village,
clan or extended family.

 - the purchase of their products at a reasonably remunerative price; some prices fixed by the Administration are at present the prices which these products would normally fetch on the free market;
 - installation, in the centre of each chieftaincy and of all large villages, of public-address systems for the dissemination of regional news. What an immense pleasure it would be for these music-loving people to hear every evening the beautiful music of the country sung by native artistes and broadcast over the magic waves!
 - the organisation under the direction of Chiefs and instructors of certain youth activities (football games, scouting, etc.).
 - some diversions could also be organised for adults (inter-village and inter-chieftaincy cycle races for which prizes would be offered, etc);
 - setting up of Social Centres in those districts which are of sufficient size to justify them.

Town-dwellers ought not to be the only people to profit by the services of welfare officers. It would be of considerable social interest if attention could be given at the same time to the cultural development of native women in the country areas;

 - each native should be given the opportunity to choose the most rewarding type of work, instead of being restricted to inadequately paid compulsory work. An exception would be made in the case of work of importance to the community generally.

The cost of organising youth activities, setting up Social Centres and installing public-address systems could be borne by the native District Funds, either in full, if sufficient funds were available, or in part.

Social Secretariats

There is an urgent need for Social Secretariats to investigate social questions and develop inter-racial and public relations.

Government officials who are actively interested in social questions have confessed to me that they would prefer to devote themselves exclusively to such a service, where they would be in closer touch with the real problems of Congolese life, instead of being tied down to paperwork which leaves them little leisure.

These voluntary social advisers would play an important part in the Belgo-Congolese Community and their work would undoubtedly be extremely constructive and fruitful. Their duties would come within the framework of the achievements of that great community, the principles of which have been worked out and accepted by all the inhabitants. The only thing which now remains to be done is to make the move towards putting these principles into practice. This requires, in addition to the good will of the Government and the people, efficient voluntary action by a few apostles of civilisation who, by their influence, their propaganda, their devotion to the common cause, would succeed in reconciling the interests of the two sections of the Belgo-African population.

There is nothing Utopian about this. My experiments on these lines in certain sectors, in collaboration with fellow workers amongst the Belgians, have produced good results which have satisfied even the higher authorities.

Alcoholism threatens the future of the Congo

Faced with the continual increase in alcoholism in the Congo, we cannot look to the future without some anxiety. The majority of the people in the urban areas seem to be passionately fond of drink. For many people the bar has become their sole place of recreation; they do not realise the grave danger which it constitutes for their people – the danger of degradation through alcoholism.

All the Government propaganda against alcohol on the radio, in the press and through leaflets, has ended in total failure.

It is impossible to prevent the Congolese from drinking by force. If the sale of beer to the Congolese were controlled and reduced, the brewers and shopkeepers would demonstrate against the Government with bombs, accusing it of "attacking the freedom of trade", and the consumers themselves would protest.

It is up to the Africans themselves to appreciate the danger which threatens their society. It is not a question of preventing them from drinking but of persuading them to drink in moderation, in their own interests and in the interests of their families and of the future of their country.

Young people straight from school, who could form a rising élite, often end up, for various reasons, by being contaminated by drunkenness. The reason for this is to be found in the proverb:

"Opportunity makes the thief"; it is the bad environment in which these young people make their contact with life: this is a phenomenon which is explained by various sociological and psychological factors.

This cancer of alcoholism is slowly eating into our people.

What will be the future of our beautiful country if the majority of our children become drunkards, forgetful of their duties to the family, to society, to the community and to their work?

A country which is dominated by alcoholism is a country condemned to degeneration and ruin.

Let us not stray from the proper path which has been marked out for us, and which our educators continue to point out to us, to follow the path of degradation.

The bars consume not only our material riches but also our riches of character and our intellectual gifts which gradually seep away as alcoholism overcomes our systems.

It is sad to note that many people, on leaving the office or the factory, instead of going home or to the library, make straight for the cafés and stay there until closing time, giving hardly a thought to their wives and children who are alone in the house, anxiously awaiting the arrival of the head of the family.

The libraries which have been opened for the Congolese in the main centre of each territory are too little used – not at all in some places. I am, myself, the librarian of a large library which has been opened in the centre of a large province, but you will be amazed to learn that there are not more than ten regular readers, and that often several weeks go by without a single reader. The books, supplied regularly by the Government, are mouldering.

There is very little interest in reading, this inexhaustible source of mental riches.

Here the examples of Leopoldville and Elisabethville are very encouraging. In these two towns, in particular, more and more *evolués* are interested in study as a means of self-improvement and are aware of their responsibilities towards society. We hope that this change will become evident in all the other towns of the Congo thanks to the influence of the élite.

Alcoholism threatens our country. Every *evolué* who cares about the future of his country should reflect on this subject and behave accordingly.

Administration of the extra-traditional centres

It would be a good thing if the duties of Chief of an extra-traditional centre were entrusted only to capable persons of sound education and good character. It is no easy matter to administer a place of thirty, forty, fifty or one hundred inhabitants or more, composed of a wide diversity of peoples drawn from all parts of the Congo, from the humblest worker to the highest intellectual. The man at the head of such a variegated township should be above the average in education if he is not to be overwhelmed and crushed by responsibilities and complex problems which are beyond his powers and his intellectual capacity. The prestige of the Chief is at stake in the eyes of the people under his administration.

Experience shows that an uneducated Chief has virtually no influence over the people, especially in the urban centres where he can only win their respect, esteem and confidence by his superior intellect, character and dignity.

CHAPTER IX

The Land Problem
and European Immigration

I cannot speak too highly of the wisdom of the policy followed so far by the Government and the honourable members of the Colonial Council in the matter of transfer and granting of land. The rights of the natives have been strictly respected by the Administration, to such an extent that it has been impossible for anyone to encroach upon the rights of the native population.

This wise policy should be maintained, particularly with an eye on the future. The land problem is the most important and the most delicate problem which can arise in the colonies. It has always been a source of numerous disputes between the settlers and the natives in certain colonies. That is why the Government should always devote to this problem all the attention it deserves, so that the interests of the settlers and the colonised do not clash. The consequences are always far-reaching.

In saying this I am not attacking the Europeans who have established themselves as our neighbours or who would like to do so. It is a question of safeguarding the natural rights of the natives against those who would try to usurp them. It is also a question of safeguarding rights already acquired by settlers or which may be acquired by settlers by due legal processes.

Much has been said recently about settlement by Europeans. I have followed the discussions very closely.

In the last analysis I find – on the basis of considerable evidence – that the settlers consider and believe that only a speedier settlement – by Europeans – on a large scale could safeguard their position in Africa. They are convinced (according to their own prophecies) that they will ultimately have to submit to the law of minorities. For them, the Belgo-Congolese Community of which the Government

talks so much, *is only a vague dream* (see an open letter addressed
to the Minister for the Colonies and published in *Essor du Congo*
on the 10th November 1956, which expresses the opinion of the
majority of the Katanga settlers.This opinion, which, has often been
expressed by various settlers' associations in the Congo, is shared
by the majority of Congolese settlers).

The letter to which we refer also contains the following phrase:
"What will be the part played by the two sections of this Community? *What will their future be if the law of numbers prevails,
as it must one day and we can already foresee to whose disadvantage?*" (i.e. to the disadvantage of the Whites).

The Congo is no longer a conquered colony to be exploited,
where people come with the sole intention of filling their own
pockets.

The task for Africa in this modern age must be the task *of
humanising and harmonising opposing interests and relations* between Europeans and Africans.

What rather disturbs us about large-scale settlement is the later
and possibly distant *consequences* which this settlement *might*
involve: *Occupation of all the good land by Europeans – impos-
sibility for Congolese to secure land in the vicinity of the large towns
or urban centres – compulsion on future African settlers (agricultural and industrial) to establish themselves in very distant parts of
the country, since the approaches to large and industrialised centres
will all be occupied by European settlers – Difficulties for the small
African tenant-farmer in developing his land by the side of the
powerful European tenant-farmer – Occupation of all important
posts by Europeans – Priority of employment for Europeans.* which
would probably cause unemployment amongst some of the African
élite or reduce them to minor functions, as is the case at present
(there are already signs of this: the Trade Unions of employees
in the public and private sector have already protested officially
against the fact that some tasks which could normally be entrusted
to Congolese élite are being given to white women, who could quite
well be satisfied with their husbands' incomes, leaving Africans an
opportunity to earn their living). Would not the effect be even
greater if the number of Europeans were two or three times what
it is today? Women certainly have the same right to work as men.
But when the husband has a good income, surely it is only fair for
the wife, in these circumstances, to give up her place to a man who
has no resources?

The Congolese, who still lack the necessary resources to set up on their own account (the activity of smallholders at the moment is limited to petty trade mainly in the urban centres), will find it physically impossible – even several decades hence – to share in the industrialisation of the country. Thus only the Europeans will be able to carry out the function of settlers in the full sense of the term, for many years to come, and the scope of their activities will continually expand. Can this progressive extension of European settlement be reconciled with the future interests of the black settler, and will it allow the latter to expand his activities?

Provided that European settlement does not threaten to destroy African settlement; provided that the black settlers place themselves under the sponsorship of the white settlers and the latter support them and help them to develop; provided that the European settlers and the black settlers live in harmony and form a unified, single group; provided that the European population fraternises with the Congolese population; provided that we can have firm and sincere guarantees; then we shall meet at the gateway to the Congo to shout a loud WELCOME to this large-scale influx of people, and wish them a happy stay amongst us.

At all events, the Government's present policy of careful selection for European immigration into the Congo should be continued; without it there would be a risk of admitting persons who would constitute a danger for the future Belgo-Congolese Community. But selection need not mean restriction.

I much prefer to have Belgians, French or other nationalities in the Congo rather than the Asians and Arabs, who come with the sole aim of enriching themselves. Their behaviour amongst the natives is often scandalous. The Congolese *evolués* have already complained to the local authorities about the behaviour of certain ill-famed members of these communities. We asked that some of them should be expelled, not merely because their conduct was scandalous, but also because they carried on subversive activities. We obtained no satisfaction.

Perhaps there will be more understanding of this problem later on.

Not all Asians are bad. We have some very good ones. But I am convinced that a large number of them bring no benefit either to the Africans or the Europeans. Many are the times that they have ruined Belgian traders by their unfair competition. They are specialists in the practice of dumping.

It is a great pity that the Congo comes under an international statute and that by virtue of the principle of freedom to trade granted by the famous Berlin Agreement of the 26th February 1885, all nations enjoy complete equality in commercial matters in the Congo, and hence even the sons of those who ravaged our country can come to exploit us once again under another guise.

Could not an amendment or correction be made to this nineteenth-century Convention?

The Congo ought not to be an international market whose gates are open even to its enemies. We want to see friendly people coming to the Congo and not just anybody who is forced upon us by the Berlin Agreement. Every one should be master in his own house. The Congo should be *nationalised*. Let the shareholders in the Congo, i.e. the signatories to the Berlin Agreement, have their shares returned to them. Let us render to Caesar what is Caesar's. No country in the world can be internationalised. We shall live with our friends and not with our exploiters.

As for settlement, it would be desirable to give the Congolese the same opportunities as the Belgians so that they could both contribute to the development of the country. We are thinking in particular of those who would like to set up on their own account, but who, although of satisfactory character and ability, cannot offer the requisite financial security (mortgage property) to obtain loans from the *Société de Credit au Colonat et à l'Industrie* (Credit Company for Settlers and Industry).

It is essential that adequate material aid should be given to the African middle classes. They must be supported in their efforts.

I hope that a solution will be found on the lines indicated here, so that at a later stage Belgian and African settlers may be found working shoulder to shoulder in the industrialisation of the Congo.

Such co-operation is indispensable if European settlement is to be stabilised. This will be unbalanced if the Africans have no means of sharing in this vast programme of development of the Congo.

The policy of establishing separate associations for the European and African settlers does not augur well for the future of the country. The best policy would have been to unite the European and African settlers in a single association in order to ensure that certain interests do not create or foment divisions and divergencies of outlook. These divisions are already beginning to appear in a latent form.

In fact, in one Province where I am in close touch with the situation, there is already serious tension between an association of European settlers and one of African settlers, and this is turning into open hostility. The connecting link between the two associations, one of which had been placed under the sponsorship of the other, has snapped. It would probably require a considerable effort to bring them back into harmony.

This situation, which is slowly developing and shows signs of spreading, presages a gloomy future in the relations between the European and African settlers.

The Minister is being asked "to press forward with the *greatest possible measure of White settlement*, because in a few years' time the *situation will be irreversible*".

This is the view of the settlers.

For them, therefore, the Belgo-Congolese Community, which the Africans are eagerly and confidently looking forward to, is only an illusion, a dangerous venture, unless this Community is kept permanently under the rule of force or of an equivalent force on the European side in order to guard against all contingencies.

As for the task of spreading civilisation – which is the basic reason for the Belgians being in Africa – has there been a change of heart? Is that the hidden aim behind the clamour to the Minister to "press forward with the greatest possible measure of white settlement?"

Since psychologically they feel powerless and incapable of creating the Belgo-Congolese Community by peaceful and democratic methods which will firmly bind the two races together, can we draw up a statement of the bankruptcy of their policy?

It is surely not surprising that the Congolese are beginning to hesitate and doubt the sincerity of the intentions of the colonists as a result of the constant repetition by their partners of proposals which clearly show that the settlement which they demand would serve private and antagonistic interests rather than the higher interests of the country.

It is obvious that these proposals will instinctively create mistrust instead of confidence.

It is a sad outlook if the colonists and the colonised have to seal their friendship by force or in fear, and if the two partners must *forever* regard each other with mistrust and always be in readiness to parry a blow from the other.

Looking at the matter coolly I think that the attitude of all

E

rational Congolese remains unchanged, and I think it would be useful to reproduce here an extract from the statement made in Belgium in May 1956 at the end of our study tour " . . . in the mind of the native people there is absolutely no thought of driving the Belgians out of the Congo. On the contrary, we all share a single desire: the co-existence, both peaceful and cordial of Belgians and Congolese . . . . "

This is the firm wish, idea, and determination of all those Africans who wish to make their country a happy one. They are anxious to use their influence to instil these sentiments into everyone, not out of fear, not to please the Belgians, but from a deep conviction; nor do they wish to show themselves guilty of gross ingratitude towards those who have helped them and are still helping them.

Those who are not sure of their motives, of the effectiveness of their actions, or of their charity towards the Blacks, can mistrust the good intentions of the latter, if they so wish.

But we ourselves have faith in the future; we hope that the predictions of the prophets will never come true, and that they will subsequently reproach themselves for having imputed to us aggressive intentions which in fact we do not have.

As for settling the country with Europeans, speaking objectively, I can see no objection to Belgians – the best Belgians – coming to the Congo in large numbers. I am inspired with the belief that the greater the number of the best young Belgians who come to the Congo, free of racial prejudice, the speedier will be the progress of industrialisation of the Congo, the more the Congolese will benefit by it, and the more rapidly will the economic and social development of the populations be achieved.

Africa will give an open-hearted welcome to these young settlers and young administrators with new and generous ideas, who, quite apart from the material gain which every man has the right to expect from his work, will bring us a new message of love, justice and friendship.

I am thinking particularly of the young students of the University Institute of Overseas Territories at Antwerp, the future administrators of the Congo. I look back on conversations I had with them on the future of the Congo during my tour of Belgium, along with my colleagues on the trip. These young people had the outlook of the future servants which the Congo really needs. They are inspired by a determination which borders on heroism and imbued with a sincere desire to place themselves resolutely in the service of Congolese development. In the Congo they want to be Africans, not Belgians, and to live closer to the native peoples, their compatriots and friends.

During the two days which we spent in Antwerp, a group of these students was always with us, accompanying us everywhere, asking us about the Congo, their second country. On more than one occasion they joined us in Brussels, and each time we parted with real regret on both sides. One of them, our friend Jacques Ryon, invited us to spend a day with his family at Hooglede, a spot some dozen kilometres away from Brussels, where we spent an evening of true friendship with members of his family who welcomed us with warm and brotherly affection.

Will the good intentions of these likeable students of the Institute be spoiled by the heat of Africa? Not unless they are exposed to other influences beyond their control. But I do not believe this would happen; they gave us their word.

We ask our friends Jacques Ryon and René Debeaune to be kind enough to act as our interpreter in conveying to their colleagues in the Institute the thanks of the delegation of Congolese V.I.P.'s who visited Belgium in 1956 for the sympathetic welcome they gave them in Antwerp. We also extend our sincere thanks to Mr. Laude, the dynamic director of the Institute for his disinterested devotion to the Congolese nation and for the valuable contribution which his Institute is making to the development of African Belgium. The Institute has become a nursery which provides the Congo with first-class administrators, apostles of African civilisation.

These new pioneers of Belgo-Congolese friendship (young settlers and young administrators leaving for the Congo) will take up and continue the work of the former pioneers of pacification.

Private ownership of land

There is no disguising the fact that the Congolese are sadly disappointed about the private ownership of land which was authorised by the Decree of 10th February 1953.

It is now four years since this Decree was promulgated and it has still not been effectively implemented. Congolese *evolués* and African settlers who wish to become owners of the land on which they have built property of durable materials, come up against all kinds of obstacles. When these native settlers apply to private organisations for loans and wish to mortgage their properties, some

of which have cost from 300,000 to a million francs or more, they
are told that the granting of these loans is subject to the registration
of their property with the *Conservation des Titres Fonciers* (Land
Registry). When they apply to this Department to have their property registered – purely an administrative formality – they are
told they must wait because the measures for the implementation of
the Decree of the 10th February 1953 in the provinces have not
yet been taken or "are under consideration", or "shortage of staff
has prevented the Administration from giving active consideration to
local measures for implementing the Decree", or "the implementation of the Decree has been deferred until after the renewal of leases
in the township by the African Townships Department and the
demarcation of plots by the Town Planning Department". These are
typical replies which have been given to the Congolese over the past
four years and will be given for years to come.

Exceptionally, in the towns of Leopoldville and Elisabethville a
total of two, three or five natives have acquired ownership of the
ground on which they have built their houses. But what does this
insignificant number of two to five owners represent amongst
12,000,000 inhabitants?

I have carried out a wide-ranging enquiry amongst different strata
of the population to find out their views on land ownership, and
especially on the purchase of land. After questioning native chiefs,
various members of the working classes and the intelligentsia, I can
roughly summarise their views as follows:

"We are very pleased with the action taken by the Government
with regard to the individual ownership of land. This excellent
measure will facilitate progress towards the individualisation of our
rights and the stability of our families. It is a good feature in civilisation. The Congo is our common patrimony. The Europeans came
to civilise us and not to usurp the natural and inalienable rights
bequeathed to us by our ancestors. These rights have always
belonged to us *collectively*. If it is a case of replacing the system
of communally-held property by the system of individual ownership,
it is obviously fair to *share proportionally* the patrimony which
belonged to us collectively, in such a way that each member of the
community receives his share. This share, which belongs by right
to each inhabitant, should be registered in the name of each family.
The rights acquired individually by each owner of a plot in the
extra-traditional Centres and native townships will be respected. But
in all this there can be no question of sale. Our forbears never

bought land to cultivate their fields and build their houses. The State must respect our ideas and our traditions. Besides, we are poor and we have not the necessary money to buy this land. The Whites have taken hold of our rights – our lands – and now wish to sell them to us for money, as if we were strangers in the country. They have become owners of our land and we, the natives, have become mere immigrants, because our own land is now to be sold to us. If they corner all our land, we can do nothing about it because we have no means of protesting. But for pity's sake, let them leave us that little portion which is our home and where we cultivate our fields, whether it be in the town or the country. Do not hustle us out. There is no objection if the State sells the land to native traders, because they have the means to buy it and they will get their money back in due course. But to sell the land to poor natives is unjust. We demand justice and understanding from the Whites."

This was the unanimous view of Congolese of all classes. This is what they passionately desire.

Some Congolese who are imbued with European ideas – and they constitute only a small minority – understand the mechanics of the conveyance and concession of land, and accept the principle of the sale of land, which is accepted in all civilised countries. But for the vast majority of Congolese the idea is incomprehensible, and it is useless to give them any explanations. Probably only the Congolese of the twenty-first century will be able to understand the idea. It will be a lengthy task.

For my part, I think it would be in the best interests of society, and a wise gesture, to reconsider this problem, taking into consideration, in particular, the very limited means of the natives and the principle of the priority of native interests.

It is quite certain that, in present conditions, the Decree on the acquisition of private land and property will be merely an illusion.

Only a few individuals – traders and people in the higher income group – could benefit by it.

Where would poor workers find the money to buy this land – even a modest sum like 2,000 francs – when, as is well-known, the great majority are hard up and even live below the subsistence level. We very much doubt if in the whole of the Congo – even in ten years' time – there will be 1,000 Congolese who could acquire private land and property. The only exception might be tenants of the African Townships Department (who have an option to purchase); but in this case it would merely be an indirect *obligation* which the tenants would be unable to escape, seeing that the price of these houses includes the real cost of the house and the price of the land on which the house is built. If one assumes that the price of the house comes to 60,000 francs and that of the land to 20,000 francs, the buyer will be charged 80,000 francs, which will, therefore, be the price of the house including the plot of land. This is what is actually being done in the sale of the African Townships Department houses, re-purchased by the Colony and sold by them to the inhabitants.

This system will not solve the problem, seeing that only a fraction of the population will be able to occupy these houses, the great majority preferring to apply to the *Fonds d'Avance* for loans, constructing houses to suit their own tastes.

Since there is no profit to be gained from the sale of land to the natives, I consider that it would be highly desirable to dispose of residential plots to the Congolese free of charge. In view of the standard of living of the natives, it would also be fair if the conveyancing and granting of land, whether for agricultural, commercial, or industrial use or for stock-rearing were carried out free of charge to a much greater extent than at present.

It seems to me to be less than fair to ask a worker who only earns 400 francs a month to buy his plot of land at the same price as a salaried worker who earns 4,000 francs per month or more.

With selling prices already fixed in certain Provinces – ranging from twenty to forty francs or more per square metre – it is only the "financially strong" who are favoured, to the detriment of the "financially weak".

Should the Administration uphold the measures taken, it would be desirable that selling prices should be related to the incomes of the inhabitants, and calculated on the basic salary of each individual. Present prices are too high for the mass of the workers.

If the system of sale is retained, could not the price of residential plots be reduced to a uniform figure of one franc per square metre or to an inclusive price of 500 or 1,000 francs?

This is a transitional measure. The first stage would permit every inhabitant, rich as well as poor, to become the owner of the land on which he is living. Selling prices would rise progressively as the purchasing power of the native population increased and as their financial position permitted. Let us go slowly to begin with. The current prices should be token prices within the reach of all and not merely of a few privileged individuals.

The private ownership of land by the natives is a big step forward and a humanitarian measure. In helping every man to acquire his own property a great service will be rendered to the Congolese people in their progress towards emancipation.

*Expropriation in the extra-traditional centres
and the native townships*

The Africans have complained repeatedly, and are still complaining, at being continually driven out every time the European quarter is extended. In some towns and centres the inhabitants state that they have been driven out as many as three times, with serious effects on their material interests and personal affairs. The compensation they receive is always inadequate by comparison with the real value of their dwellings and crops and the physical effort they have put into developing their plots of ground and their township.

A native township is situated 500 metres from the European quarter. After X years the European population has doubled or trebled and the quarter becomes too small. In order to find homes for all its people, the European quarter, in accordance with town-planning decisions, has to extend for one or two kilometres. The town-planning order recommends that the African township, situated 500 yards from the European quarter, should be moved a specified distance in order to make room for the latter. The Africans sadly leave their former township. Expropriated and given a ridiculous compensation, they set to work to clear the ground in the new area allocated to them, and build new homes – with the greatest difficulty, since the compensation is quite inadequate to cover the cost of all the materials for building a new house; then they fit out their new village and settle in.

If, after ten or twenty years, the European quarter extends again, the same procedure will be repeated. Another removal and further worries and financial loss for the inhabitants. In this way the African townships suffer repeatedly as a result of the extension of the European quarters. Thus, as the years go by, the African townships give way to make room for the extension of the European quarters and withdraw to the most remote corners of the urban centres.

Take the example of Stanleyville; the inhabitants of this town have had to uproot themselves three or four times and quite

recently the Saïo quarter – which was developed by the natives only
a few years ago – has just been shifted, in spite of opposition on
the part of the inhabitants, not for reasons of public interest, not
in the interests of the inhabitants, but always for he same reason,
to serve the interests of others. All the inhabitants of this quarter
have been compelled to take up residence in houses built by the
African Townships Department because, as was announced at the
time in the press, a thousand of these houses were without tenants
as the natives did not wish to live in them.

Again, there is the case of the Arab chieftaincy, situated some
distance from the European town and which is in process of being
moved, again in the face of the protests of the population. In fact,
there is a general outcry. The sector chief and the inhabitants are
unwilling to move; but the Administration will compel them to pack
their bags. It is alleged that the removal of this chieftaincy has been
decided upon by the Health Department (that is what I have been
told by the native authorities in the chieftaincy). But the inhabitants
will not accept this reason, insisting that they have always inhabited
this district since the foundation of Stanleyville without any trouble
of any kind. We are certainly not being moved for reasons of health,
they say, for we are very healthy here – but in order to make room
for European projects. That is what the Arabs think. They are still
deeply worried about the transfer of their chieftaincy.

Are all these massive and continual expropriations *always* in
conformity with the law, as laid down in the Colonial Charter?

I have a clear impression – and this is the general opinion – that
although certain expropriations may be justified in the public
interest, others are certainly not. And it is against these unjustified
expropriations that the population is beginning to protest.

The Africans complain bitterly about this state of affairs, but
they dare not protest openly. They have to be satisfied with complaining amongst themselves. They see that there is something
wrong. In all the extra-traditional centres the natives have the conviction that they are not "on their own ground", and this is made
clear to them. The authorities explain that the land in the extra-
traditional centres belongs solely to the State, that the Congolese
do not own the land on which they have built their dwellings, and
that the Administration has a perfect right to move them whenever
this may be considered necessary.

The Congolese who have left their traditional areas to work for
the Whites in the urban centres should be assured of some perm-

anence in the quarters which they occupy and which they themselves have developed. It is essential that they should be contented and secure, as if they were in their own villages.

They confidently expect that their wishes will be realised, and that their worries will be dispelled once and for all; that the European quarters will extend in virgin areas and the sacred concept of private property will be respected in the best interests of the African community.

CHAPTER X

Basic Education

An uneducated man, however well trained, counts for nothing. On the other hand, a man of character but with less training, is superior to an extremely well-trained man who lacks character.

What form of education should be given to the Congolese people? As I have said repeatedly, it should be an amalgamation of Western and African civilisations, without any of their decadent elements.

The education hitherto given to the Congolese seems to be too much imbued with abstract precepts which are not only foreign to the Bantu mentality, but sometimes beyond their understanding. This explains the precarious and ineffective nature of some of the methods which, in spite of the willingness of the teachers, rarely produce the expected results. On the other hand, anything practical is more likely to capture the attention of the masses, hence empiricism is worth more than dogmatism.

This empiricism also explains why the African has benefited much more from the material side of European civilisation – its "outward" form – than from its moral or "inward" aspect.

In actual fact, the Congolese copy more from the external forms of European civilisation (style of dress – going at times to quite ridiculous lengths – bearing, ornamentation, etc., gestures which are sometimes misunderstood), than from the *transcendent qualities* of the colonising nation, whereas true civilisation lies in the manner of thinking and living, not in the outward trappings of materialism.

Go into the large towns and you will see how elegantly the Africans dress, their well-kept houses, their clean and correct behaviour. This magnificent result is the product of imitation. The African is a great observer whenever he has the means; he quickly imitates everything he sees the European do, looking upon them as his daily pattern.

As a result of this imitation, which is frequently slavish, the faults of the European are more often copied than his inward qualities, for the simple reason that the Congolese lack social contact with the *best* Europeans, contacts which would enable them to assimilate the inner qualities of their masters – qualities which are more evident in intimate society than in the artificial relations of work, limited as they are to orders given by the boss to the employee. In general, the African seizes upon the outward gestures and minor faults of the European, which the less experienced assume to be virtues.

Apart from these workaday relationships, strictly limited to the office or workshop, friendly relations between Black and White are generally speaking practically non-existent.

I am not speaking here of cultural relations in such associations as "Belgo-Congolese Clubs" which bring Black and White together. These clubs have such a cultural and artistic tendency that their members generally meet only to attend a lecture, cinema show or theatrical performance. Occasionally a little dinner is arranged.

These multi-racial associations could play a valuable part in the sphere of human relations if they were shorn a little of the rather excessively academic atmosphere which they exhibit at present. Meetings and gatherings take the form of academic sessions where the time is often spent in sterile discussions on racial topics. At every meeting and in every discussion, racialism can be sensed at the tip of certain tongues, European as well as Congolese. I know this from my experience as one of the chief founders of one of these associations and from having taken part in its management.

The main purpose of these inter-racial groups should be directed towards the social and civic education of the Europeans and the Africans, the improvement of their mutual relations in all their forms and in all spheres of social life, and as a secondary consideration, to the intellectual training of those who need it.

But to get back to the subject. At the end of the working day every one goes home: the Europeans to their quarter and the Africans to theirs. The two quarters, as can be seen in all the towns of the Congo, are separated by a certain distance which forms a barricade between them. This segregation is normal – indeed necessary. Each must live in his own "atmosphere" since habits and customs are not identical.

I put this question to every Congolese, a question to which only
conscience can give the answer: are there any Congolese (I am not
speaking of a few members of the élite who have become "westernised", who would like to live side by side with the European if they
had the opportunity, not out of vanity, but merely with the object
of being completely absorbed into the European civilisation which
they have deliberately chosen, not because they despise their own
race whom they have always served, but to avoid the risk of certain
bad influences, inherent in the life of the African township, which
hamper the sound education of their children) who would be
genuinely at ease if they were placed in an urban area among the
Europeans where they would be under the austere discipline of a
civilised life quite foreign to their nature; where they would no
longer be able to organise "matanga" evenings or other ceremonies
to the beating of the drum; where they would be required to
"respect other people's peace, sleep and rest", ideas which are the
outcome of a long European tradition and are quite foreign to the
Africans who have grown up in the native township under the
influence of tribal disclipine; where every man is absolute master
in his own home and can shout and sing as much as he likes without
any complaint; where they will live in a dead, silent city, in which
music has to be muffled, whereas African life is full of noise, loud
music and shouts of joy? There are many other reasons which I
cannot go into here. Everyone must give his own reply.

Basically, then, the separation of the two quarters is justified by
sociological factors in the interests of the Africans themselves as
well as of the Europeans.

Besides, the Africans are happy in their own quarters, where they
are free.

Some deserving Congolese undoubtedly wish to live in the European quarter and adapt themselves to its life, and conversely there
are Europeans who would like to live side by side with their African
friends. I can see no objection to this. On the contrary, this would
be the symbiosis of that Belgo-Congolese Community which is so
much desired, and the prelude to the fusion of the races in Belgian
Africa.

Whose task is it to educate the Africans? Clearly, their Belgian
teachers and the African élite.

The little African boy leaves the paternal roof minus any particle
of European civilisation (this is not uniformly true) and goes to
school where he has to learn the new standards of civilised life

which have not been taught to him by his parents in his own home. He is taught to read, to write and to do arithmetic. By way of education (European style), his masters teach him ideas, which, although sometimes "memorised", take no hold on him, because these ideas have no application in practical life (parents lead a completely different life and inculcate in the child ideas which are in contradiction with those taught at school).

In these circumstances – and this is the present position for the majority of Congolese children – the black pupil finds himself caught between two conflicting forces: the standards of the school and those of the family. The parents who know nothing of these European standards undo the work of the school.

To be effective, a child's education must above all be inspired by *example* rather than by sermons and lectures. The same applies to African adult education.

Experience shows that Africans who have had the opportunity to be in permanent contact with Europeans often come under an extremely salutary influence with regard to the refinement of their habits. Amongst other things, I have observed that the homes of house servants (boys waiting on the Whites) are often run in a more orderly manner and with more taste than those of many clerks. The explanation for this is that the servant sees day and night how his mistress runs her house, and he does the same thing at home in imitation. He arranges his own home as he has been taught to arrange his employer's home. But the clerk, who has never lived with the European, who has never been in a European's home, does not always have an idea of order; sometimes articles are placed the wrong way round.

The same thing can be observed in the case of Congolese women who live with European men. After several years these women – even if illiterate – are changed greatly for the better and are far and away in advance, from the point of view of habits, domestic and family training, of women educated at the school desk but living "the native way".

Taking my own case, I have to admit that the fragment of education and social training which I have acquired up to the present – a training which is still inadequate – I owe above all to the practical teaching I have received from many European friends, sympathisers and teachers with whom I have had friendly contacts and who have been good enough to guide me further in my education. Like any other Congolese, I certainly received some theoretical ideas at school, which I am always enlarging; but what one acquires by practical methods is often more valuable and more lasting than any abstract ideas. Without these closer and more fraternal encounters at the personal level, without this practical teaching derived from daily contact with better educated and more experienced persons, in intimate discussions, in the gentle school of life, without the sympathy of these benefactors in the truest sense of the word, benefactors who were willing to help me and receive me in their homes as a member of the family, I should certainly not have had a fraction of my present modest education and I should not be what I am today. I cannot give sufficient thanks to these mentors who continue to improve my education, as indeed other European sympathisers are doing for other Africans.

When the African has completed his studies and starts work, he often receives no further education except from his immediate circle, from the companions with whom he lives and discusses his ideas and feelings. He soon forgets many things which he learnt at school, owing to lack of use and application, and only retains a little book-learning which is strictly necessary for his work.

The Europeans who are in contact with the Congolese outside working hours are generally *the less reliable* sort who frequent the Congolese quarters with no good motives or, to put the matter briefly and frankly, to get what they can out of it: to go drinking in the bars where beer costs less than in European cafés (sometimes half the price) and to establish relations with Congolese friends with the object of procuring women at a reduced rate, women whom they almost invariably abandon when they become mothers.

In the native township these "doubtful characters" are warmly welcomed by all the Congolese, who are pleased and proud to be visited by their seniors and friends; they then exhibit in front of the watching Africans all their faults and vices: wild gestures, bad language, indecency. This often occurs when they are under the influence of drink (and there is perhaps some excuse for them in this case, when they are no longer in control of their actions; but it is all the same regrettable). These are the "good" ways of speaking and the "good" manners which these mentors bring to the Congolese who, most unfortunately, adopt them blindly, because, for the majority of the Congolese, who are even less well-educated, everything brought by the European, the bearer of civilisation, is GOOD and FINE.

If an intelligent African blames a less intelligent companion for some attitude, way of behaving, remark or language, the latter will retort "But the Europeans do it too, I saw such and such a European do that, so it can't be bad." They forget that Europeans are men like any others, and that there are ill-educated people among the Europeans just as there are amongst the Congolese and in any group of human beings. The colour of the skin does not confer the seal of civilisation or of infallibility.

For the average African, the White man has no faults. Everything about the White man is as pure as the pigmentation of his skin. The European is often called "son of God". This is a false conception of the White man which explains the slavish imitation of the large majority of the natives.

These doubtful characters among the Europeans do the African a great deal of harm, the effects of which are demoralising.

I hope that these gentlemen will realise the danger of their actions and will mend their ways amongst the native population. They bear a heavy responsibility and have a mission to fulfil amongst these people, a mission which they cannot ignore without failing in their duties as educators.

I understand and readily admit that they are men like the rest of us. I do not expect them to be angels; there are no such things in this world. But I do wish to avoid scandal and discredit falling on the good name of the Europeans, because the native masses are not always able to distinguish the good from the bad. And I am anxious to ensure that the efforts made by people of good will for the education of the Congolese people shall not be undone.

Those Europeans who mix with the Africans for good motives can be assured of their sympathy, for the fraternisation of the two races has become the watchword of the Africans.

The best type of Europeans rarely frequent the Congolese quarters. This is not from any feeling of contempt – in fact some of them are beginning to frequent these districts – but because they have no particular reason or motive for going there. They cannot go into the African township in the evening just for the fun of going unless they have a *purpose*. Neither can an African go into the European quarter in the evening unless he has some reason or motive for going. Why then should we ask others to do what we cannot do ourselves?

Hence I do not see how we can condemn these Europeans for not visiting the native areas. Perhaps they ought to go there in groups like tourists or welfare workers, stroll along the roads of the township, shake the hands of passers-by and organise propaganda processions in support of inter-racial relations.

I am not referring here to human relations and the propriety which must be shown by White and Black in their everyday contacts. This is another aspect of the problem. What I am speaking of here is friendly *social intercourse*. I am in favour of this, but it must never be forced. We shall never unite by blaming each other but only by getting to know each other as persons and individuals. This affection must appeal to the heart and the emotions.

There is no law or principle which requires one man to like another.

What we can do is to express a wish, since the great and increasing need of the Congolese is for education through contact with the better Europeans.

How shall we be able to benefit from the qualities of the Whites, acquire their good manners, their tact and ways of thinking, and become acquainted with their customs, if we lack opportunities for close contact with the best Europeans? This is something which cannot be learned in the office, where everyone, White as well as Black, is confined to his desk.

It seems to me that the best formula is that of personal relationships, which means that every Congolese who is aiming towards a certain ideal must make a serious effort to become more closely acquainted with any European with whom he is in contact. This European would be both his friend and mentor or his "sponsor". This kind of contact is better than group contacts on café terraces or occasional propaganda meetings.

In human relationships, whether among the Africans themselves or among Europeans, it is always up to those in a lower position to make a greater effort in order to become better acquainted with those in a higher position, and if the man in the lower position behaves properly and wins the liking of those in a higher position, he will quickly be accepted by the latter and absorbed into their company.

The same applies to us. From their point of view, the Europeans have virtually nothing to gain from our company. It is not up to them to leave their homes and come to see us in our homes in order to make friends with us. We are the people who are *primarily interested* and it is up to us to stretch out the hand of friendship. The Europeans are not going to receive us because of speeches or recriminations but because of our behaviour, our conduct and our propriety. Only these three words will open for us the door of friendship with the Whites.

The Congolese élite also have an important role to play in the education of their people, their less advanced fellow Africans. It is only by the scrupulous fulfilment of this lofty social mission that we shall be able to serve our people. Let us not be egotistical; what we have received from the European as a result of our personal efforts we must be willing to pass on in order to help others who have not had the same opportunities as ourselves. This is a heritage which must be passed on from one individual to another.

Whatever our family, business or other obligations, each one of us must keep constantly in mind the mission he is called upon to fulfil in the education of his people. It is not a question of performing miracles or making spectacular sacrifices, but of setting a persuasive example by one's actions, advising and guiding those who need advice and guidance. Pompous speeches are of no use whatsoever.

Let us, the élite of the country, set to work so that our country does not remain backward. Let us give our mentors our support; they are greatly in need of our effective collaboration.

The education of Congolese children

Many Congolese pay little attention to the education of their children; they take greater care of themselves than they do of their babies. In a good many families – even those of *evolués* – the wife has to look after the rearing and education of the children on her own, whilst the head of the family, forgetful of his duties, has nothing better to do than to spend all his leisure hours in the cafés and dance halls in the neighbourhood. He comes home for three purposes: to *sleep* when it is late and he is sleepy; to *eat* when he is hungry and to *change his clothes* when these are dirty.

For such people the daily time-table is as follows: in the morning, leave for work; at mid-day, return to the house to eat; at two o'clock, return to work; at four-thirty or five o'clock (office closing time or end of working day), return from work and go straightaway in search of excitement; at 7.20 p.m., or later, return to the house to eat and sleep. This is the programme of the fast set who lead the same sort of life from Monday to Saturday, from the first to the last day of the month, from January to December, always at the expense of their wives and children.

Apart from the three things which I have just mentioned, there is nothing to keep them at home; their interests lie elsewhere. Once or twice a week they stay out all night.

Conduct of this kind inevitably has its effect on the character and psychology of the children who will suffer almost irreparable damage.

The poor mother who ought to be able to rely on her husband as her mentor has to make the best she can of the humble resources at her disposal; for education, she will pass on to her children the rudimentary ideas of tribal education which were taught to her by her parents.

The education of these unhappy children who have had the misfortune to be born into an indifferent home often suffers. The sound instruction given to them at school is ruined by their own parents, and the father is most to blame. It is, indeed, a pity that parents should themselves ruin the education of their dear children.

Children are not like mushrooms which grow at random. Education in the home is the most valuable and lasting form of education which any man can have. The school can do no more than supplement and improve it.

If it is to have a firm foundation the education imparted by the mother must start when the children are aged between three and six, and continue throughout their school life.

The foregoing applies only to parents who fail in their duty and not to those many conscientious parents who do everything in their power to provide a better future for their children.

The work of the school will only be effective if it is backed up by the efforts of the parents, efforts which must always follow the same lines as those of the school.

When once a bridge has been formed between family and school there will be harmony and purpose in the education of Congolese children.

I appeal to the good will of all parents, and especially to all members of the élite who must set an example in order to encourage others.

All our efforts must be directed towards this one end: to transform our children from little savages or beings on the same level as ourselves, into culturally developed children who will be the future leaders of the Congolese people.

The education of Congolese women

It is common knowledge that the education of Congolese women has been neglected and is still neglected in certain schools which obstinately refuse to improve the syllabus for girls' education, and especially in rural schools.

The responsibility for the backward state of Congolese women falls on teachers, parents and husbands.

On the teachers, because they have neglected the education of girls – specially at the start; this is the cause of the regrettable disparity which is found in the homes of the *evolués,* a disparity in education, habit and outlook. This disparity, which creates a gulf between husband and wife, is one of the main sources of disagreement in the home, a disagreement which often leads to separation or divorce.

In saying that girls' education has been neglected, I refer to the fact that the syllabus of girls' schools was considerably inferior to that of boys' schools in the same grade and that French was not taught in these girls' schools possibly because it was considered that a Black woman had no need of this civilised language. Here I am leaving out of account the improvements which have only just been made by the widening of the syllabus in certain girls' schools. Moreover, the inadequate education of our wives goes far to explain the obstacles which often stand in the way of the education of our children. When an *evolué* husband wishes to educate his children in accordance with the standards of Western civilisation, his wife, whose mind is completely in the grip of ancestral customs, will set her face against the idea and undo all that her husband has done. When the husband says white, the wife says black. I have come across some really dramatic cases of husband and wife coming into conflict over the type of education given to their children.

I have noticed that almost all Congolese wives – even those who have been educated by the Reverend Sisters – have an unshakeable faith in native fetishes. Even in Christian families you will almost invariably find small boys wearing greegreb – protective amulets to which their mothers attach supernatural power. In the teeth of the opposition of their *evolué* husbands, some wives will insist on their children wearing these good-luck charms which preserve babies against evil.

There are, of course, exceptions, but this is the mentality of the majority of Congolese women.

In their search for a woman who is somewhere near their ideal, or rather level, some Congolese have been divorced two, three or four times. Some of them are philanderers, but there are others for whom life with a particular woman has become impossible and was an obvious handicap to the advancement of the husband and the education of the children.

The inadequate education of African women has considerably retarded the cultural development of the Congo. We cannot lay claim to any kind of civilisation as long as our wives remain in this state of stagnation.

When you civilise a man, you only civilise an individual; but when you civilise a woman, you civilise a whole people.

Teachers have recognised these facts, and there are signs of an improvement thanks to the mixed system of education adopted by the State schools and the widening of the syllabus in girls' schools. Boys and girls are thus placed on an equal footing and will be able to receive the same level of primary and post-primary education. This is an excellent measure which will not only help to raise the status of African women but will also contribute to the stability of our families.

I am especially proud to note the tremendous progress made by the Reverend Sisters at Leopoldville and Banza-Mboma in the Lower-Congo in giving girls a sound primary and domestic education. The more gifted girls speak an impeccable French when they leave these schools.

I pay a sincere tribute to the directors of these institutions and I give every encouragement to the parents.

I appeal to the future husbands of these girls not to disappoint their hopes of being *evolué* wives, respected by their husbands.

Responsibility also falls *on the parents*, who refuse to send their daughters to school, preferring to keep them at home as material assets to get them a dowry. Here is the argument used by parents in the villages: "Of what use is it for a girl to go to school if she cannot afterwards work in an office to earn money? We do not want to send our children to the Sisters because, once they are baptised, they will be compelled to enter into 'chapel marriages' (that is, religious marriage); then they will be regarded as 'slaves' because, even if they are ill-treated by their husbands, they will no longer be able to leave them in order to marry another man. We should be selling our daughters if we allowed them to go to the Mission in order to enter into that kind of marriage."

I often heard these very words spoken when I was a small boy living in the village.

It is a fact that many natives were suspicious – and some still are suspicious – of religious marriage. It is simply a question of the mentality peculiar to each country.

From the creation of the world until the time of the arrival of the White man in the heart of Africa, the Congolese did not accept the indissolubility of marriage. The native people considered marriage not as a life contract, but as a simple, revocable agreement which can be broken by mutual consent, at the wish of the parents of one of the partners or of one of the partners themselves when life together no longer runs smoothly.

Moreover, according to the Congolese conception, the woman – even when she is married – still remains under the authority of her parents.

The intervention of the parents in the life of the household is often harmful; many marriages have come to grief in the past, and still do so today, owing to the whims of the parents.

This age-old conception of the revocability of the marriage contract – an idea which is firmly held by the great majority of the Congolese, even those who are Christian – is sufficient to explain the spate of divorce and separation among partners in religious marriages.

Many people contract religious marriages, not from any religious convictions but often for reasons of expediency. This has frequently been admitted to me quite frankly by both husbands and wives whom I have questioned on this subject during my investigation.

A man who wishes to have an educated and *evolué* wife must approach the Reverend Sisters and enter into a religious marriage. Without this, he will not be able to have the wife he desires. On her side, the fiancée will demand a religious marriage to avoid being "made fun of" by her companions; this is because such a marriage provides an opportunity for more elaborate ceremony than traditional or civil marriage. Some girls consider that marriage outside the church is a humiliating sign that the husband has not sufficient money to meet the cost of all the ceremonies and that they will be regarded as "pamba" girls (girls of no standing).

The plain fact is that for many people religious marriage is simply a luxury marriage.

Both the girl and the young man are desperately keen to make a show, and to do this they have to be married in church, the usual place for the celebration of these luxury marriages.

To achieve their object, the young couple will squander all the modest savings which might have been used for the purchase of equipment for their home and, in fifty per cent of the cases, they will even run into debt. Both bride and bridegroom have outfits made in the latest fashion.

The big day of their dreams arrives – the day of the nuptial blessing. Five, ten, fifteen or twenty cars are taken. After the marriage ceremony, the long procession leaves the church with a great deal of show, following the main roads of the European quarter and the busiest roads of the African township. The car conveying the happy couple leads the procession, followed immediately by other cars conveying all the women who took part in the marriage ceremony and who belong to the two families of the married couple. The bride's schoolfellows congregate together in one or more of the cars which have been specially placed at their disposal.

One might imagine that it was a royal wedding, accompanied as it is by a degree of luxury which would be beyond the reach of many Europeans in comfortable circumstances.

The cars roll along at twenty or twenty-five miles an hour, the occupants waving headscarfs from both sides all along the route until the home of the married couple is reached. This is to attract the attention of passers-by and announce the happy occasion.

No sooner have they left the priest's house than the occupants of the cars start up tuneful songs; sometimes there is an orchestra; the sound can be heard five hundred or a thousand yards away; it brings every passer-by to a stop and even rouses the birds which are peacefully sleeping in their nests.

As soon as they set foot on the ground, the bridal pair are welcomed to their home by cheers and enthusiastic cries from the relatives who have been eagerly awaiting the arrival of the procession.

The marriage feast, to which an impressive number of friends and relations are usually invited, begins in the afternoon, almost always in a large bar specially fitted up and decorated for the event. The beer flows in rivers.

The music intoxicates the music lovers, over-excited dancers struggle for floor space, and then there is the "atmosphere", as everybody calls it; gaiety, charm, the whole room given up to rejoicing.

The bridal pair change their clothes three or four times in the course of the same evening in order to display to all present the extent of their wardrobe.

In some households these ostentatious ceremonies are followed by a long period of hard living because the improvident husband has to work a long time before he is in a position to repay the debts which he has imprudently incurred in his youthful folly in order to have a princely wedding instead of marrying simply and modestly but with the same dignity.

And what happens later on in a good number of these marriages? We have only to look round and the same situation is seen all over the Congo. After the honeymoon, the husband becomes enamoured by some fly-by-night and makes a mockery of the marriage ceremony in which barely a few weeks, a few months or a few years ago he made a formal promise of fidelity, and abandons his deceived victim to go off in search of excitement.

If, after a few years, the wife has not given him any children, he will put her away without more ado, either at the instigation of his parents or at his own sweet will. He will apply to the District Court to seek the dissolution of the traditional marriage which always follows the religious marriage (The religious marriage is, of course, still in force but, for the Congolese, once the wife's name has been struck out in his identity book, the two marriages – both religious and traditional – automatically lapse.) If he does not obtain a divorce from the traditional marriage quickly, he will simply live in concubinage with his second wife.

If the couple stay together for a long time or for the whole of their lives, this will not be because they have made a religious marriage but because they *get on together* (and this can also occur with non-Christians), or because the husband is in Government service and fears that there may be trouble and he may lose his job if his conduct is not above reproach.

Hundreds of Congolese religious marriages are continually being dissolved on the arbitrary decision of the husbands or the parents, who do not appreciate the seriousness of their conduct or the very bad example which they are setting.

The foregoing is based on countless observations and surveys carried out among young married couples in order to find out what they think of religious marriage and why they so frequently separate; it is intended to show that the indissolubility of marriage has no meaning for the majority of the Congolese.

This state of affairs confirms the apprehensions of the wise old men of the village; it was for fear of seeing their daughters unable to separate from their husbands if they proved unsuited that many parents, who were still strongly attached to tribal customs, prevented their daughters from attending Mission schools because they were convinced that every daughter educated in these schools would end by making a religious marriage. The second reason was that these non-*evolué* and somewhat mercenary parents saw no need for their daughters to be educated instead of being married quickly in order to bring in a dowry. The third and final reason was to keep their daughters away from the influence of the Whites; they argued on these lines: "Once our daughters have been educated by the Whites, they will no longer be willing to plough the earth and to go out and work in the fields, work to which they will not have been accustomed. They will no longer respect us" (this is explained by the fact that a girl who has had a European education will no longer accept without question certain tribal ways of living which her parents wish to impose on her). "They will become lazy and no one in the village will want to marry them."

These are the three reasons which I heard the old people of the village invoke throughout my childhood.

A considerable change in mentality has now taken place. In country districts and in towns parents no longer maintain the same attitude as before with regard to the education of their daughters; in fact the latter, not wishing to be known as *"basendji"*, themselves express a wish to go to school in order to become *evolué* wives and to marry *evolués*. Every girl has this desire, but unfortunately, in some cases, this noble desire is thwarted by the parents.

In the towns, almost all children, both girls and boys, attend school.

The present generation must pay more attention to the education of girls so that they may become good mothers and true educators, who will make their husbands and their children happy—*evolué* wives who will be able to carry out their duties and, in so doing, be true mentors for their husbands. This is the task to which every parent is called.

It must not always be left to the Europeans to educate our daughters; we must take the lead.

We must all have the pride and the ambition to make our daughters the "modern" women needed by the Congo of tomorrow.

Finally, responsibility for the backwardness of women falls on *husbands*, some of whom will do nothing to educate their wives. A large number of Congolese husbands care little for the education of their wives, whom they regard – and this symbolises the ancestral ideas which are still strongly held by many Africans – not as their companions and their closest friends, but as *servants* whose function in the home is only to bear children, to enrich the clan, to prepare meals for the army of lazy parasites who are continually sponging on the household, to keep house for the master and to do all the work of the household whilst the husband lives like a little king, watching his servant toil. This is particularly the case with the *evolués*.

Leisure hours are often devoted to other people, to friends, to idle strolls, instead of being devoted to the life partner and to other more profitable activities.

When the servant has prepared the *tchop*[1] she lays the table and the selfish husband eats alone (in the European manner), whilst his life partner (excuse me, his servant) retires to eat in the kitchen – sometimes with the children – eating, with her hand, from the saucepan which has been used in the preparation of the meal.

When the boss wants to have water on the table, instead of going to get it himself – even when it is within reach of his hand or only three yards away from the dining table – he barks to his wife "Marie, mai" (Marie, water!) even when Marie, completely worn out by exhausting work (going to the market which may be several miles away, looking after the children single-handed, doing the washing up, sweeping the house and yard, in fact everything which falls to the lot of the African wife in her hard married life) is in the kitchen resting and having her meal. She must leave her *tchop* at the mercy of the hens in order to go and serve her master, and sometimes, as soon as she returns to the kitchen, she has to chase off the parasites who have taken her place or run after the dog which has gone off with her piece of meat. She will have to leave her food once or twice in order to wait on her master who is sitting at the table like a statue and refuses to move, thus showing the despotic authority which he has inherited from his forebears.

This is how many Congolese behave.

Such is the hard life led by many Black women in their homes. Obviously, it is part of their tradition, but does not this tradition belong to the past? Ought we not to abandon this tradition, which

[1] *Tchop*: More familiarly rendered as *chop;* A word of Oriental extraction introduced by the Portuguese to describe food. It is used both as a noun and as a verb: to chop, meaning to eat.

reduces our wives to a form of disguised slavery?

Who will deny that this situation prevails amongst a large number of us? Examine your conscience to make sure that you are not
guilty before condemning me for making this criticism. It is not
exactly a criticism since it is a natural state of affairs, gladly accepted by the wife. But is not this custom of treating our wives as
servants completely out-of-date for *evolué* men?

How can our wives improve their cultural status in the conditions
to which we subject them? It is easy for us to reproach the teachers
for not having taught our wives to speak French, and so forth and
so on, but what have we done ourselves to improve the lot of our
women? Some of us are so critical that we forget our own faults.

— Can we honestly claim to be *evolués* when we leave our wives
and children to eat on the ground like savages whilst we ourselves
eat at table?

Is not this a strange contradiction? Let us admit quite sincerely
that, in the circumstances, our culture is merely a veneer.

And what can one say of the other type of husband, who leaves
his own home every evening and only comes back late at night
after he has been thrown out of the café at closing time? And when
their wives ask for an explanation for these frequent and lengthy
absences from home, the despotic husbands reply rudely, instead
of soothing their wives' hurt feelings. Many wives who have had
the misfortune to fall into the hands of these night-bird husbands
are like sentries: they have to wait up for the master and open the
door for him.

If the wife grows angry at this treatment and refuses to open the
door, she can expect to receive a hail of blows as punishment. Such
is the sad life led by many wives, a life of anguish, disappointment
and care, their minds turning endlessly in search of consolation.
What a sad existence, to be neither loved, respected nor helped by
their husbands.

A husband may neglect his wife every evening, possibly to stay
out all night, but if she gives way to despair and does what she ought
not to do or goes for a walk to visit friends, the husband will tear out
her hair. For him she is a statue with neither heart nor rights, who
must guard the house without respite just as if she were a watch dog.

There are other wives who are very progressive but unfortunately
do not apply the ideas and skills which they learnt at school, for the
sole reason that their husbands give them no encouragement or show
hardly any interest. This applies particularly to the art of cooking

(variety of dishes), embroidery, dressmaking, knitting, etc. They often lack the money to buy materials for this or that little domestic accomplishment; their husbands have an adequate income but spend it on beer and other extravagances.

Other husbands devote all their attention to buying luxury clothing, radio sets and spirits, rather than to improving their diet and giving their wives sufficient housekeeping money.

For them, civilisation starts at the top instead of at the bottom. Many of them will buy cars and radio sets while still living in a hovel. Would it not be more appropriate to start by acquiring a rather more suitable home to give the family decent accommodation?

Women married to this type of husband may have been to school but they lead the same sort of life as our old mothers did; instead of advancing, they remain tied down in such conditions of slavery that it is difficult for them to make any progress.

With typical illogicality these same husbands who had the good fortune to marry educated girls, criticise the teachers, saying: "Our wives are not civilised, they do not speak French."

There are, of course, some wives about whom nothing can be done. Any efforts made by the husband are doomed to failure. But it is quite certain that some wives would not be what they are today *if they had been sincerely helped and guided by their husbands.*

The husbands are most to blame for unfaithfulness in the home. It is they who very often begin to show a bad example to their wives. The wives often retaliate only after a long period of patient suffering followed by despair. There are extenuating circumstances for the unfaithfulness of some wives: the husband constantly spends the night away from home or keeps another woman (at the expense of his wife); he fails to support her and keeps her short of money for clothing; he fails to show her affection; and all the other things which affect the morale of any human being.

A wife who lives in harmony with her husband (in good psychological conditions) *generally* behaves irreproachably.

Other husbands seem to be so wrapped up in themselves that they tend to neglect their wife and children. They are always dressed up to the nines; they have a varied selection of suits and shoes – in fact everything necessary for their daily "adornment", whilst their wife and children go barefoot and ill-clothed.

Is it logical to live in luxury oneself and to leave one's family in an inferior position like servants? This contrast can be observed even in some families which are *outwardly* cultured; does it really give proof of cultural development on the part of the fathers?

All this applies only to those husbands who neglect their family and social duties, and not to those others who discharge their duties most conscientiously. To the latter, I extend my sincere congratulations for their commendable efforts. My remarks are addressed not to them but to those who, after reading these lines, examine their consciences and admit the error of their ways.

Having apportioned the responsibility, let us now consider each of the parties responsible: teachers, parents and husbands; and particularly parents and husbands since the teachers ask nothing better than to be able to hasten the cultural development of Congolese women and to remedy the present defects in accordance with my wishes.

It now only remains for me to express the hope that every *evolué* husband and every father will make an effort to bring about the cultural development of the women of the Congo.

We must have more respect for our wives than for ourselves, our friends, and our uncles and aunts. This does not in any way detract from the affection which we have for our relations.

Our wives share our misfortunes, our anxieties and our bad times. It is they who bear the main burden of looking after us when we are ill or in difficulties.

Our wives are human beings with the same rights as ourselves to human dignity. More than any other material gift or rich velvets, they need our respect, our affection, our moral support, our constant presence at home, our whole-hearted assistance. Material gifts have no value in the eyes of our wives if these other conditions which make for harmony in the home are lacking. If they are to be appreciated by our wives, these gifts must be a symbol of true love in the highest sense of the word.

Our wives suffer whenever they see that we are neglecting them. We do not always realise the extent of their distress.

We ourselves must look after our wives. If we do not respect them, no one else will do so, not even members of our family.

Whenever we are away from home, let us think of this bosom friend to whom we are called by the mysterious voice of inward love in our heart. Let us be considerate towards our own wives and towards all other women.

In bars and public places, in the streets, let us always show deference to our wives without any distinction based on their physical beauty. We must inculcate the same sentiments in our sons; this should be part of their education.

As far as is possible, let us go out in the company of our wives as the Europeans do. In going out with them, we shall draw them into discussions and conversations which we have with our friends. We shall explain to them the normal customs of society so that they will not feel too much out of their depth, especially with regard to courtesy in the street and in public places. In short: *good behaviour*. We shall show them how to receive visitors in the house, and we shall invite them to join in the conversation.

By such practical instruction, which requires no special effort on our part other than the willingness to give it, we shall succeed in overcoming their shyness and so gradually complete their social education.

Before marrying, let us think very seriously and, once we have made our choice, let us give up everything else for the companion whom we have freely chosen. Of course, she has, and always will have, faults which will often annoy us, but there is no such thing as the ideal wife, except in our imagination. The important thing is to choose a wife who comes nearest to our ideal. We ourselves have the same minor faults which we shall find in her.

In any union between a man and a woman, just as in ordinary friendship, one must know how to be tolerant and to be as forgiving as one possibly can.

Let us be teachers as well as husbands. It is for us to complete our wives' domestic, family and social education. Let us teach them to run the home of which they are the lawful mistresses, especially in regard to household management, giving them a sense of order, cleanliness and the rudiments of child-rearing; then, as they acquire more competence, let us leave the full control of the house to them.

In gradually giving them these responsibilities, we shall create in them a feeling of the dignity of their responsibilities, and an awareness of the important role which they have to play in the home. If we demand that our employers shall give us responsibilities and grant us the rights which are essential for human dignity, why should we not give our wives their responsibilities and especially their natural rights, since the running of the home is the wife's responsibility.

Surely it is both tyrannous and selfish to reduce our wives to the role of mere servants who only have to obey orders?

Some of us – and I have had ample evidence of this – go through a religious marriage ceremony for reasons of ostentation rather than from sincere conviction. Are not these marriages merely marriages of convenience and a cynical mockery of religion? What a scandalous example we set by such unprincipled conduct. Either one gets married and wears the Cross to show one's love for Christ or one does not. Why should a man ruin the life of an innocent girl and wantonly abandon her for another when this girl, who may be an orphan, must needs rely on him for protection. Does not this show a complete lack of human feeling?

Why should a man ruin his own life by going through a religious marriage ceremony when in his heart of hearts he has quite different ideas and is unwilling to accept the principle of the indissolubility of marriage?

Husbands will never be saints: they will always fall and rise again. A couple can always have recourse to legal separation and divorce (in the case of civil and traditional marriages) for really serious and convincing causes. That is quite normal. But what we are discussing are these frivolous marriages, separations and divorces, which are not justified by any specially serious circumstances.

When, after careful consideration, we have made a decision, we must show ourselves capable of standing by it.

Whether it be a traditional, religious or civil marriage, the wife is not like a shirt which one can change at will: marriage is "a life contract" which cannot be broken except for valid reasons.

Let us, as far as possible, give up the practices of our forebears: we belong to a different generation.

I also appeal to wives – and particularly to those who are still at school – to listen to what I am saying and to break away from the harmful influence of their uncles and aunts. Once married, they are no longer dependent on their relatives but come under the authority of their husbands. They should do everything possible to avoid bad company, which is often the cause of tension and discord in the home. They must also give up the stupid habit of constantly wanting to leave home in order to spend long and lazy holidays with their own families: their place is in their home.

I also rely on the good will of White women, not only the nuns and welfare workers, but also married women. I pay tribute to the devotion of all those who voluntarily give their time to the service of African women.

This joint effort of teachers, parents and husbands, directed towards a single goal, will do much to ensure the cultural development of Congolese women.

CHAPTER XI

Disagreement between the Belgian Political Parties in Matters of Colonial Policy

It is becoming more and more obvious that the three large Belgian political parties are not completely in agreement on certain aspects of African policy. Nevertheless, they are in agreement on many points. All these three parties and their leaders have the most laudable intentions.

What seems to me to be rather dangerous is that the Belgians themselves contradict one another in public. These contradictions – not to mention exaggeration on the part of certain persons – are unlikely to maintain the prestige of the Administration either abroad or amongst the indigenous population under their administration.

When one party has held its Congress and defined the principles of its colonial policy, the other group attacks – at times without any relevant reason, or merely because of political rivalry. As a result of these continual petty partisan intrigues the most trivial decision is the subject of interminable and exhausting discussions, some of which – and here I do not wish to give offence to anyone – are an indirect means of causing obstruction.

Thus many fine projects, which might have been carried out if the initiative of a particular government in power or a particular official had not been perpetually obstructed by the poisoned arrows of political ambition, have had to be abandoned or suspended or left to moulder in files.

In the circumstances, I doubt whether this political manoeuvring is always in the interests of the colonial people and of Belgium herself.

What has been, and what is, the result of these contradictory policies? To create confusion in the minds of the Congolese, to create doubt as to the sincerity of the government's intentions and to postpone the solution of certain problems since these contradictions automatically involve interminable discussions.

When one party says "Let us do this for the Congolese, let us give the Blacks such and such a right which is justified by their present stage of cultural development", the other party replies: "No, don't let us do this for the Congolese, don't let us give the Blacks such and such a right because this would be premature". The Congolese are at a complete loss to understand what is going on, and their minds are thrown into utter confusion. For them, Belgium is a single entity and Belgian policy is also a single entity. The Christian Socialists, the Socialists and the Liberals are all Belgians and they all follow the same policy: *the government policy* of education and emancipation of the Africans.

I said "policies" in the plural, because it seems to me that although in theory there has been a colonial policy from the Free State to the present day – a traditional policy which has always been followed by our Ministers – this is no longer fully accepted in its present form by all the Belgians and in particular by those who, in Belgium, are entrusted by the nation with the direction of public affairs.

As I have clearly shown, this policy is due for revision, a revision which is demanded not only by all the Congolese but also by all those who are closely following the evolution of the Congo.

The success of the new policy depends upon a fusion of the new principles which must be freely accepted and scrupulously respected by the three parties, by all the governments which take over at the Colonial Department, and also by the authorities in Africa.

The result of this fusion of viewpoints and ideas will be to give birth to a *unity of direction* in the administration of the Congo, a unity which will extend from the most humble official of the General Government in Kalina to the Place Royale and will guarantee the success of Belgium's colonial mission. This unity will make the task of our rulers an extremely simple one and will save them from unnecessary fuss and bother.

It is essential to disarm certain demagogues or malevolent people who take advantage of the divergent views prevailing amongst the big Belgian political parties and cast discredit on the good name of the Belgian administration by intrigues and propaganda of all kinds. Their manoeuvres must be frustrated.

As long as the three parties are unable to agree on the new aims

F

of African policy, Belgium will be faced with a situation which will
in no way redound to her honour. It is absolutely essential that in
matters of colonial policy there should be not two or three policies
but a *single policy*.

I am confident that those who are in charge in Africa will co-
ordinate their efforts and that their one aim will be to serve not
their respective parties but metropolitan Belgium and overseas
Belgium, for the greatest good of the Congolese people.

The clash between White and Black

The reasons for this clash are primarily economic and social and
secondarily racial.

Firstly, economic: these are due to economic factors. When the
"economically strong" wish to enjoy a higher standard of living and
earn more at the expense of the others, the latter – i.e. the pro-
letariat – revolt against the capitalists and the bourgeoisie, thus pro-
ducing a clash of interests.

The struggle of the poor against the rich is a continuous process
which is evident in all human groups and has nothing to do with
race. These tendencies can be seen even amongst people belonging
to the same race.

The attitude of a Black employer towards an employee of the
same race is no different from that of a White employer.

Is there any African or European who would not be happy to pay
his domestic servant the lowest wage possible?

This is an inherent tendency in human nature: man's selfishness
and his inclination to exploit his fellow-man.

The complaints which the Congolese level against their White
bosses are exactly the same as those which the European workers
direct at their employers through their powerful trade unions. It is
these trade unions which, in Europe, have noticeably improved
the standard of living of the workers. There is a perpetual struggle
which sets employers against employees and which will last as long
as humanity itself and as long as one man has to work for the
account of another: in short, a fierce competition created by the
natural law of existence.

It would, therefore, be Utopian to believe that the clash of interests will ever disappear from the world. The important thing is to
reduce the causes of tension and to make it possible for each person
to obtain a reasonable reward for his work which will enable him
to live in tolerable conditions.

Social causes: These are injustices resulting from the perpetuation of excessively marked social inequalities, injustices which produce a serious impact on the weaker members of society.

Since these conflicts, which are of a purely economic and social character, arise in Africa between White and Black, the latter regard them as a form of racial discrimination and they consider they are being victimised because of the colour of their skin. This is a regrettable misunderstanding mainly due to ignorance of economic laws.

When these same conflicts set the citizens of the same race against each other, as happens in Europe, they are given a different designation, such as *capitalism,* etc.

In sharing out the profits of an undertaking it is normal for the owner to have a larger share than the workman because it is the owner who has provided the capital. But when the owner wants to live in opulence whilst the workman, who is the producer of the profits (because it is he who does the work), lives in poverty, this is sheer selfishness.

Social inequality arising from ineqaulity of aptitude is quite normal – indeed it is necessary for the proper organisation of society – but when it arises from an arbitrary "monopolisation" of privileges to the exclusive advantage of a single group, this is class selfishness. Such an attitude is the source of innumerable social conflicts.

Lastly, racial: when there is no other valid justification, the differentiations noted both in the economic and social sphere clearly assume the troublesome form of racial discrimination. Let me explain: when a White and a Black are equally efficient in regard to both quantity and quality of work, and there is a considerable variation in pay because of the colour of the workers, this is racial discrimination. When the Black shows himself the equal of the European by his training, maturity, character and way of living, his behaviour and his skill and he is treated not on the same level as the European but on the level of an inferior being, because he is ethnically a member of a so-called "inferior race"; when by reason of blind racial prejudice he is rejected by the "superior" society to which he applies for admission for quite legitimate motives: in the bar, restaurant, hotel, shop, cinema, schoolroom, etc.; when he is jeered at by those who are sometimes less well-educated, less well-trained and less civilised than he is himself; when, in spite of his aptitude and ability, he cannot rise and take the place in society which is his due; when, by ingenious arguments and racial theories,

F*

a limit is set to his rise in the social scale and it is impossible for him to occupy a position of authority over a White, even if he is more capable than the latter; when he is deliberately refused his fundamental rights as a citizen of this great human family; all this amounts to nothing more than the disease from which the African soul is confusedly suffering, the disease of racial discrimination.

These social conflicts arise from the anxiety of the dominant race to safeguard its economic interests, its prestige and its superiority. It is the outward expression of selfishness, that failing which is common to all the human species.

It is natural to protect one's interests and one's prestige, but only on condition that one does not thereby harm anyone else and that the interests of others are also protected.

These, briefly, are the causes which, in my opinion, often set White against Black; causes which are mainly economic and social in character.

As for racial feelings, it is undoubtedly true that, amongst certain persons, both European and African, there is an instinctive racial antipathy. These "racialists" are affected by a kind of emotional ailment and are, generally speaking, beyond hope of conversion.

I think it can safely be said that the majority of Belgians do not in their heart of hearts harbour any racialist feelings. I have drawn this conclusion after lengthy observation. The attitude of certain colonials towards the Africans is not that of the majority of metropolitan Belgians. It is an attitude which is specifically "colonial".

The attitude of the colonials towards the colonised people stems from the quite natural desire of any person in a privileged position to preserve a certain distance, economic and social, between himself and persons of an inferior rank.

The colonial who today maintains the distance between himself and the Congolese would, if met tomorrow in Belgium, receive you with open arms as a brother and a sincere friend, and you would never notice the slightest difference between his manner towards you and his manner towards any other Belgian. Everywhere, in all circles, you would enjoy perfect equality.

What is the reason for this duality of attitude in the colonist? It is because he has been *advised* to avoid all familiarity (certain colonial Belgians have confided this to me) with the colonised people, so as not to lose his prestige, which is to a certain extent necessary; secondly it is because he must protect his economic interests. But, once he has left the Colony, there is no longer any reason for this attitude, and the Belgian will resume his normal attitude which is basically friendly.

When a Congolese tours Belgium, from east to west and north to south, he is given a brotherly welcome by all Belgians, men, women and children, no matter what circle he enters. All this proves the absence of any racial prejudice in the make-up of the Belgian.

During my stay in Belgium, I met a group of French Africans which included some university students from the University of Paris. At the time this group was touring European towns to give theatrical performances. One of the leaders of the group expressed himself as follows: "Having been to London, Brussels and other places, not to mention Paris where we are living, we much prefer to live in France or Belgium because the French and the Belgians look upon us as friends. In London, for instance, we were not very kindly received; the English have racial feelings even towards Europeans of other nationalities."

This assessment of the situation by Africans living in Europe is ample proof of what I have just stated.

In all educational work, it is essential to maintain a certain distance between the teacher and the person being taught. This distance does not indicate disdain, but simply the need to maintain a certain discipline, since excessive familiarity between employer and worker or between a father and his children is not conducive to the maintenance of authority and discipline. Hierarchy is necessary in all human society and every sensible man must respect it.

Moreover, we must not lose sight of the fact that, despite the good will of men, the Congo will never be a paradise where all men are equal and where everything runs smoothly without friction. The important thing is to reduce the causes of conflict to a minimum and to establish a climate of undertsanding so that co-existence is not only peaceful but friendly.

In the Congo the Blacks would be helpless without the Whites, and the Whites would be helpless without the Blacks.

What in effect would happen if the Whites left the Congo today? It would spell complete ruin. And what would happen if the Africans withdrew completely from the Europeans, abandoned them and returned to till their own fields? The Europeans would be able to do nothing with their capital and machines; they would go bankrupt and would have to pack up their bags and go home.

This interdependence should suffice to bring together White and Black, not merely for their immediate material advantages but in a spirit of genuine human solidarity.

The bond of common interest would be frail indeed if it were not strengthened by the bond of sentiment and mutual affection.

The interpenetration of races and the fusion of interests form the only foundations for a firm and lasting Euro-African society.

CHAPTER XII

An Appeal to the Belgians

Dear Fellow Citizens: you have set your hand to a magnificent and humanitarian task in Africa which, today, is crowned with success; this work is not completed and there is still a tremendous amount to be done. We are only at the first stage.

Our gratitude to you is not merely a courtesy; it comes from the bottom of our hearts.

Whilst you are in this land of Africa, put aside your Western ideas whenever they are incompatible with the advancement of indigenous peoples.

Realise that you are, and will always be, among men who have a different philosophy, different customs, a different outlook, a different code of behaviour from your own. Whatever form of civilisation they may receive from you, they will continue to be Africans and at bottom they will retain their Bantu nature just as you have your nature; it is placed in their sub-conscious minds by the Creator.

Do not destroy the African's soul by attempting to make the African a superficial caricature of a European, a black-skinned Westerner. That may give good short-term results but they would have no firm foundation.

In the sphere of religion, philosophy or politics, always bear in mind the African mentality in your civilising work and do not think solely of the principles and ideas imported from Europe. Your principles and ideas may be good for you but they do not all suit the Africans.

A Belgian who is naturalised as a Chinese or Greek will always have the Belgian mentality and the same is true of Africans.

We admire the greatness of your civilisation because it is superior to our own. We have a passionate desire to become civilised people

like you but we wish to keep our own personality and our originality; to Europeanise ourselves artificially would be to deny our
own race.

We want to create a new civilisation, taking the good and fine
elements from yours, keeping the good and fine elements from ours
and fusing them, both European and African, to create one single
civilisation.

Let poor Belgium keep its ideological squabbles. The Congo
needs something other than petty wrangling. Let us all unite,
Catholics, Liberals, Socialists, Christians, Protestants, Atheists, to
achieve real peace in this country.

The missionaries of all the churches must pursue their sacred task
of uplifting the native people; their work must be backed up by
moral and material support. We believe that this support is available, both from the Government and from private bodies. Moreover,
all the religious or charitable institutions and activities have enjoyed
the special protection of the Government since the beginning of the
work of colonisation.

The Government should devote itself to the mission for which it
has sole responsibility to the nation. All the inhabitants – colonists,
missionaries and natives – must facilitate the work of the Government, not hampering the task of its representatives because they do
not belong to our camp or because of any other subjective considerations. When a Government official makes a mistake in carrying out
his duties, we ought not to make an outcry and stir up unnecessary
trouble with the sole aim of furthering certain sectional interests or
of injuring a political adversary.

We must realise that they are only human and that they can make
mistakes just as we could make mistakes if we were in their place.
No one is perfect in this imperfect world; that is a fact that we must
not forget.

Let us settle our differences amicably, always practising the principle of Christian charity taught by religion.

Each person should keep to his own field of activity without
squabbling or interfering unnecessarily in other people's affairs.
Relations between the various sectors should be restricted to a
trusting and fraternal collaboration in the management of public
affairs and in the defence of common interests. The colonists must
be helped as far as possible in their difficulties and their problems,
for the Congo would not be what it is today without their capital
and their co-operation. They give substantial assistance to the rural

population, providing in their concessions schools, clinics and medical care – often without charge – which are available even to natives not in their employment.

As far as this can be done without endangering the interests of the natives, encouragement should be given to young Belgians to come to the Congo, provided that they can give adequate proof of their good character, and that they have previously been educated in citizenship and made aware of the need for fraternal collaboration with their African fellow citizens. We believe that these young people, with their wide vision and generous ideas, will have a contribution to make towards the advancement of African society which is quite distinct from their own personal interests.

Have no hesitation in entrusting the African élite with responsible posts suited to their ability; by so doing you will convince them of the sincerity of your intention to make them your collaborators and allies. This will strengthen their confidence in Belgium, the protector of their destiny. They will regard you not as foreigners who have come to exploit them but as elder brothers and fellow citizens.

Let us show tolerance in our mutual relations, for without tolerance life in a community would become impossible.

People cannot all have the same opinions, the same ideas, the same ways of thinking. There is no uniformity of views and opinions in any human society.

It is for this reason that the Belgian Constitution and the Colonial Charter expressly lay down that "freedom of worship, in private and in public and freedom to express opinions on all matters are guaranteed, subject to the punishment of any crimes which may be committed in the course of exercising those rights."

The same fundamental principle underlies Articles 18 and 19 of the Universal Declaration of Human Rights: "Everyone has the right to freedom of thought, conscience and religion; this right includes freedom to change his religion or belief and freedom, either alone or in community with others and in public or private, to manifest his religion or belief in teaching, practice, worship and observance.

"Everyone has a right to freedom of opinion and expression; this right includes freedom to hold opinions without interference and to seek, receive and impart information and ideas through any media and regardless of frontiers."

I recall these elementary principles, with which you are all well acquainted, because I have recently noted the growth of certain absolutist tendencies and of a certain intolerance, all of which poison social relations and give rise to ceaseless quarrels.

The Congo belongs collectively to all its citizens, Congolese and Belgians of all shades of opinion; these citizens do not all subscribe to the same principles; this is normal and natural – there would be something wrong if it were not so.

So let us have political clubs in which every citizen can quench his thirst; I see nothing wrong in this, provided that these clubs all have a single aim, that of the general interest of the population, and maintain friendly relations with each other. But they no longer have my approval if their aim is to destroy society and to stir up sterile and partisan quarrels.

The tendencies which can be observed in a secular society can also be seen in the religious world. Christians all follow what is, in effect, the same objective – eternal salvation – but they are divided into various religious bodies such as the Society of the Priests of the Sacred Heart, the Premonstrants, the Fathers of Scheut, the Passion-ists, the Jesuits, the Marists, the Calvinists, Methodists, etc. All these different religious societies have a common background, but each one specialises in the study and practice of a particular dogma. The same concerns and tendencies can be seen in secular society. But we do not deny that there are abuses and defects. The following lines occur in the work of Jacques Maritain entitled "*The Rights of Man and the Natural Law*": "At the same time, the very fact that every person as a person should normally be able to give expression to his thoughts and his wishes in the political field also makes it normal for the members of the political society to group themselves according to the affinities of their ideas and aims into political parties or political schools. Much criticism has been level-led at political parties, and these criticisms are justified by all the abuses which have impeded their working and which have paralysed and corrupted the political life of the European democracies. But these defects are not inherent in the concept of such groups, the variety of which reflects the natural variety of ideas and methods found among the members of the political community. It has also been rightly pointed out that the rule of a single party instituted in the totalitarian states maximises, instead of curing, the vices and tyranny which the opponents of democracy lay at the door of the party system. The totalitarian single party system is the worst and most catastrophic form of the party system."

Again, Pierre Aubry, a doctor in the legal, political and economic sciences, writes: "The steady development of the means of communication between the different countries of the world has led to a vast movement of peoples of all races, colours and religions which has put completely dissimilar human beings cheek by jowl in some regions and in some great centres of population. Will this continual contact between Westerners, Americans, Asiatics, Yellow races, Whites and Negroes lead to a mixture of races, a gradual fusion from which new types of men will emerge, social groups better adapted to all the conditions of life on the planet and integrating harmoniously the various conflicting tendencies and aspirations which today lead all too often to conflicts and wars?

"Either these inescapable contacts between all the varieties of the human race are a prelude to the dissolution and ruin of Western civilisation, or else they will merge into a fuller form of civilisation which will open the way to a new stage of human evolution.

"In so far as human evolution is dependent upon political evolution, we may consider that the trends towards nationalist and protectionist imperialism which caused the great wars of modern times are a symptom of the forces of dissolution opposing the forces of creative and regulatory evolution embodied in international agreements. If the latter are to prevail, and if security is to be definitely established over the whole face of the globe, it is to be hoped that the governments of the great colonial states who possess armies and fleets will once and for all give up any thought of conquest and colonial war, and that the statesmen who guide opinion in all countries will use their intelligence, their activity and their political good sense to harmonise the peoples' desire for peaceful progress with their attachment to sound national traditions.

"Let the patriots of all these countries come together. The disappearance of political antagonism between the peoples does not presuppose, and will not involve, the abandonment of their rightful desire to spread their own philosophies. The juridical association of the great political states will merely reflect their common need for security and it need not result in, or be dependent upon, the establishment of a universal republic and the creation of administrative, economic, intellectual and spiritual uniformity. On the contrary, it must be regarded as the abolition of an obstacle to that harmony, always so desirable, which arises from the diversity of physical surroundings, and the variety of economic needs and abilities, intellect, character and judgment.

"And human progress does not occur otherwise than by an

increasing specialisation of hand and brain, by a growing competition in the assessment, implementation and living-out of that
progress, and lastly by the increasing intensity of the exchange of
goods, ideas and feelings beween all the inhabitants of the globe."

Jacques Maritain writes again: "The aim of society is its
common good, the good of the body social. But without the realisa-
tion that the good of the whole is a common good of human beings,
just as the body social itself is made up of human beings, this
formula in turn would give rise to other mistakes of the national-
ising or collectivising type.

"The common good is the basis of authority because, in order to
lead a community of human beings towards their common good,
towards their general good as such, it is essential that some of them
should be in charge of this operation and that the directions which
they give, the decisions which they take in this connection, should
be followed or obeyed by the other members of the community. An
authority of this kind, leading towards the general good, is directed
towards free men; it is the absolute opposite of the domination of
human beings by a master for the particular good of that master.

"Everyone, Catholic and non-Catholic, Christian and non-
Christian, from the moment of recognising within his own field of
vision the human values of which the Gospel bids us to be aware,
the dignity and the rights of the individual, the nature of the moral
obligation which is inherent in authority, the law of brotherly love
and the sanctity of the natural law, would thereby be swept up by
its dynamic force and would be capable of co-operating for the
common good.

"If such a society is to be called Christian, not in its outward
appearances but in its inner substance, this will be due, not to a
system of privileges, outward compulsion and pressure, but to inner
forces developed within the people and issuing from them; to the
devotion and self-sacrifice of men giving their services to the common task, men whose moral authority will be freely accepted; it will
be due to the institutions, moral standards and customs of that
society.

"In any evolving society we can observe the natural aspirations
of human beings towards freedom of development and towards a
political and social emancipation which will free them increasingly
from the shackles of material nature. This movement leads towards
a steady fulfilment in social life itself, of the aspiration of all men
to be treated as persons. It is an ideal which can only be put into

practice by the development of law, justice and honour and by an increase in friendship.

"It is the duty of every political society to secure the common weal, to ensure strength and peace, to give every individual positive assistance in the steady achievement of that freedom of development which consists, above all, in a flowering of the spiritual and intellectual life, and of those inner activities which are the expression of the intellectual and spiritual virtues."

This is the goal towards which we should be bending our efforts.

Some of you – fortunately not many – vilify the Government in the Press and insult its representatives; this makes a bad impression on the Africans, the majority of whom have not yet acquired the critical spirit which is essential for discriminating judgment of the written word. Some of your "open letters" to the Governor General, the Minister, etc – and particularly the tone in which they are sometimes written – give the natives the impression of an attempt to obstruct the Government and revolt against it. The unfortunate thing is that some of you mischievously incite the natives to revolt against the representatives of the Government; you do not realise what such actions may lead to later on. By so doing, are you not teaching the Congolese, who read your words and imitate you slavishly, to revolt in their turn against the Government whenever the claims of a particular sectional interest are not met?

Every citizen has, of course, the right to address petitions to the authorities, and the Colonial Charter sanctions this; but this right must not be abused and its use should be restricted – particularly in the case of petitions published in the Press – to really important matters in which the public interest is at stake. But it is most undesirable to rush into print for purely demagogic purposes in "open letters" with the aim of inflaming passions, undermining the prestige of the Government or harrassing political opponents.

We want a democratic government but not a bad democracy.

Our country has much greater need of "builders" than of squabblers, pamphleteers and purveyors of communist slogans.

Do not be aloof from us because, in that way, we shall not get to know each other better, to appreciate each other, to work together.

When you go to a Government office, or any office where an African is in charge, talk to him as correctly as you would to a fellow countryman, and use the same accepted formulas of courtesy; men should not be treated in two different ways; the rules of civility are the same everywhere.

The work of educating the Congolese is not merely the duty of the Government and the Christian missions, but of all Europeans living in the country. For whatever reason you may be in Africa, regard yourselves as teachers and play your part in building up the Congo.

It is not easy to do this; you will have many difficulties, even rebuffs, from some of my fellow Africans, but do not lose heart; have patience.

We Africans say to you from the bottom of our hearts, without fear or flattery, that we love you sincerely, because you have greatly helped us, and also because we are all brothers; apart from the skin of our bodies which divides us into Blacks and Whites – a pure matter of chance – the difference in our language and civilisations, our social conditions and our racial origins, we are all descended from a common ancestor; we have a common soul: a human soul; we have the same destiny, the same mission to fulfil in this world. We expect from you the same love which we show to you and which is manifested in the hospitality offered to you in this country for more than three quarters of a century.

The children of this country have no feeling of hatred towards the Belgians or the Whites in general for the very good reason that, as I have already fully explained, they helped us in our most tragic moments, they gave us back our dignity, they educated us and continue to educate us as good citizens. It is thanks to them that the Congo is recovering.

It would be culpable ingratitude to drive you out of this country, even if we had reached complete maturity and were capable of administering the country ourselves.

We shall always need your technical assistance just as you will need our help. No country can be self-sufficient, not even rich America which, incidentally, is supplied with uranium by the Belgian Congo.

If the Congo should obtain its independence or autonomy tomorrow, why should you leave us and why should we drive you out, so long as our co-existence gives rise to no friction and so long as we continue to treat each other not as neighbours linked by the mere ties of courtesy but as true friends in the fullest meaning of the term.

Have confidence in this country as we have confidence in you.

If one day you should lose the Congo or quit this hospitable country, it would be your own fault and not the fault of the natives, who ask nothing better than to live in harmony with you. And it would not be the fault of all of you, for we have become convinced of the goodwill shown by many of you, particularly in the last few years; it would be the fault of a few saboteurs who are cunningly undermining your work or, rather, our joint work. It is impossible to condemn too strongly the attitude of these few people who are jeopardising the social order.

There are some prophets who foretell the end or the decline of Belgium's achievements in Africa. We believe that, in many cases, their prophecies must be regarded as a skilful campaign, a screen for jealousy and vindictive ambitions. But we thank the men of humane outlook who have such a disinterested concern for our fate.

We shall not call for outside help unless an amicable agreement proves absolutely impossible. At the moment, outside interference is unjustified and the offers of our "liberators" should be ignored. We need not worry too much about the little games of our Jeremiahs and fishers in troubled waters.

Nevertheless, there are certain just and constructive comments which we should accept, because they can enable us to avoid mistakes which might have regrettable consequences.

There will never be a lack of critics, destructive and constructive, among foreigners, Belgians and Congolese. The Africans read more and more; they are aware of what is being written and said to their disadvantage or advantage.

The reactions of certain journalists are sometimes clumsy and do more harm than good. For instance, when a public figure in Belgium or a journalist who is favourably inclined towards native interests claims some benefit or right for the Africans or criticises a particular attitude adopted towards them, the Congolese jump for joy on finding a "defender". But then, unfortunately, a colonial journalist or journalists will react strongly and protest every time someone wishes to take up the cudgels on our behalf or do us a favour . . .

And so all colonials, without distinction, are treated as anti-African; the innocents are suspect because of the blunders committed by a single person, and with some justification!

The fact is that the Congolese as a whole tend to generalise and the plural is often used instead of the singular.

Take the arguments often put forward: "We colonials know the situation in the Congo best and we follow its development. Our advice in matters of native policy and African emancipation should be given more weight than that of V.I.Ps from the Home Country

who know nothing about the Congo." The Africans pay no attention
to arguments, however valid they may be; they are concerned with
what will improve their lot. Thus they have more confidence in
those who demand rapid emancipation than in those who counsel
prudence and deliberation and who, in their eyes, wish to hold back
their development as long as possible under the cover of specious
arguments.

This is not a personal judgment; I am simply giving the opinion
of the Congolese on this point. I myself recognise the considerable
efforts made by certain newspapers in the Congo to further the
advancement of the natives, and certain improvements are often due
to the disinterested action of the Press.

Although some journalists cause the Government trouble by their
rashness, there are others who aid the Government in its task.

In a young country like the Congo, the Press has a delicate part
to play. The journalist's role is not restricted to the provision of
information; it is also educational, and for that reason it is essential
that every journalist should be conscious of his responsibilities.

Newspapers with racialist tendencies will have the most harmful
effect on the relations between Blacks and Whites.

Moreover, attacks on our work must be countered not by violence
or philosophic dissertations but by the force of persuasion and by
calm. Only a solidly-based union between Belgians and Congolese
can forge a powerful enough weapon to withstand storms and outside influences.

CHAPTER XIII

To My Congolese Compatriots

What should be our attitude towards the complex and agonising problems which confront us and which involve the future of our country? It must be one of calm, level-headedness, correct behaviour, impartiality, objectivity, justice, patience, perseverance, constant faith and continuity of effort and action. We must not give way to discouragement if we are to complete our difficult journey with its many hazards, disappointments and rebuffs.

Problems exist, and will continue to exist, as long as the world exists. The solution of these problems often depends on many factors which are not always evident to us. Let us not always jump to the conclusion that these problems are due to ill-will on the part of the authorities or of our rulers.

Every time that we *evolués* discuss these problems, we must think of the mass of our fellow-Africans, for our task, like that of the Government of the country, is to concern ourselves not with a single class but with the population as a whole.

Let us not stand aloof from our brothers because they are less educated, less cultured, less fortunate than ourselves; this would create an unfortunate gulf between us. We want to bridge the gulf which separates us from the Whites but we must not create another one behind us. Who will work for them if we abandon them? May they not one day turn against us? Our concern must be not to satisfy personal ambitions but to achieve the harmonious development of all Africans. We must give up any activities which may cause cleavages within our society.

Our success depends above all on our unity. This can only be achieved if we manage to rid our minds of excessive clannishness, to face up together to our patriotic duty and, above all, to be aware

of the absolute necessity for each one of us to achieve the harmonious development of the Congo by means of a united and
unselfish effort.

The reforms which we are seeking must be achieved in a spirit
of agreement and harmony. Anyone who plans rebellion or con-
spiracy will endanger the country and bring it into disrepute.

It is easy enough to shout slogans, to sign manifestos, but it is
quite a different matter to build, manage, command, spend days
and nights seeking the solution of problems.

Some Europeans of the less desirable kind exploit the credulity
of the still largely uneducated Africans by urging them to claim
immediate independence; they go so far as to suggest that autonomy
will never be obtained without the spilling of blood, that all the
Western countries had to fight in order to obtain their independence
and that the Congolese must do the same if they wish to free themselves from the Belgians. This is indeed a sad state of mind!

We must reject these ideas, from whatever source they may come.
The Congo will obtain its independence with dignity and not with
barbarism. Civilisation and war are incompatible.

Some nations may have obtained their independence by means
of atom bombs and bloody wars, but we shall obtain ours by words,
by intelligence, by reason. It would be an act of the greatest barbarism, an act of banditry, to sacrifice human lives, the lives of our
fellow-countrymen who are so dear to us, in our zeal for independence. No, the Congo shall not be kept on apron strings. Let us spare
our country this misfortune, which humanity would hold against us.
Instead of imitating other warlike nations, we shall give them an
object lesson.

This is no childish phrase. There is no moral justification for war,
with its slaughter and pillage, and those who commit such barbarous acts, except under extreme provocation, do not deserve the
name of civilised people whether they be white, yellow or red.

Let us also bear in mind that these wonderful "liberators" who
promise heaven and earth are not always striving for our good; they
are often swayed by other and more sinister motives. We must not
be deceived. It is no help to anyone to preach disorder; what is
needed is order in ideas, in personal conduct and in the life of the
community.

Let us, on the contrary, make friends with those who sincerely
wish to help us.

We need not complain too much about our fate. By comparison

with some other nations, our situation is not as bad as is sometimes believed.

In the course of my brief visit to Belgium, I took the opportunity of visiting some towns in France and the Netherlands, spurred on by curiosity and by the desire to obtain information for the benefit of my fellow-citizens. I can assure you that quite a number of Congolese are in a much more comfortable situation than many Europeans in their home countries. We often have the mistaken idea that all Europeans live in the same conditions as the Europeans of the Congo, but this is a serious mistake. Anyone who could travel in South Africa, in the southern United States, in Italy, India, in China, or in any country of the world, would realise the position and would discover that the standard of living of the Congolese is considerably higher than that prevailing in certain other countries.

This is only a straightforward comparison and not a piece of propaganda. Nor does this comparison prevent us from claiming certain improvements which we feel to be essential.

In our daily relations with the Whites, we shall sometimes be annoyed or hurt by certain ill-natured people, but we must not generalise and attribute to all Europeans the misdeeds and mistakes committed by some of them. If the facts are sufficiently grave, we may react soberly but we must never dramatise things.

In putting forward our claims, let us avoid the use of violent language which wounds the self-respect of the people to whom we are speaking; instead of obtaining what we want by means of a polite approach, we shall meet with a refusal caused more by anger than by ill-will. Should we not do the same if we were in their place? It is only human. More can be obtained by polite persuasion than by shouting like Hitler.

As we work for the defence of our rights, we shall find ourselves blamed, rightly or wrongly, and we shall run up against obstacles and difficulties. We must not always ascribe these setbacks to racial discrimination. We must realise that Europeans very often encounter the same difficulties. If we imagine that all of them are always happy, it is only because we do not know their problems and do not live with them. Some of them encounter more difficulties and troubles than we do.

Let us tell the Belgians frankly what we want, opening our hearts to them and they will do the same to us. Frankness and sincerity must be the keynote of our mutual relations in this freely contracted Belgo-Congolese marriage, because those qualities are indispensable

if the union is to be a lasting one. Let us give up all tendencies to
hypocrisy in dealing with Europeans. Many Congolese tell the Europeans not what they think or feel in the depths of their heart but
what they think the Europeans would like them to say. We must
realise that the Europeans who devote themselves to our problems
have no desire for flattery or excessive and hypocritical praise, nor
is this in their interest. On the contrary, they want to be told
frankly what our problems are. How can they get to know us, find
a solution for our troubles or correct our judgments (many of us do
in fact still lack reasoning powers) if we conceal our true thoughts
from them? There are many people who say that one should never
tell the truth to a European because this will not be appreciated and
your frankness will later cost you dear. It is, of course, a fact that
some of us have suffered and still do sometimes suffer for our frankness and sincerity, either because we have boldly put forward a valid
point of view which is not accepted by the Europeans concerned, or
because we have defended a just cause; but that is no reason to
lose heart, to take refuge in silence or, worst of all, to dull our wits
by hypocrisy . . . [illegible] This dumbness is a serious handicap
to the liberation of our minds because, instead of discovering the
truth and correcting our false judgments, we remain prisoners of
ignorance and fear – very often imaginary fear.

There is no question of saying everything that comes into our
heads; that would be stupid. The essential point is not to violate
truth and commonsense. We must set ourselves to search ceaselessly
for truth in all its forms. Truth is the only means by which we can
contribute to our spiritual and intellectual development.

Some Congolese, being jealous at the promotion of their colleagues (although the latter are more capable and deserving than
they are themselves) have no hesitation in making slanderous statements about them to their employer or to Government officials.
Since these revelations (which are often of their own invention)
cannot be verified, or because they are trusted employees, their
allegations are taken at their face value. Cases have occurred and
are still occurring of thoroughly loyal people who could have
worked closely with the Belgians becoming the victims of calumny
and being put on the black list by the security organisation . . .

These bearers of false witness who specialise in hypocrisy and
calumny know how to pull the wool over the eyes of the Europeans
and gain their confidence and sympathy. In front of the Europeans
they are tireless in their praise and their professions of loyalty and

gratitude but, elsewhere, Judas-like, they make treacherous remarks about the Europeans, sow confusion in the minds of the unsuspecting natives and destroy their confidence in the Belgians.

These flatterers pass themselves off everywhere as "saints" and loyal supporters, which they are not . . . These slanderers and tale-bearers have done a great deal of harm to their victims; their method is simply to betray their rivals and seek favours and honours without regard for commonsense and charity.

All the Congolese are aware of this regrettable situation, which prevails particularly in the large towns, where alleged agents of the security forces (we are not referring to the Security Service proper, whose vigilance is of great benefit to the community) carry on their self-seeking activities.

It is to be hoped that those who indulge in such shady practices will mend their ways; these activities do them no credit – they lower their reputation.

Let us not always have our hands outstretched to receive, but always make a personal effort to obtain what we want. We shall achieve nothing by folding our arms, indulging in perpetual lamentations and recriminations or philsophising over a glass of beer. We shall never achieve anything except by working feverishly, struggling fiercely for our existence, and searching for constructive solutions. Life on this earth is hard, very hard, and bristles with difficulties; it often requires sacrifices.

Civilisation is not handed out like alms; nor can it be poured into men as one pours water into a bottle; it must be acquired by personal effort.

We must sacrifice all that we have in order to teach and educate our children, for the future of the Congo is in their hands; we must be very exacting in regard to them, watching over their studies, their outings and their walks, keeping in close touch with their teachers, so as to bring to light and remedy in good time any difficulties in their school life, and we must subject them to very severe discipline.

In every town, we must establish common classes (Study Funds) to collect the necessary money for the grant of scholarships to our most gifted children, so as to enable them to go to Europe for specialised training, particularly in technical subjects and the professions. We must ask the Government to establish a special compulsory tax to yield the necessary funds for this purpose.

If every inhabitant paid ten francs a year, which is the cost of a bottle of beer – one bottle for the whole year – we should have an enormous sum, which would enable our children, both boys and girls, to study in Belgium or in Africa and obtain specialised training in the various branches of knowledge. Let us suppose only one million taxpayers out of the thirteen million inhabitants were to pay ten francs, that would give us ten times one million, i.e. 10,000,000 francs. With this money it would be possible to send as many students as necessary to Europe every year, paying their maintenance and tuition fees.

In this respect, Ruanda-Urundi is ahead of the Congo. Recently, dozens of boys and girls have been setting off for Belgium, and the same applies in all the other African colonies. Are we to be left behind our neighbours?

The inhabitants of Ruanda-Urundi achieve this result mainly because the students' travel, tuition and maintenance expenses are borne by its local funds, sometimes independent of Government control.

Surely, we have the same resources as our neighbours, both material and intellectual, and we can make a similar effort. This depends on our initiative and determination. It can be done.

We must not continue to live like spoilt children, always awaiting magnificent gifts. We must take action so that the Congo shall not lag behind the other countries of Africa in regard to education and political emancipation; we must realise that this emancipation depends on a real maturity of its citizens.

When the Congo has its own technicians in every trade, its doctors, agricultural specialists, engineers, businessmen, geologists, administrators, contractors, skilled workers (this does not mean that we have no skilled workers at present; I am referring here to highly-qualified workers like those to be found in the big factories in Europe), social workers, nurses and mid-wives, *then and then only* can we talk of independence or autonomy, because we shall then be strong enough, intellectually, technically, and materially, to administer the country on our own if necessary.

Some Congolese like to keep on recalling past errors. But what is gained by this? Virtually nothing. Let us leave to the past what belongs to the past and look at the future from another angle.

No one denies that these mistakes have been made. They were errors due to inexperience. But we must remember that those who made these mistakes, the pioneers of colonisation, were not saints and had not the gift of infallibility. Yet it is to these brave pioneers of the Free State, these heroes who obtained little or no benefit from their labours, that we owe our present position.

These pioneers of the Free State left their fair country to answer the call of conscience; they left behind them their families, their closest friends, their pleasures, in order to cross the seas and rescue us from chaos and from the yoke of the man-hunting pirates; they crossed trackless and perilous country to establish lines of communication. These humanitarians, who lived in the greatest discomfort and shared our sorrows and our food, were closer to us than the "modernists" of the epoch of refrigerators and American cars.

Some of them, worn out and demoralised by countless disappointments, undoubtedly made some mistakes, but are not those mistakes outweighed by the immense amount of good which has been achieved and is in the process of achievement?

No human activity is entirely free from blemishes and mistakes. It is often these blemishes and mistakes which show the correct route to be followed in the future.

I readily admit that not all colonists are inspired by philanthropic motives. Many of them come to the colonies only with the object of earning their living and having a comfortable life which they could not have had in their own country. There is nothing unusual about this.

If a Congolese is invited to go today to Poland and earn two, three or four times what he is earning in his own country, he will go like a shot, even if this means sacrificing his friendships and family ties, at a moment's notice, in order to secure the counterbalancing benefit of a more privileged position.

But this financial incentive does not, of necessity, exclude a valuable contribution to the process of civilisation, provided that the colonists have human emotions and that their colonisation programme has a social or humanitarian side to it, as well as an economic one. This is exactly the position, and people who claim that the Whites are in Africa solely to exploit the Blacks seem to be mistaken in their judgment. There are, of course, some who exploit the Blacks but it is wrong to claim that all Europeans exploit the Blacks.

Is the African to show ingratitude by reviling the pioneers of the civilising process who sleep their last sleep in this country which they loved and served? Certainly not. We must not lay ourselves open to such a charge.

When we pass the graves of these heroes who gave their lives for our safety, and thanks to whom we can now utter the words "independence – autonomy", let us be silent for a few moments and bow our heads respectfully in their memory. Together with our fellow countrymen they gave their lives for the defence of the country. May the mingled blood of the Belgians and Congolese, which was spilt in their common struggle and formed an undying bond of friendship, cement Belgo-Congolese friendship for ever.

CHAPTER XIV

We Must not Confuse Government and Men

It sometimes happens that a particular government servant fails in his duty and does not apply the instructions which have been given to him, either by the Government or by his superiors.

It may also happen that he treats us unsympathetically. In this case, we must not criticise the Government as such, by laying at its door faults committed by some of its servants. We must regard these acts and these errors as individual acts for which their authors alone bear responsibility.

Similarly, when a European behaves badly towards us, we must not make the hasty general deduction that ALL Europeans are bad, as some people often do.

The same thing applies in the field of religion: the fact that one priest behaves badly does not prove that religion is bad or that all priests should be condemned. Men in Holy Orders are human beings, just like laymen, and they cannot escape from the law of fallibility.

From these few explanations, the conclusion can be drawn that everyone must be held personally responsible for his acts. That is a simple question of logic.

To illustrate my ideas, I shall give some examples, taken from among many others, which may perhaps convince those who are sceptical.

The right of access of Congolese to public premises

Belgian Colonial policy is opposed to racial discrimination. Since the Belgians first reached the Congo there has never been any legislation forbidding the Congolese the right of access to public premises frequented by Europeans as is the case in certain countries, including South Africa and the southern United States (it should be emphasised that the situation there has begun to change in the last few years), but nevertheless, owing to the unwillingness of the proprietors, access to these places – restaurants, hotels and certain shops – has been, and still is, forbidden to non-Whites irrespective of their stage of civilisation and their behaviour.

It required an energetic decision by the Governor General in 1955 to put an end to these manifestations of racial discrimination. It will not be forgotten that the Governor General was roundly criticised by those who wished to maintain racial prejudices.

In spite of the appeal made by His Majesty King Baudoin, who laid particular stress on the improvement of human relations between Whites and Blacks, in spite of constant exhortations by the head of the colony and by the Minister for Colonial Affairs in all their official speeches on social policy, in spite of a Press campaign, some racialists persist in ignoring the instructions and recommendations of the administrative authorities.

Since the views of these racialists have been frequently repudiated, both by their fellow citizens and by the authorities, it is clear that the Government is in no wise responsible for these personal conflicts about which we so often complain.

Since persuasion – even by the King! – is not enough to convince these diehards of the absurdity of their prejudices, a special provision should be added to the penal code for "affronts to human dignity", so as to punish the illegal actions of these obstinate racialists who are jeopardising the social order and the equilibrium of relations between the races. They constitute a danger for Belgium's work in Africa, and they will cause the Government difficulties later on.

When a European living in this country disagrees with the policy of the Government and despises the Africans, we consider that his place is elsewhere, and that it would be advisable for him to return to the paradise whence he came. It is impossible to live with people whom one does not like.

People who only like the material side of the Congo (the facilities for growing rich) and not its human side, are exploiters whom the country does not need.

The days of the ivory hunters are past.

*Relations between the African public and government
servants or Europeans in general*

First of all, let me quote the legal and official texts on native
policy setting out the obligations of Government servants towards
the natives " . . . they (the Government servants) must watch their
attitude and their language and avoid anything which might bring
them into disrepute and expose them to ridicule. In dealing with the
natives, they must never forget their educational function puts them
under an inescapable obligation to set a good example everywhere
and at all times. Any misconduct, any undesirable attitude or word
can destroy at one blow the efforts of many years . . . They must
be inspired by a real sympathy for the natives, and must manifest
this to them at all times if they do not wish their work to be fruit-
less."

Reference to these duties is made frequently in administrative
circulars. Thus the good intentions of the Government are clearly
proved.

If these instructions were observed in letter and in spirit by ALL
Government officials, I consider that there would be little ground
for complaint in this field.

The Government is not to blame if an official speaks to us con-
temptuously in the second person singular (I am not referring here
to a friendly use of that form between a superior officer and his
colleague, between the European and his African friend), refuses
to shake hands with us, receives us coldly in his office, or will not
offer us a chair, as he would do to any European coming into a
private or public office.

On the other hand, the fact that in the same quarters we meet a
considerable number of officials at all levels who are well-disposed,
kindly, attentive, modest, impartial, who treat us humanely as
friends, on the same footing as people of other races – all this again
proves that the Government is innocent and sincere in its intentions.

Does this mean that the Government is a "saint" and makes no
mistakes? I am far from holding this idea. I simply wish to draw a
fair distinction in order to avoid misunderstandings. There is a place
for everything and everything has its place.

CHAPTER XV

Independence—Autonomy—Federation ?

What form of Government should be given to the Congo? The question is asked with increasing frequency because the form of Government provides a fairly clear pointer to what the Congo is to become and what its political future will be.

We have, of course, the right – and it is a sacred right – to choose the form of Government of our own country. But let us right from the start avoid all slogans and catch-phrases.

The pre-requisite of independence or autonomy is an adequate political maturity, a suitable level of organisation and people of real ability to administer the country. Has the Congo yet reached this stage? If it has, we are right in demanding immediate autonomy; if not, we must avoid rushing things.

Have those who demand *immediate* independence today given the matter serious reflection?

In every process of development, as in the growth of a child or a tree, there must be transitional stages; these stages are essential, and they are determined by the inexorable law of nature. It would be a wrong move to attempt to dispense with this law and raise a premature cry of "independence".

The words "independence" and "autonomy" have little meaning for us at the moment. What the Congolese people greatly need at present is social reform, an improvement in the standard of living of the natives, peace, harmony between Belgians and Congolese, the root and branch elimination of all causes of friction, and the democratisation of the country.

The higher authorities are closely concerned with these questions. The problem of human and social relationships has become the favourite subject of the Head of the Colony. Our Minister for

Colonial Affairs, M. Buisseret, is a great enthusiast for social problems, which he brought to the fore recently in an interview with a correspondent of the African programmes of the Belgian Congo Radio; the interview was reproduced in all the Congolese papers, and here are the principal passages:

" . . . It is above all by the contact of hearts that relations between Blacks and Whites must develop . . . There also exists between Blacks and Whites a discrimination which runs counter to our desire to see the establishment of a Belgo-Congolese Community in which relationships between Whites and Blacks will be human relationships in the highest sense of the term, characterised by that fundamental equality proclaimed by the French Revolution with no distinctions other than those of 'virtues and talents'.

"We have decided to abolish unfair discrimination. The Government Council dealt with the subject a few weeks ago. There is an impression in some circles that the question is one of settling relationships between employers and employees. In fact, however, it is a question of implementing freedom of association and of giving that freedom a legal framework and regulation, thus working towards the inter-racial policy which will be the law of the Congo in the future.

"Whatever may be said in some circles, the views of those who, in Europe and Africa, bear the duty and the responsibility of carrying out policy, are crystal-clear. Our programme is a continuation of the work which Belgium has carried out in Africa for more than half a century, but adapted to new situations. Those who have taken the trouble to read, not only the two speeches by His Majesty the King, but also the parliamentary debates of 1955 and 1956, will know that it has been stated repeatedly that our policy follows the same broad lines which have been followed by Belgian policy since the earliest days. These constant factors of policy are: an economic expansion which is intended to give the maximum benefit to Whites and Blacks; an intellectual advance which has now led Whites and Blacks to the gates of the universities; the education of the mass of the people in administration and then in politics, starting at the local government level.

"These are wise and effective methods, methods of emancipation, progress and peace, whatever may be said at home by the over-hasty or ill-informed and abroad by some people whom one cannot but suspect of being informed if not lacking in good faith.

"Dear M. Godfroid, you are going back to Stanleyville to resume your fine and noble task as representative of Belgian Congo Radio. Please tell our fellow countrymen in Africa, Black and White, that we are backing them up with greater determination than ever in the task of bringing progress and prosperity to the wonderful country in which they live and which we shall defend against the predatory designs, the risks and the dangers which may threaten it. Our Africa, the Africa of the pioneers, has always been self-confident, grappling with life and progress, and this is what we want it to be in the future."

How reassuring these words of the Minister for Colonial Affairs are! His recent gesture in appointing a Congolese to a high post in the Colonial Department – something which has never previously happened in Africa, where no high post in the administration has ever been given to an African – is an admirable proof of the sincerity of his intentions and of the Belgian Government in regard to the advancement of the Congolese élite. The gesture made by this great Minister who devotes himself to the service of African Belgium with a sincere sense of vocation will always remain engraved on the hearts of his African friends.

The Congolese consider this gesture today as the official start of that policy of promotion which has been so long awaited and desired by the Black élite.

Now that the symbolic ribbon has been cut by the representative of His Majesty the King, we trust that the door to integration will remain open and that every citizen will occupy a place in society appropriate to his abilities and knowledge, both in the public and the private sector, from the foot of the ladder to its highest rungs. This is the great wish of all Africans.

The achievement of the Belgo-Congolese Community is inextricably linked with the advancement of the Congolese élite, without which the Community will only be a sham.

Congolese of all shades of opinion regard the Minister's gesture not as a symbolic or political appointment intended to hoodwink them but as a practical implementation of the policy of emancipation preached by Belgium for many years, a policy which has been clearly laid down by all the ministers who have occupied the Place Royale; we still recall the very progressive ideas which another minister, M. Wigny, put forward on this subject. This is the policy of the King and of all the leading Belgians; it marks the beginning of the advancement of the Congolese élite, an advancement which should have taken place long ago.

The Belgian Congo is surely lagging behind in the integration of the African élite.

Finally, this message from the Minister for Colonial Affairs, followed shortly afterwards by a solemn act giving concrete expression to the sincerity of Belgium's intentions, has dispelled the clouds of despair which hung over the Congo. There is a new light everywhere: in their meetings and their conversations, the Congolese – even the most disillusioned – are beginning to look to the future with optimism. More than ever the Congolese offer their loyal devotion and all their confidence to their Minister, whom they have called "the Great Friend of the Congolese", to their Governor-General and to all Belgians who, regardless of colour or ideology, are looking after their interests from near or afar.

CHAPTER XVI

Conclusion: Crisis of Confidence

Ever since the Belgians first came to Africa, the Congolese have shown themselves to be docile, obedient and grateful to their mentors. Their confidence has been put to the test for over seventy-five years.

The social peace which reigns in the Congo and which foreigners call the "Belgian Miracle in Africa", is a dazzling sign of good administration and of the high morale of the native population.

The first stage of the colonisation has been completed: the stage of the conclusion of treaties, construction of roads, liberation of the people, etc. After these three-quarters of a century of hard work, of groping steps which have now led to success, the people of the colony put forward a confident and dignified plan to leave this stage, which has been out-dated by the course of development, and to enter stage two.

Will Belgium disappoint them? I do not think so, because there is no valid reason to justify such a refusal and because Belgian policy as a whole is sincerely moving towards the steady emancipation of the Congolese under Belgian trusteeship.

What is this *second stage*? It is the stage of *integration* (not of assimilation which involves the absorption of one people by another) of the *democratisation of the country* and of the *Africanisation of the leadership*.

This integration is the task of our rulers, in whom I have every confidence. In this book, I have mentioned some transitional stages which may facilitate the immediate advancement of the Belgian Africans.

In their co-existence with the Whites, the Africans are greatly worried, not by the fact of living alongside them, but by the idea that they may never be able to attain complete emancipation and liberty whilst under European domination.

Hence the African's dream of independence does not arise from hatred for the Whites or a desire to drive them out of Africa, but simply from the wish to be not merely a free man but also a citizen in the service of his country and not perpetually in the service of the European. He believes, moreover, that, even if he is able to obtain complete emancipation under white domination, it will only come after centuries, because the European will hamper that emancipation by all sorts of tricks and political schemes, and that the Blacks will therefore be kept in a state of inferiority as long as possible. Finally, he believes that once the country becomes independent, the emancipation of the inhabitants will be much more rapid than it would have been under the system of tutelage and colonialism.

"We shall certainly have difficulties at the beginning – like every other nation – but we shall overcome them thanks to the help of the Europeans to whom we shall appeal and who will come, in this case, not to dominate us but to help us and to serve Africa. With these Europeans we shall always maintain neighbourly and fraternal relations."

This is what the Africans think in their heart of hearts.

This general impression prevailing among the Congolese, which they do not pass on to Europeans for fear of reprisals – a fear which is often imaginary – arises out of the following considerations:

Since the European occupation began, some eighty years ago, no African in the Congo has been accepted for any post – even the lowest – of European officer grade in the administrative services, the law and the army, even if he has had a full secondary education and studied philosophy for several years. (I am leaving out of account the two Congolese from Leopoldville who recently finished their studies in Belgium and the native priests.) A European (I refer here to temporary officials, some of whom have had no secondary education) is *always* superior to an African even if the latter has studied longer and hence is better educated.

There are, in fact, some cases of this kind.

Except for the priests and the two or three Congolese who have studied in Belgium, no native, however competent, occupies the post which is his due and which he could have occupied long ago or could take over now *if the leading administrative posts were Africanised.* Even if he holds a responsible position, he does not have the same prestige as a European official. He is only a minor assistant, always dependent on a European official.

As a justification for refusing him the position which should by rights be his, the African will be told that he does not hold the European secondary education certificate or some other academic document, or that he must go to university, even though everyone cannot go to university even in Europe or America; or, if he is employed in the Government Service, he will have to wait twenty, twenty-five or thirty years before getting to the rank of chief clerk, Grade I, assistant drafting officer or assistant territorial officer, although a short three- or five-year course would be amply sufficient to give a really capable person the competence to do the work of a territorial officer or drafting officer. Many people can do these jobs long before completing five, ten, fifteen or twenty years of service.

Example: A Congolese with six years of secondary education is at present taken on in the rank of a clerk, third class. He must have a minimum of eighteen years' service (with good reports and regular promotion) in order to enter the grade of chief clerk, first class; to become an assistant territorial officer or assistant drafting officer, he must serve for a further three years, making a total of twenty-four years. Thus, it is only after twenty-four years of good and loyal service that a Congolese with a certificate of secondary education can take his place among the European officers, just when he has reached the end of his career or is about to do so.

At the moment when the Congolese is admitted to the lowest grade in the European hierarchy, a European who has had the same education (secondary) and who was initially engaged in the rank of area officer or drafting officer, will, after the same period of service of twenty-four years, be a director or head of some department.

And yet the same Congolese could very well carry out the duties of a territorial officer or drafting officer immediately on recruitment, or at least after a normal probationary period; there is no need for him to wait for this excessively long period of twenty-four to thirty years.

The fact that Ruanda-Urundi, a territory which has been under Belgian mandate since 31st August 1923, is more favourably situated than the Congo from the administrative point of view is not without influence on the Congolese.

"Whereas Ruanda-Urundi, which had the great good fortune to be placed under international trusteeship in 1923, is taking giant strides towards autonomy, we Congolese, who have been under the *same Belgian administration* for more than three-quarters of a century – much longer than Ruanda-Urundi – are far behind our neighbour. In Ruanda-Urundi, the position of the chiefs and under-chiefs has been *enhanced*, their authority is respected and there are two kings, but, in the Congo, the authority of the native chiefs is reduced to the point where they are no longer real chiefs in the etymological sense of the word but mere V.I.Ps, government servants working under the authority of territorial officers and agronomists." That is the authentic view of the Congolese on this matter.

There is a contradiction in methods, particularly between the political principles enunciated by the Government and the higher authorities in all their official statements on colonial policy, and the application of those principles – sometimes in a contrary sense – *by the executive* officers. Some lower-grade officers apply these principles in a reactionary fashion *whenever* they are not personally in favour of a particular measure planned and enacted by their superiors for the benefit of the African.

These contradictions have created, and are still creating, a most regrettable confusion in the minds of the Congolese who draw the illogical conclusion that "The Government is scheming and intriguing with its officials to hoodwink us. The Government promises us this or that, enacts its laws and regulations and makes spectacular speeches, but the Government officials go in the other direction; perhaps they have received secret instructions. Even at school in Europe, they are taught to be cunning in dealing with the Blacks. Before they come to Africa, they are told that they must always live a long way away from the Blacks. This is proved by the sharp line of demarcation between the European and African quarters. The so-called green belts which separate the European and African quarters are barricades but, in order to fool us, they plant trees and flowers there to look like nursery gardens. If what they tell us is true, it should be put into practice by the high-ups and by the lower-ranking officials.

Let me explain: If, for example, the Governor General, gives instructions to European officials, advising them to behave towards the natives with all due correctness, and if no change takes place in the behaviour of a large number of these officials, so that the Africans still do not obtain satisfaction, the latter follow this train of reasoning: "It is inconceivable that a minor official can ignore the instructions and recommendations given by the Head of the colony. As these instructions do not always give the results which we expect them to give, we doubt their sincerity. The policy is designed to trick us."

When some Congolese find difficulty in obtaining a loan from the Colonial Advancement Fund to purchase a decent dwelling, they reason as follows: "They don't want us to have nice houses to suit our taste. They refuse us loans so as to compel us indirectly to live in the houses of the African Townships Department, houses which are not to the taste of most people but for which funds are provided without any hestation. All this is so that the Blacks shall not have houses of the same taste and style as those of their 'masters' (the Whites)."

When the "King's Fund'" does not give the satisfaction which Congolese families expect, their reaction is the same: "Our dear King has seen with his own eyes that we are poor and badly housed and he has SENT money to enable us to have decent dwellings. The Whites have misappropriated this money and are using it for projects which are of benefit only to them. We are being deceived."

I note that quite a number of settlers (though there are exceptions) hesitate or even protest sometimes whenever the Government or the high-ups decide on the smallest increase in salaries or confer some benefit on the Congolese in the economic or social sphere or elsewhere.

There is an impression that anyone, be he minister, governor-general, governor, administrator, or mere official, in the public or private sector, who concerns himself actively with native interests and inter-racial relations and lives in close contact with the Africans, often ends up by being looked at askance by the others, *simply* because he takes a greater interest in the advancement of native society and has no axe to grind. Thus there are some people who pay dearly for espousing the cause of the natives and who forfeit sympathy in many quarters.

This idea can be illustrated by a few notable examples: "M. Jungers, who, in the opinion of the Congolese, was the first Governor General to advocate, in his historic speech to the Government Council in 1952, (the last Council over which he presided at

.. ¹ *King's Fund*: *Fonds du Roi* – instituted on 18th October, 1955 by King Baudouin to promote social welfare in the Congo. The number of beneficiaries from the Fund in 1955 was 777 on a budget of about £60,000; in 1958 it provided for 2,608 beneficiaries from a budget of more than £4,600,000.

the end of his term of office) the establishment of the Belgo-Congolese Community and the total assimilation of the Congolese *immatriculés*, was hotly criticised, regarded with disapproval in some quarters and described as a *madman* by certain organs of the Press" (I have irrefutable proof of this in the form of Press articles) "because he was bold enough to express progressive ideas in front of people with conservative ideas."

Then Governor General Pétillon, who won the approval and appreciation of the protagonists of African advancement, was frowned on by a considerable number of people because of his moving speech at the opening of the Government Council of 1955, dealing with human relations between Whites and Blacks, and also because of the authorisation which he gave to the Blacks to enter public premises which had previously been reserved for Europeans only.

One section of the Press threw back at M. Pétillon the idea which he had put forward in his speech that "Anyone who disagrees with the policy of the Government is respectfully asked to pack his bags," and invited the Governor General "to pack his bags".

I still recall the tension which prevailed in the Congo following the decision of the Governor General to allow the Congolese entry to public premises, Fortunately, this tension was eased when the Africans, with great reasonableness, withdrew from these places voluntarily.

I must add that a number of public premises were, and still are, glad to welcome Congolese.

"M. Buisseret continues to be the object of malicious partisan criticism, not because he is administering the Colony badly but because he attaches a great deal of importance to the social factor; because he never ceases to preach and defend the principle of equal rights and equal prestige; because he invites the Africans to come and discuss their problems in Belgium instead of confining them to the Congo and leaving all matters which concern them to be decided on the spot; because he wants to "go quickly" with the Africans instead of crawling along at a snail's pace and slowing up the emancipation of the natives by excessive delays; and because he introduced state education for the Congolese. But the establishment of state education for Europeans (the Royal Athenæums) roused no protests; protests only come when Africans are concerned, and yet this education is giving great satisfaction to Congolese parents. The reason why protests are made against this education is that French

G

is taught from the first year of the primary school. The curriculum is similar to that of the European schools, so that the Africans will soon have enough education to compete with the Europeans. There is opposition to M. Buisseret because he has won the hearts of the Congolese who regard him not as a Minister, a Belgian, a Catholic, a Liberal, a Socialist or a Communist, but a sincere FRIEND of the Blacks, just as they do in the case of all other Belgians who champion their cause. Some people are afraid that the unanimous liking which the Congolese of all shades of opinion, Protestants, Catholics and pagans, show for a Liberal Minister, and their great confidence in him, will lead all the Africans of the Congo to become Liberals; but this is completely false, since the African masses are not interested in the label – Liberal, Catholic, Socialist or Communist,—but in their *material, intellectual and moral welfare*. We will turn to anyone who can secure these benefits for us, or help us to obtain them, and we ignore questions of dogma or freemasonry, which are of little interest to us as they will bring us no material advantages. Finally, there is opposition to M. Buisseret because he wants the Blacks to advance instead of leaving them as servants of the Whites." These opinions have been expressed to me by ninety per cent of the Congolese, and I do not wish to make any comment on them.

If an official who is popular with his African colleagues is transferred to the interior or to another post, they exclaim: "Look, he is being moved because he gets on well with the Africans, and his superior officers frown on this."

"A good European who likes us and who sometimes visits us at home never stays long in the department (or the office or firm) because people who have the same outlook towards the Blacks are preferred. In order to keep his job, even the most sympathetic White will refrain from being at all intimate with the Blacks. One particular European was kept on in his post because we sent a petition to the Authorities to demand that he should be sent back amongst us." These words can be heard almost anywhere, both among office workers and manual workers, but they will never be spoken to a European, for the very good reason that there is a fear of reprisals."

I have reproduced these remarks just as I took them down in the course of my enquiry. I give them as they are, out of regard for impartiality, so as not to distort the opinions of the people I interviewed.

This general impression, which I have illustrated by a few concrete examples, is current among the majority of Congolese. That explains why they are becoming increasingly suspicious of all the promises made to them and all the official speeches, even when the latter express quite sincere intentions.

This suspicion is due partly to the fact that certain firm promises made to the natives have proved impossible to carry out owing to one difficulty or another.

Another unfortunate thing is that a large proportion of the natives cannot wait in patience; they imagine that a promise made today will be put into effect tomorrow, without always realising that it sometimes cannot be carried out without a preliminary study of the question, which may take some time.

If the promise is not followed immediately by action it is described as a fraud.

This does not mean that the natives are not right in some cases.

This unfortunate atmosphere of suspicion must be dispelled as quickly as possible by the best efforts of the White and Black élite before the gulf widens further. This sombre situation must be remedied.

Before going further, we must say that the King's Fund still does not seem to have adequate resources. Some companies continue to contribute to it. The administrators have paid due attention to the conditions for making grants. Nevertheless, it is quite certain that all Congolese families cannot make use of it.

We ought not to cast suspicion on the King's noble intentions. The money has certainly not been diverted to other purposes. On the contrary, the authorities are constantly appealing to the generosity of the Belgians to contribute to the Fund and enable it to extend its range of activity.

The Government's intentions, as expressed in statements and in legislation, are sincere. The few mistakes which have been found here and there can be attributed solely to the officials concerned.

These mistakes will be eliminated and we must have confidence in each other.

Much has been said recently about the "crisis of confidence". I must say frankly that this crisis is the inevitable consequence of broken promises, of past faults, of the *unjustified* perpetuation of certain discriminatory measures (I say unjustified because there is such a thing as justified perpetuation) particularly in regard to the élite, and of the clumsiness of certain settlers. All these together finally gave rise to despair and a weakening of confidence. These discriminatory measures, these broken promises, these faults, are the sole source of the crisis and of all its potential consequences.

Local officials have not always paid attention to the justified protests made by the Congolese against these unjust measures. Some Africans who were defending the common cause by acting as intermediaries between the population and the authorities have often been misunderstood and accused of being "revolutionaries and nationalists", whereas they were in fact valuable collaborators who should have been received with open arms, loyal leaders who were fully informed of the latent discontent building up in the minds of their brother Africans and anxious to warn the authorities in order to avoid trouble with the natives.

Instead of these loyal spokesmen who enjoyed the confidence of the inhabitants, collaborators or representatives of the Congolese were chosen among particularly "reliable" people, "mutes" and, I venture to say, hypocrites. (Not all, but the great majority of these representatives, are not respected by the population. A little public opinion poll will prove this to anyone who likes to carry out the experiment). These people, although they were themselves aware of the wave of discontent forming in native quarters, failed to bring these facts to the attention of the responsible authorities. Or else they concealed the truth and abused the trust which was placed in them, misleading the authorities by hypocritically singing their praises instead of informing them. They helped neither the Whites nor the natives, but only themselves.

Thus the rulers and the ruled lived and often still live in an atmosphere of misunderstanding, which is partly created by untrustworthy intermediaries. Certain rash judgments would not have been made, both on the European and the Congolese side, if the two partners – coloniser and colonised, governor and governed, or White and Black – had informed each other, in an atmosphere of mutual confidence, of the problems which confronted them and which, if solved, would have spared them continual strife.

In addition to these internal difficulties, which still continue, there are certain outside influences which are continually stimulated by modern means of communication.

The *evolués* read, discuss and are fully aware of everything which goes on in the world. They take an increasing interest in political life. They are not unaware of the movements which are growing up in the other African colonies, where their neighbours are demanding autonomy and independence. They envy the position of some colonies and want to secure a similar position in their turn. They are eager to enjoy the benefits of one or other of the systems prevailing in certain African territories.

The candidates for the liberation of the oppressed races (this is the term which they use) give concealed, discreet support to these aspirations without weighing up the possible consequences; these aspirations are all quite legitimate but whereas some are reasonable, others are somewhat capricious (in the case of certain hastily or prematurely expressed wishes). This support, which is sometimes given by people who are hostile towards the Belgians or simply by communist propagandists, contributes to the mental unrest of the natives.

I am not referring here to the beneficial work of level-headed writers who sometimes make comments in good faith on particular aspects of the colonial system, and who are only concerned with the higher interests of civilisation and with safeguarding national sovereignty.

These various influences which I have been condemning have such an imperceptible yet irresistible force that they cannot be stopped by any coercive military measures.

How can we dissipate this unhappy atmosphere and produce ultimate harmony?

There are some who believe that only firm measures can restore a better atmosphere. Do they mean by this police measures? Others suggest that the frontiers of the Congo should be patrolled to prevent the penetration of Eastern influences among the Congolese people. It is also suggested that the activity of the Security Service should be redoubled so as to keep watch on all suspect characters who may have nationalist tendencies.

All this seems to me pointless. The solution is not to be found here. Possibly it might yield some short-term results, but even if every Congolese was kept under surveillance by a police officer, even if the Congo was surrounded by iron bars, emotions and thoughts could not be kept down.

The more the natives are given the impression that their wishes are frustrated, their actions kept under surveillance, the stronger will be their conviction that there is a desire to restrict their development. This will only rouse them and cause an increasing loss of confidence.

I myself feel that the solution must be found elsewhere. The problems are within us and it is up to us to solve them in an atmosphere of mutual understanding.

Solutions achieved as a result of freely-negotiated agreements will be more deeply rooted in the hearts of the people. They will do more to strengthen their loyalty and attachment to the Belgians than any military solutions.

Some people, who certainly do not know the Congolese mind, although they claim to do so, declare that the crisis of confidence, which is so much talked about throughout the Press, is due to the interference of Belgian politicians in colonial matters and to their contacts with the natives.

I myself, with full knowledge of the facts, feel that these allegations are incorrect. Either the truth is being concealed and the blame being thrown on the innocent people of Europe, or else the doctors of colonial sciences and the experts in African psychology have not properly diagnosed the heartbeats of their patients.

On the contrary, all the Congolese believe firmly that the increasing vigilance of these parliamentarians in the Home Country, and of the head of the colony, has restored confidence, or is in process of doing so, at the critical moment when the atmosphere of the Congo has been darkened by storm clouds. It is thanks to the healthy rivalry of these Belgian politicians, who are accused of all the sins of the Israelites, as though they had not a single virtue and were scheming the destruction of the Congo, that substantial improvements are in process of being carried out in the life of the Congo, in the interest not merely of the natives but also of the metropolitan Belgians.

It is because of their confidence in Belgium that whenever the Minister for Colonial Affairs or any other V.I.P. from the Home Country comes to the Congo, the Congolese provide a smiling welcome, express their sympathy for their protectors' fellow countrymen and friends, and enter into cordial discussions.

The Africans do not trust some of the settlers because of their lack of tact and sympathy. But there are some settlers who are closer to the Congolese, treat them with humanity and justice and enjoy and will continue to enjoy their confidence.

In the interest of truth it must be admitted that some irresponsible people (some Whites) have carried on propaganda to incite the native population – particularly the *evolués* – against the Government in power.

This is proved up to the hilt by some shamefully insolent communications which were addressed to the authorities by certain *evolués*. But it was Europeans who were using these Africans as a screen, to cause difficulties for the Government.

No African in the Congo has ever had the slightest idea of rebelling against authority – particularly against the high authorities.

Is there a single Congolese *evolué* who, off his own bat, would conceive the idea of addressing manifestos to a Minister for Colonial Affairs? Is there any group of *evolués* who, *on their own initiative and without being egged on by Europeans*, would produce the telegrams, petitions and pamphlets, which have flooded the Ministry through the Press during the last years?

It is not so long ago that every Congolese was convinced that the slightest resistance or insolence towards the authorities might involve him in punishment. Even when he wanted to draw attention to some irregularity in the person of an ordinary Government official, or any other irregularity, he often dared not do it. Even if he wanted to draw attention to the position through the Press, he very often contented himself with anonymous letters; the fact is known to all journalists, as they have received articles from Congolese reporting exact facts but unsigned. This anonymity was, and is, frequently the result of fear even among the higher *evoluès*.

Whenever one or more Congolese takes issue publicly with the authorities, you can be sure that, in ninety per cent of all cases, they are being encouraged and supported by a European or Europeans.

Article 136 of the Penal Code (Volume 2) states: "Anyone who, by acts, words, gestures or threats, attacks a magistrate, civil servant or official of the administration or of the police force *in the exercise of, or on the occasion of the exercise of, his functions,* shall be punished with a maximum of six months' penal servitude and a fine of from 25 to 200 francs or one of these punishments only."

If those Congolese who, at the instigation of certain persons, have rendered themselves, or are still rendering themselves, guilty by publishing insults directed at the Minister and the authorities, were not "protected", they would certainly have been punished. This is not a question of the freedom of the press but of the respect due to the authorities.

When the Minister, *in the exercise of his functions,* and by virtue of the powers which are conferred upon him, appointed an African as a departmental assistant, a certain section of the native Press described him – or rather insulted him – with the epithet RUDE, the reason given by that section of the Press was that the Minister had not consulted anyone, that he had shown a want of common courtesy (does this common courtesy permit public insults at the expense of a representative of the authorities . . . ?): because he had been *rude* towards *all* those who wielded any authority . . . ?

One may naturally make some comments to a civil servant when he makes a mistake. But these comments must be polite. Insults are not permissible. This is sheer flouting of authority.

Instead of receiving congratulations for his action, the Minister is criticised at every turn. The inhabitants of the country, Belgians and Africans, instead of offering their sincere congratulations to their fellow countryman on his promotion, ridicule him because (according to the same paper) he is a Liberal.

I am not defending anyone, and I am not against anyone, but the principle must be defended, the principle of loyal respect towards our representatives.

Where Europeans see party colours, we Congolese see in all the Belgians, Catholics, Liberals or Socialists, our mentors and our brothers.

What would happen if, every time a Minister or a Governor-General was appointed, he was opposed by a particular clique, depending on whether he was a Liberal, Catholic or Socialist? For instance, if we had a Socialist Minister, all non-Socialists would oppose him and, when we had a Catholic Minister, all non-Catholics would be up in arms against him in the same way.

Every Minister or Governor General, irrespective of his party allegiances, is entitled to the esteem and respect of all the inhabitants of this country.

Finally, it is we who have shaken confidence in the authorities by our bad behaviour. The instructions may have come from Europe but we Africans do not know this.

There are certain Whites in the Congo who are responsible. I state this categorically. I personally have made myself unpopular by refusing to take part in these petty intrigues which I was asked to take part in and to lead.

Of course it is urgently necessary to re-establish confidence once and for all, and I desire this wholeheartedly for, without this confidence, the Congo would be exposed to the hazards of an uncertain future.

Is that the future which we want to lay up for our dear children?

Are we not delighted today to see Belgian and Congolese children, free of any colour prejudice, frisking about together in the class-room and on the playing field? Have we any right to ruin the future of these little innocents, a future which they are already building for themselves in common accord? Why should we struggle for years and then suffer such defeat? What good will it do us to persist in these sinister and dangerous paths, the outcome of which may ultimately be fatal?

We must build up this confidence by every possible means, other-wise we shall live to see the birth of extremist national tendencies which would bring misfortunes in their train, and from which neither Whites nor Blacks would profit.

Does Nationalism exist in the Congo?

Undoubtedly everyone, White or Black, has inherent nationalist tendencies, the strength of which vary from one individual to another. These natural tendencies, which bind the individual to the soil of his country, which inspire him to deeds of heroism for its defence, are basically only patriotism and national pride. Is there any people in the world which is without nationalist sentiments? Without nationalist tendencies, without patriotism, it would be impossible to conceive the bravery of those great heroes who, in all countries from ancient time up to the present-day, have sacrificed and continue to sacrifice their property and their lives for the defence of the interests of their own countries.

Let us not quibble over words. Let us look at the real facts as they are and examine these problems in their true light.

A man without any nationalist tendencies is a man without a soul, because the soul in its essence contains all the feelings which the Creator has placed there, and I believe that, among those sentiments, patriotism occupies a leading place in the heart of every human being.

What we have to avoid in our country is false nationalism: the cramped nationalism which conceals forms of racialism and hatred for those of another race. This kind of nationalism, whether among the Congolese or the Europeans, must be combated because it gives rise to racial hatred and dissensions which we must abolish at all costs.

This struggle against racialist nationalism can only be effective if we are able to abolish its causes. No disease can be conquered unless the microbes which transmit it have first of all been destroyed.

The nationalism displayed by the Africans is often, if not always, the result of provocations and injustices from which they have suffered. There is an irresistable law of nature which leads men to react against aggression, unhealthy influences and social injustice.

When we look at the different methods of government adopted by the various colonial powers, we see that reactionary nationalism is always the price paid for a racialist policy practised by the colonising government at the expense of those who are colonised; sooner or later they will end by revolting.

When one compares the different colonies in the world, it will be seen that the colonisers are often responsible for this situation. The racialism of the colonised people is always preceded by the racialism of the colonising country. It is always the stronger man who blazes the trail and the weaker only follows.

The policy of racial segregation practised by England in South Africa and by the Americans towards the coloured people in the south of the United States, a racialist policy which gives rise to ceaseless social conflicts between the colonisers and the colonised, is the monument to European racialism in reverse or, in other words, to blind nationalism.

Is it reasonable to blame the colonised people or the South Africans if they react against a continual infringement of their human dignity and of the social order by adopting legitimate means of defence just as any human being would do? Those who, by their own errors and inhuman acts, have given rise to racial hatred lay the fault at the door of the innocent colonised people when things get out of hand, probably with the aim of covering up their own errors.

I sincerely hope that this sort of nationalism will not appear in the Congo. On the contrary, I seek a Belgo-Congolese nationalism which will unite Belgians and Africans in the defence of their common patrimony.

Until this veil falls from our eyes and our minds, we shall always be subject to social crisis. This veil, which often prevents human beings from understanding and co-ordinating their actions under the control of reason and friendship, is man's petty pride, this pride which, if we are to believe the Bible, drove the first man out of the garden of Eden.

We can observe the exteriorisation of strange selfish tendencies which prove that, from the psychological point of view, men are generally governed by their feelings and passions rather than by reason.

Is man the enemy of his fellow man?

If man is by nature a social animal, how can we explain these social qualities when the men who form human society cannot agree among themselves? Does this mark the decadence of humanity?

Discord, unjustifiable racial hatred, wilful slights inflicted in order to belittle other people, the desire for domination, the exploitation of the ignorant and weak by those who are cleverer and stronger, the subjugation of one people by another, bloody wars which spread terror and pitilessly crush human lives by causing irreparable harm, both mental and physical, in innumerable families: are those who behave or tend to behave in this way giving proof of civilisation or savagery? Men certainly are not saints. We are not living in an earthly paradise. Nevertheless, it is regrettable to note that materialism is coming to dominate life more and more at the expense of those values of the mind which ought to be at the very base of every healthy society worthy of the name.

For many people – and materialists are most prone to this temptation – the dignity of man and of human life no longer has any meaning. Their only creed is the pursuit of Mammon, of material possessions, of personal vanity, at the expense of the rights of others.

Let us hope that the Congo will escape this crisis, which threatens certain countries of the world; it has already proved its capacity to do this since its union with Belgium.

The reason why the Congolese have remained backward by comparison with other nations is simply that, for many centuries, very unfavourable geographical conditions have made all contacts between the Congo and the West difficult if not impossible.

If every country in Europe had been thrown back upon itself and had had to rely on itself without any outside aid, those countries would not have seen the progress which they have done. We have the clearest proof of this: all the scientific inventions and discoveries of the past and present are the result of the work of a few research workers and scientists. Their inventions and discoveries are of benefit not only to the inhabitants of their own country but also to all the other countries of the world.

Thanks to the removal of the obstacles which hindered communications with Europe, Africa is now beginning to take part in the same world-wide competition; it will not escape from this law of inter-dependence and it will follow the path which all the other nations have followed. We Congolese must never for a moment think of breaking our links with Europe and particularly with Belgium which will always be the source of energy for the Congo.

However great our skills and the natural riches of our lands, we shall always have need of others, of those who have preceded us in the path of progress, just as the young are always in need of the wisdom of their elders.

Our progress and our success are dependent on our solidarity with Belgium, and on the continuation of financial, economic and technical assistance even after the Congo is granted autonomy. Such assistance will always be indispensable for the Congo.

Our precursors will still be our technical and intellectual advisers for many a long year.

The success of the Africans – and of the work undertaken by Belgium in Africa – will depend mainly on the way in which relations develop between the Africans and the Belgians.

Those who lay claim, or would like to lay claim, to political hegemony and who oppose the governmental principle of the *priority of native interests*, diminish the stature of Belgian achievements and are trouble-makers. It is these very troublemakers who, by means of all kinds of cunning manoeuvres, obstruct government policy and the steps taken by its representatives to improve African living conditions and to promote their welfare; it is they who, whenever the authorities grant African workers a trifling increase in wages, concoct selfish and fallacious reasons for keeping the Africans permanently at the bottom of the social scale.

By the priority of native interests the Congolese do not envisage a system which will work solely to their own advantage, but one which will offer legal protection and a fair distribution of the country's income between Congolese and Belgians. The priority of native interests must henceforth be interpreted as a priority of Belgo-Congolese interests.

The Congo is waking up. Her sons are emerging from their age-long sleep and trying to clear a way out into the light of day, still under the enlightened guidance of their elders.

In reply to these legitimate African aspirations some paternalists cry: "Don't force the pace." That is true in certain well-defined cases. But the Africans no longer seem to be in agreement with this principle when their *reasonable* claim for the abolition of certain obsolete and outmoded measures is refused with the excuse: "You must not force the pace."

This phrase contains much wisdom, but it must not be applied as a generalisation in all cases or whenever the colonial people put forward wishes which do not meet with the approval of the colonising power.

To rule a people in accordance with the personal views of those in power, and not in accordance with the views of the governed, is dictatorship, the exact opposite of a democratic system of government. The only colonial governments which can hope to succeed in their task are those which take the legitimate aspirations of the colonial people into account in all their activities.

Not all the aspirations of the colonised people are reasonable, of course. They have to be educated, and they must not be spoiled by a defeatist attitude. To govern a people is to guide and educate them. But when the people express aspirations which are worthy of consideration, then the government should take note of them and give the people satisfaction.

I favour a policy of prudence. The task is not as easy as it seems. There are certain spheres in which, despite the wishes of the colonial people, patience is required and there has to be a normal waiting period before a particular reform is initiated.

Precipitate action must be avoided. Conservatism must also be avoided, as far as this is compatible with the overriding interest of the advance of civilisation.

The majority of the African élite complain that they are not always encouraged to use their initiative; they are often the victims of unfortunate misunderstandings, due to lack of contact, of opportunities to exchange views in free discussion, and of possibilities of intellectual collaboration.

The tremendous determination now being shown both by Europeans and Congolese will soon remedy this situation and greatly improve social relations between the two races.

Alcoholism – this social scourge which hampers the much-needed development of the Congo – seems, in the last analysis, to be caused by the poverty of the native population.

In general the Africans earn inadequate wages and live in conditions of relative poverty. In order to forget their worries they try to "console" themselves with drinking and dancing, and the ones who earn the least drink the most. Those who are somewhat better paid live in decent conditions; they have pleasant homes which make them reluctant to go out, a modest standard of comfort which gives them a feeling of dignity, and on the whole they behave well.

A man who has to live from hand to mouth must always be struggling with his baser instincts. A minimum of comfort has a beneficial effect on the character of the individual.

The policy of low wages is a serious handicap to the advancement of the native workers.

An under-nourished man (because he lacks the resources to feed himself and his family properly), inadequately housed, falling asleep at the work-bench or in the office because he has not had a square meal the day before, always a prey to innumerable cares, drifting every evening to the "Nduku" [1] to beg for a bite to eat – such a man will have difficulty in increasing his efficiency and will rarely do well at his job.

"Wage rates", said Novikov, "depend on economic, not psychological factors, and the colour of the skin and the contours of the face are irrelevant in this connection. It is not enough to belong to the same race to earn the same wages."

What is the use of industrialising the Congo if it is to be mainly for the benefit of the Europeans, whilst the labouring classes stagnate in relative poverty?

The Congolese workers want to be paid adequately, to learn how to manage their own affairs, and to try to find their own way, instead of continuing to receive inadequate wages and, as compensation, benefiting from collective paternalistic favours specially designed for the "low wage-earners" (free hospital treatment, medical attention and all the other associated advantages).

In the interest of the community these benefits should be reserved for those who are out of work or have inadequate means, and who thus deserve to receive public charity.

Social relations are only possible between people who are in more or less the same circumstances and have similar interests. These are the prerequisites of social intercourse, whether between White and White or White and Black.

So long as these glaring differences persist between White and Black, in the social as well as the economic and intellectual sphere,

[1] *Nduku*: possibly a regional variant of 'ndeke'. 'Going to friends to beg a meal' [?].

so long will the Belgo-Congolese Community remain only a dream, because friendship between two people with diametrically opposed interests and standards of living is impossible. Except, that is, for the simple relationship between a superior and an inferior who, while displaying a certain degree of cordiality, hold each other at a distance.

Feelings of friendship between men can only arise out of an identity of outlook, feeling and situation; from common interests instead of blows, decrees and official injunctions.

Whatever may be said to the contrary, there is no such thing as platonic love.

Once these differences, the product of certain official discriminatory practices, are abolished, the Whites and Blacks, or Europeans and Africans, will merge, and the problem of race relations will solve itself.

When the employer, or the European, meets Africans, he sees only smiling faces, little knowing that these faces sometimes hide sorrow and anxiety. They will not readily confide these anxieties to a European, for fear of acquiring the reputation of being revolutionaries or agitators and falling out of favour. In order to keep his job and his good reputation every employee or worker will hide his discontent, his anxiety, and his worries, to avoid any move which might irritate his employer and lead to his dismissal. He will complain only out of earshot of his employer.

All this gives rise to mounting grievance and suspicion. If only it was possible to say straight out what is wrong, we should be spared much misunderstanding and many wrong judgments which are often due to misunderstanding.

Many employees fail to understand their employers, who may be very kind and considerate, and credit them with opinions which they do not hold.

There are few thoroughly bad men among the colonists. There are far more who lack understanding; this is an undoubted fact. And this lack of understanding is very prevalent amongst us Congolese. Let us not always be trying to throw the blame on others. There are faults on both sides.

The colonists are undoubtedly making tremendous efforts to further the moral well-being of the colonial people, which must inevitably come as a result of education and Christianity. But do they appreciate the mental torture which the Africans suffer as a result of certain injustices to which they are often exposed in their relations with the Whites? Do they also realise the gulf which sometimes exists between certain European principles of education and the nature of the Bantu people?

It is useless to continue with methods which ultimately can only produce illusory results. The civilisation which the Congolese require is still the same, but the methods of imparting it should be adapted to the realities of life. We ask for effective methods, which take account of the mental make-up of the African, and rather more democratic ideas.

When the colonists have learnt how to cure this mental sickness from which the Africans suffer all the time, it will be possible to describe the process of civilisation as philanthropic, because it will be concerned not only with the material and mental well-being of the colonial people, but also their moral well-being. We must eradicate not merely the epidemics and diseases from which the Africans have suffered but also their mental diseases – the distress of mind which is partly the result of colonisation.

Before the arrival of the White man in Africa, the African suffered from physical diseases. The White man has cured the African of his physical sufferings by the use of medicine. Now that he is cured in his body, the African is begining to suffer increasingly from another sickness: this is *mental illness*. In certain respects this is a more acute form of suffering than a physical illness.

Only an African, living among the Africans, can fully appreciate this. Day in and day out, at their meetings, in their conversations and confidences, the Africans discuss their future, complain about the behaviour of their departmental head or some other European, or about the unfair treatment they have suffered in some sphere or another of social life. As soon as the boss leaves the office or work-shop, the employees gather together to discuss his attitude and behaviour, any injustice of which he may have been guilty, the bias he shows in a dispute between a European employee and an African worker. But as soon as they see the boss coming, they all rush back to their work as if nothing had happened. Any disciplinary action, whether deserved or not, is often regarded as "racial discrimination, spite, cruelty". There is an unfortunate confusion in the minds of many poorly educated people.

When the employer or the European meets Africans, he sees only smiling faces, little knowing that these faces hide sorrow and anxiety; anxiety which they will not readily confide to a European.

When we have learned to cure this disease of the mind, from which the African suffers all the time, the process of colonisation will acquire a philanthropic as well as an economic aspect, because it will be concerned with giving the colonial people moral as well as material and intellectual well-being.

The colonists are undoubtedly making considerable efforts to further the moral well-being of the colonial people, which must inevitably come as a result of education and Christianity. But do they appreciate the gulf which sometimes exists between European principles of education and the nature of the Bantu people?

It is useless to continue with certain methods which ultimately can only produce illusory results.

I am not pleading here for a negro form of civilisation, which would be absurd, but I do ask for effective methods which take account of the mental make-up of the Africans; these are obviously the only methods which will be successful in the moral education of the native population.

I appeal to the good will of all to ensure that the old colonial outlook is scrapped. This attitude is out of date, including its vocabulary of "conqueror, right of occupation, subject peoples, civilised masters, savage people," etc. A new outlook is required which is more in keeping with the dignity of the Africans, and with universal ethical principles.

These terms do not appear in the official vocabulary but in a certain private language which is not used among cultured people, but by certain people who make a show of their alleged racial superiority by the use of clichés.

I stress these trifling facts, to which no intelligent African attaches any importance, because they offend the majority of the native population. It is not a question of susceptibility, as will be immediately alleged; has not every man, whatever his status, the right to protect his human dignity and to ask his fellows to pay him the respect which is his due?

Is it not for the protection of human dignity that the penal code in all countries lays down punishments to be meted out to any person who wounds the honour and dignity of another?

Whenever the Congolese complain of lack of consideration towards them, the Whites reply: "The Blacks are sensitive."

It is not a question of sensitivity, but of *mutual respect.*

The new Euro-African society which we are building today must be administered and directed *jointly* by the Belgians and the Congolese. Neither of the two sections of the Belgo-Congolese Community must dominate or persecute the other. In every department and office, African and European officials can be found working side by side in the administration of their country.

Administrative paternalism and all official measures which unintentionally or incidentally favour the superiority of the White over the Black, in the social, economic or political sphere, should in so far as it is compatible with the advancement of the natives, be replaced by rather more liberal measures, more democratic and more in keeping with the basic principles of the Belgo-Congolese community which is in process of being built up.

This humanitarian task, in which we have to work together, should be removed as far as possible from the field of politics. A piece of work which is essentially humanitarian is best carried out in a spirit of brotherhood, civic friendship, charity and tolerance, and not in an atmosphere of political intrigue.

The only workable policy is one which guides social and civic activities and relations between citizens; not an obscure, abstract, ideological policy which tends to cloud the issue.

The Congolese need something better than ideological pipedreams. The work of civilisation is not a philosophical process; it builds on precise and concrete facts, in the light of reality.

Is European religion suitable for Africans?

The European religion is a good one.

Everyone is free to believe or not to believe, to be a Christian or not to be a Christian, to be a catholic, protestant or atheist. Ethical principles recommend absolute tolerance in religious matters.

The important thing is to base the whole of our life on high ethical standards, which give a society its strength. A man who is poor, but who has high standards, is superior to a rich man who lacks them.

The Africans have their own moral code, of course, but I have to admit that we can obtain great benefit from *all that is best* in European ethics. It is this ethic which has made Western civilisation great. Any African who wishes to profit from Western civilisation, must also profit from its ethic; an ethic which, it must be admitted, is far finer than our Bantu ethic.

Our moral code is good, too, but that must not prevent us from gathering enrichment from another source.

We must obtain this moral wealth from our teachers in the schools which are available to the people.

Both the State and independent schools must be increased in number, not only in the towns, but also in the most remote country districts. There is still much more to be done in these neglected areas than in the industrial centres.

The improvement of education in the country districts will go some way towards stopping the exodus of young people to the towns, where they often go to find good education. Many of them have told me that they came to the big centres with the sole aim of obtaining a good education, "of learning French because this language is not taught in the rural schools." I am speaking here of schoolchildren and not of agricultural workers who come to look for work.

What legal form will the Belgo-Congolese Community assume? That is a matter of prime importance.

In the first place, taking into account the present and future state of affairs, I do not think that it will be possible to harmonise the Belgian Constitution and the Colonial Charter. This is not due to any bad faith on the part of either the Belgians or the Congolese, but to a whole series of profound differences in the social pattern and customs of the two races.

If all the Congolese were won over to Western civilisation, in the same way as the few members of the African élite, it would be an easy matter. This is not the case, however, and will not be for many years to come. There are other Congolese who, whilst making the most of the fruits of Western civilisation, prefer to keep their African civilisation and customs.

Two tendencies can be discerned in Congolese society: that of the progressives evolving towards Western civilisation, and that of the traditionalists, turning towards African civilisation whilst coming under the influence of European civilisation. Both these tendencies are legitimate. Everyone has the right to opt for the civilisation of his choice.

In my view, as long as there are TWO Constitutions (the Belgian Constitution and the Colonial Charter) and different laws, there will also be TWO separate States, each with a distinct personality, but firmly *united* by bonds of friendship and brotherhood, and coming under the rule of ONE KING, the King of the Belgians and of the Congolese.

In the light of the new policy of Belgo-Congolese association, the Colonial Charter, which dates from 1908, should be replaced by a new Constitution, more in harmony with the principles of this new democracy.

This change is justified and urgently necessary.

If the Belgo-Congolese association is to be built effectively and on firm foundations, its principles must be accepted by both the contracting parties: Belgians and Congolese.

In an article on Belgian colonial policy which appeared in the magazine *The Reporter* (replying to one by Mr. Chester Bowles, published in the same periodical dated 12th July), Mr. Claeys-Bouuaert, former Governor of Ruanda-Urundi and Belgian representative at the Trusteeship Council wrote, amongst other things: "The Government feels unable to define at this stage the future political structure of the African territories under its administration, as this would involve an arbitrary assessment of the wishes of their inhabitants. But is is totally untrue to assert that my Government's only aim is to perpetuate the *status quo* or that it rules out the possibility of independence.

"The important thing is not to speculate on remote issues or future political formulas, nor to fix a time for dealing with them, but to work for the gradual achievement of the various aspects of political, economic and social emancipation . . . If the method of laying down stages in advance is adopted, this should only be in the form of plans of campaign worked out by the authorities, in collaboration with the representatives of the population, and submitted as working programmes.

"If colonialism is taken to mean the thirst for political domination, the desire to perpetuate privileges or to exploit the weakness of other peoples, Belgium is as anti-colonialist as any other nation. She is aware that the pursuit of the general good is the only justification for authority, and that the consent of the governed is the indispensable condition without which any government will cease to be legitimate and effective. These principles are the guiding rule of her policy in Africa."

It is most desirable that the Congolese élite should be associated in the drafting of the Statute which is to govern the Congo in the future. This would spare us controversy later on.

In view of the complexity of the various problems which I have discussed in this survey, the wisest solution would be to set up a mixed Reform Commission, consisting of leaders of colonial policy and of some exceptionally competent members of the African élite.

These representatives of the people should not be selected from amongst the big native Chiefs (I mention this because they are usually the only people chosen as representatives of the people) the majority of whom lack the trained minds required to discuss with competence and objectivity, and to give sound advice on these complex problems which are beyond their powers; the representatives of the people should be chosen from amongst the intellectual élite who have studied these problems closely. These representatives would work in close touch with the native authorities and the different sections of the population and obtain their views on various subjects.

The task of this Commission would be to reform the old laws which at present give rise to innumerable disputes. After consulting public opinion, it would repeal existing laws where necessary and add new laws. Or rather, it would submit its conclusions to the legislative power, which alone has the right to amend the laws.

Fundamental reforms are essential in view of the present state of development of the African population. These changes in the law will, in fact, represent the first transitional stage in preparing the Congo for autonomy.

All legislation must be brought up to date in *good time* as each stage is reached, so that in future years there will no longer be a wide gulf between the stage of development of the population and the legislation to which they are subject.

A final possibility, which might meet with general approval – and here I am basing my judgment on various opinions expressed during my survey – would be the restoration of the former CONGO FREE STATE, which existed before the Congo was annexed by Belgium in 1908.

This would give the Congo internal autonomy. The autonomous republic or Congo Free State would form a federation with Belgium. It would be placed under the command of a Belgian High Commissioner, and would be administered jointly by Congolese and Belgians in accordance with mutually agreed conditions.

When the Congo has reached a more advanced stage of civilisation, and the requisite political and administrative maturity, at a time which only the future can decide, it should be raised to the status of an autonomous country, because the Congolese, as free men, have the same fundamental rights as the citizens of all nations of the world.

This autonomy would be the final aim of Belgium's colonial mission.

Even after this autonomy has been granted, the Belgians will stay with us, since the Congo has become their country by adoption.

I would remind those Europeans and Africans who are called upon to watch over the destinies of this country, of one matter of the utmost importance:

- To attempt to build Africa or the Congo in the image of Europe is to deny the youthful Africa, the youthful Congo, its originality and to take away its sensitive character, to build on foundations of sand a pseudo-European democratic society in defiance of African ideas.

Euro-Africa, or the Belgo-Congolese Community, must be a fusion of tastes, feelings and ideas, in a word the *interpenetration* of Western and African civilisations.

Any attempt to build up the Congo independently of the contribution of the West would lead to chaos; it would be a retrograde step which would hold up the development which we all desire and towards which we are moving.

Let us work together, White and Black, to construct Africa in harmony and mutual affection; these are the indispensable conditions for any firm union.

Let us construct in the Congo a new society to which our European compatriots, exhausted by the worries and vicissitudes of the home country, will come to breathe good air under tropical foliage, and where we shall give them the warm welcome of this hospitable country.

An aggressive partisan spirit and the exaltation of racial feeling do not and will not make any constructive contribution to the goal at which we are aiming, which is that of our common good.

Let us not waste our time in trifles, whilst forgetting the essentials. Important matters and problems demand the collaboration of all men of goodwill, from the most humble to the greatest. Let us all meet this call to our consciences, like faithful believers setting out on a pilgrimage.

The hour of brotherly collaboration has come.

In this first investigation I have confined myself to certain aspirations which have been expressed by Congolese opinion for some years. The preceding pages represent the opinions of a large number of Congolese.

In my next survey I shall deal with the *Future of the Black Race*.

I hope that this brief survey may have helped in the search for a solution to the numerous problems which burden the African heart. I hope also that it will enable our mentors to understand and know what their pupils think about certain matters which have not been brought to their notice.

After a patient investigation I have analysed the graph of Congolese discontent, ascertaining what brings them so often into conflict with the Whites. I have had long discussions with them, recorded their anxieties, and done my best to clarify those anxieties. This work has been done without haste, but with a sincere desire to show understanding and impartiality.

I have preferred to speak frankly and straightforwardly, without twisting the truth by means of ambiguous circumlocution. My aim has also been to enlighten our rulers and compatriots.

I have told Europeans, as well as Congolese, what I personally think about the future of the Congo.

I apologise to my interlocutors – because this is simply a discussion – for having been brusque and rather naïve in the expression of certain ideas, thereby giving away my thoughts. These thoughts are clear: I wish to see a better and more prosperous Congo in a union of hearts and minds with Belgium.

I cannot close without repeating the praises which I have expressed throughout this work and elsewhere, regarding the meritorious efforts which Belgium has made and continues to make for the advancement of the Congolese.

It is thanks to Belgium that we are what we are; it is thanks to her that our country, risen from nothing only yesterday, is destined to rise in a few decades to the ranks of the civilised nations.

I have taken the liberty of passing some comments on particular situations or of expressing certain hopes: I did not intend to denigrate what has been done, or to under-estimate the splendid and admirable work which has been accomplished in this country and which bears the stamp of true humanism; those remarks were made out of affection, because I do not wish any error or errors, whether on the part of the Belgians or of the Congolese, to involve my country in social conflict which no one desires, or to bring about an unhappy

separation from Belgium as a result of mistakes made by irresponsible elements.

Only by a joint effort of understanding and brotherly collaboration shall we succeed in building our empire.

The Belgian motto "Union is strength" must penetrate into the
hearts of each one of us. In future this noble motto will read "The
Belgo-Congolese Union", that Union which will set the seal on
eternal friendship between Belgians and Congolese, a Union no
longer of White and Black but simply of PEOPLE, which will prove
to other nations that *friendship* is not just a word. There will be no
limit to this friendship which will last over the centuries as long as
the two friends of today live. Hand-in-hand, these two friends will
bring happiness to this country.

The farsighted policy pursued by the Belgian Government,
especially in recent years; the very special interest shown by the
Colonial Minister in the social factor and the emancipation of the
Africans; the concern of the Governor General and of the colonial
authorities for improvements in the living conditions of the native
people; the increasingly marked attention given by Belgian Members of Parliament to Congolese affairs, as well as the very cordial
relations existing between them and their Congolese friends both in
Belgium and during visits to Africa made in order to acquaint themselves at first-hand with the aspirations of the people under their
administration; the gradual improvement in human relations between White and Black; the substantial improvements which are
evident with each passing year; the concern shown by His Majesty
the King for his African subjects; all these factors will have an
increasingly beneficial effect on the future life of the Congo and are
undeniable proof of the sincere and unselfish determination of the
Belgian nation to achieve the advancement of the Congolese community.

I hope that my modest voice will be heard by all those who
sincerely love this country and wish to serve it loyally by guiding it
steadily forward to freedom.

I firmly believe in the determination of the Belgians and the
Congolese to build in concord a truly democratic and brotherly
society in which friendship, love, peace, social justice, liberty and
equality will reign for ever, a society free of racial hatred in which
Belgian and Congolese will unite with undivided hearts in the
service of Euro-African Belgium and for the greater good of future
generations.

To the question "Congo, land of the future, is it threatened?"[1] which is the title of this survey, my answer, after mature reflection, is that THE FUTURE OF THE CONGO IS ASSURED; it is full of promise and I look forward to it with optimism.

[1] The title of this book when orginally published in Belgium.

Author's Notes

This addendum takes up in a different form the ideas expressed round about pages 163 *et seq*.

Here are a few random examples to illustrate these ideas:

1. M. Jungers, the first Governor General, who, in the opinion of all the Congolese, foresaw in his speech to the Council of Government of 1952 (the last Council over which he presided at the end of his period of office) the creation of the Belgo-Congolese Community and the total assimilation of the Congolese *immatriculès*, encountered strong disapproval at the time from many European colonists (I have irrefutable proof of this in the form of newspaper cuttings), for having boldly expressed very progressive ideas (in the presence of people with very conservative ideas) and courageously defended the cause of the Africans. It is sufficient to read his historic speech of 1952 to be convinced of this. In an article entitled "The Governor General exaggerates" – which appeared in a certain colonial paper in 1952 – M. Jungers was described as a *madman*, when in fact he was being very sensible. Did not M. Jungers, a man of great wisdom, prophesy "The hand held out too late may be refused"? Are these prophetic words those of a madman?

All Congolese who still remember what a great administrator we had in M. Jungers, declare that if he had been at the head of the Colony from 1952 to 1956 the Congo would not be in its present position. This does not mean that his successor has not worked well; quite the reverse. But we cannot conceal the opinion held by the Congolese about M. Jungers, which is confirmed by the memorandum submitted by the Association of Native Public Servants (A.P.I.C.), Léopoldville, to M. Pétillon in 1954, in which this big union of State officials recalled the merits of M. Jungers and regretted that his policy had not been continued.

2. Again, the Governor General, M. Pétillon, although he won the approval of some supporters of native advancement (I dare say "some" since the majority of colonists do not seem to endorse the Government's policy in this field) also encountered disapproval – as did M. Jungers – because of his moving speech at the opening of the Government Council in 1955 (a speech similar to that made by M. Jungers in 1952), particularly on the subject of human relations between White and Black. And the decision which he made in 1955, authorising Congolese to visit public premises, access to which had until then been reserved for Europeans only, met with no enthusiasm from the majority of European circles. All the *evolués* – including the Congolese *assimilés* – know about this because they were turned out of these places. Energetic intervention was required by the local authorities in order to ensure that the decision of the Head of the Colony was respected.

In an extremely unpleasant – even malicious – reply, a certain newspaper in the East of the Colony flung back at M. Pétillon the phrase he had used in his speech "if anyone is in disagreement with our policy, we beg him to pack his bags" and invited the Governor General to pack his bags and leave the Congo.

One day in August 1955 an influential person was heard to declare in the course of a conversation at the Commercial Fair at Stanleyville; "M. Pétillon was a good Governor General, but he is now taking a very queer line."

I can still remember the tension which prevailed in the Congo as a result of this decision by the Governor General to allow Africans to visit public premises. Fortunately the tension was eased thanks to the sensible action of the Africans in withdrawing from these places.

It should be noted, in passing, that certain establishments opened and still do open their doors with pleasure to African customers. I thank them most warmly for this and offer them the thanks of all the Congolese.

3. Since his appointment to the Colonial Department, the Minister, M. Buisseret, named (by the Congolese themselves) "Great Friend of the Blacks" has also been subjected to continuous criticism and vicious attacks. It is not for me to know whether or not M. Buisseret has committed certain errors. I can only judge the facts

which can easily be verified.

Let us allow the soul of the Black to speak. In the opinion of all Congolese (I am categorical about this because for two years now I have heard the same statements, the same opinions and the same judgments expressed by catholic, protestant and pagan Congolese), the reasons for the attacks on the Minister, M. Buisseret, are as follows:

– because the Minister attaches great importance to the social factor and courageously preaches the principle of equality of rights and status between White and Black, which has never existed in the Colony;

– because the Minister invites the Africans to go and discuss their problems in Belgium (the A.P.I.C. affair) instead of confining them to the Congo and leaving everything which concerns the natives to be decided *locally*, whereas the Africans in the other African Colonies (French and English colonies) frequently visit Europe at the invitation of the Government (or at their own expense) to have personal discussions with the metropolitan authorities about the problems which affect their respective countries.

All the colonists claim that to invite the Congolese to Belgium to discuss their problems would affect the prestige of the colonial authorities.

As for the Congolese, they adopt the following line of argument:

"All the reasons put forward by the Europeans are pretexts. The Colonial authorities will lose none of their prestige if they continue to administer the Congo properly. The Africans are prevented from going to Belgium to discuss their problems with the high authorities in the mother country so that they will not disclose certain conditions which prevail in the Colony and of which the authorities are ignorant. The European colonists are determined to stifle the desires and aspirations of the Congolese and to send reports to Europe which are not in accordance with the real facts. They want to ensure that they will always speak in our name (to conceal the truth) and not we ourselves, who are better acquainted with our problems. The colonists are determined that everything affecting us shall be discussed and decided in Africa, so that they can influence the decisions of the colonial authorities by all the means at their disposal. They are determined to preserve at all costs the present state of backwardness in regard to native policy. This is the reason why they disguise their intentions, why they violently attack the Minister for having, for the first time in the history of the Congo, invited a delegation of African civil servants to go and put their point of view to him on the problems which concern them. They attack the Minister violently, because he wishes to break this long-standing tradition of paternalism which has furthered the interests of the Europeans at the expense of those of the Congolese."

Because the Minister, in accordance with our resolution – which was submitted to the Council of Government by M. Pascal Luanghy, the native representative, long before M. Buisseret took over the Colonial Department – had instituted state education for the Congolese. Whereas, when state education was instituted for Europeans (Royal Athenæums) no one protested. They only protest now when the Africans are involved. And yet this education is giving full satisfaction to all the Congolese parents, and the opinions of every pupil are scrupulously respected. There are even punishments laid down for any teacher who tries to influence his pupils or convert them from the practice of a particular religion adopted by their parents. We are very pleased with the lay schools because of their tolerance for the liberty of conscience and their co-educational system which enables our daughters to make up for lost time and receive the same education as the boys. We are very pleased that our wish has been fulfilled and French has been adopted as the working language for these schools, starting from the first primary year. We are especially pleased that the syllabus for these schools approximates to that of the schools for European children, and also that inter-racial Athenæums have been established. Thus any-one who is against the state secular schools is also against the emancipation of the Africans.

"There is opposition to M. Buisseret because he has won the hearts of the Congolese. We do not regard him as a Minister, a Belgian, a Catholic, a Liberal, a Socialist, a Communist, but as a *sincere friend of the Africans*, as indeed are many other Belgians, like our great defender, the Very Reverend Father Van Wing, who has defended our interests on the Colonial Council and in all his missionary and extra-missionary duties for many years past, like Governor General Jungers, like Governor Peigneux, present Chair-man of the African Townships Department, who was recently appointed a member of the Colonial Council, like M. Pétillon, who allowed us to visit public establishments (and there are many other names, too numerous to reproduce here). Some people may perhaps fear that this unanimous sympathy and tremendous confidence shown by Congolese of all shades of opinion towards a liberal Minister, may lead all the Africans of the Congo to become Liberals, but this is by no means true since it is not the label – Liberal, Socialist, Catholic or Communist – which interests us, but our *material, intellectual and moral* well-being. We shall put our trust in anybody who can obtain these benefits for us. or help to obtain them, and not in ideologies. The latter are of very little interest to us."

"There is opposition to M. Buisseret because he wants to force the pace instead of crawling at a snail's pace and using political manoeuvres to delay the emancipation of the native populations and leave them as long as possible under European domination."

"There is opposition to M. Buisseret because he has a great liking for the Africans and recommends the Whites to change their attitude towards us so as to encourage fraternisation between Belgians and Congolese, which is, of course, our most ardent wish. It is also the wish of our well-loved King, a wish which he expressed during his visit to the Congo."

"Finally, is it because we show the same affection to M. Buisseret as we do to His Majesty King Baudouin, Our Protector, that the Europeans are displeased? Would they be happy if every time the King or the Minister for the Congo passed by, all the Blacks hid away in their huts or showed indifference and ingratitude towards the representatives of Belgium? Have we not a duty to show the same sympathy and the same confidence towards any Minister of the Colonies, towards any Governor General, and towards any leading Belgian who is interested in us?"

This is what the Congolese have told me.

These words are heard almost everywhere. But they will never be confided to a European. And with good reason! For fear of reprisals – often imaginary.

I have reproduced these statements as they stand, as I recorded them during my enquiry. I do this out of scruple for impartiality, so as not to distort the intentions of my "interviewees".

This general impression provides an explanation for the doubts which are to be found mainly among the evolving classes. This impression explains why many people are becoming increasingly distrustful of the promises made to them and of official speeches, even when these speeches express sincere intentions. They distrust them because they are convinced that these promises, as experience has shown, are not always translated into action, or are often sabotaged by officials entrusted with their execution.

This distrust is partly due to the fact that certain firm promises made to the natives have proved impossible to carry out or have been postponed indefinitely owing to some difficulty or other which the natives are incapable of understanding.

This distrust is also affected by the fact that the natives are often impatient. For many of them, any promise made today, for example, must be put into effect *tomorrow* or very soon. If it is not implemented within the period of time they expect, they regard it as "trickery", not realising that its implementation sometimes requires a preliminary investigation of the problem which may, in some cases, take a long time.